Lab Manual for

Linux+ Guide to Linux Certification, Second Edition

Ed Sawicki

COURSE TECHNOLOGY
CENGAGE Learning™

Australia • Brazil • Japan • Korea • Mexico • Singapore • Spain • United Kingdom • United States

COURSE TECHNOLOGY
CENGAGE Learning™

Lab Manual for Linux+ Guide to Linux Certification, Second Edition
Ed Sawicki

Managing Editor: William Pitkin III

Product Manager: Manya Chylinski

Developmental Editor: Rebecca Holmes

Production Editor: Summer Hughes

Manufacturing Coordinator: Trevor Kallop

Quality Assurance Technical Lead: Christian Kunciw

Marketing Manager: Gayathri Baskaran

Associate Product Manager: Sarah Santoro

Editorial Assistant: Jennifer Smith

Compositor: GEX Publishing Services

Copyeditor: Mark Goodin

Proofreader: Sue Forsyth

For product information and technology assistance, contact us at
Cengage Learning Customer & Sales Support, 1-800-354-9706

For permission to use material from this text or product,
submit all requests online at **www.cengage.com/permissions**
Further permissions questions can be emailed to
permissionrequest@cengage.com

ISBN-13: 978-0-619-21620-7

ISBN-10: 0-619-21620-4

Course Technology
5191 Natorp Boulevard
Mason, OH 45040
USA

Cengage Learning is a leading provider of customized learning solutions with office locations around the globe, including Singapore, the United Kingdom, Australia, Mexico, Brazil, and Japan. Locate your local office at **international.cengage.com/region**

Cengage Learning products are represented in Canada by Nelson Education, Ltd.

To learn more about Course Technology, visit **www.cengage.com/coursetechnology**

Purchase any of our products at your local bookstore or at our preferred online store **www.ichapters.com**

Printed in the United States of America
6 7 8 9 10 14 13 12 11 10

ED172

Table of Contents

INTRODUCTION

Hands-on learning is the best way to master skills necessary for both CompTIA's Linux+ exam and a Linux-related career. This book contains hands-on exercises that apply fundamental Linux concepts as they are applied in the real world. In addition, each chapter offers review questions to reinforce your mastery of each chapter's topics. The organization of this book follows the same organization as Course Technology's *Linux+ Guide to Linux Certification* and using the two together will provide a substantial, effective learning experience. This book is suitable for use in a beginning Linux administration course. As a prerequisite, students should have a fundamental understanding of general operating system concepts, and at least one course in operating systems. This book is best used when accompanied by the Course Technology textbook *Linux+ Guide to Linux Certification*, or another Linux+ textbook.

FEATURES

In order to ensure a successful experience for instructors and students alike, this book includes the following features:

- **Linux+ certification objectives**—Each chapter lists the relevant objectives from the CompTIA Linux+ Exam
- **Lab Objectives**—Every lab has a brief description and list of learning objectives
- **Materials Required**—Every lab includes information on access privileges, hardware, software, and other materials you will need to complete the lab
- **Completion Times**—Every lab has an estimated completion time, so that you can plan your activities more accurately
- **Activity Sections**—Labs are presented in manageable sections; additional Activity Background information is provided where appropriate
- **Step-by-Step Instructions**—Logical and precise step-by-step instructions guide you through the hands-on activities in each lab
- **Review Questions**—Questions help reinforce concepts presented in the lab

Hardware Requirements

- 400 MHz Pentium CPU
- 3 GB of hard disk space
- 256 MB of memory (RAM)
- CD-ROM drive
- Floppy disk drive
- One PCI Ethernet network interface card
- Internet connection

Software/Setup Requirements

- Fedora Core 2
- Any Web Browser

Acknowledgments

Thanks to Merryl for putting up with me for all these months, to Mark for being a pal, and to Beth for being her usual zany self. Chuck Quesenberry helped me with some of the Red Hat-specific issues—I'm more of a Slackware, Debian, and roll-it-yourself Linux geek.

David May provided me with interesting intellectual diversions when I was bogged down and needed a break. These discussions, research, and experiments resulted in Sealed System™ technology that you'll hear about in the future.

Thanks to Richard Stallman for giving birth to the Free (Open Source) Software movement back in the 1980s. His contribution is being unjustly minimized by some in the community because of his views. Thanks to Linus Torvalds for creating Linux and the many thousands of people who contribute ideas, software, documentation, and support.

Thanks also to Course Technology, Cengage Learning. Deb Kaufman and Becky Holmes are exceptional editors and eased the burden of using Microsoft Word—Unix people use less troublesome tools for publishing. Thanks also go to Manya Chylinski for her relaxed but supportive approach to Project Management.

CHAPTER ONE

INTRODUCTION TO LINUX

Labs included in this chapter

- Lab 1.1 Become Familiar with Squid Proxy Server
- Lab 1.2 See How Linux Is Used by Vendors
- Lab 1.3 Explore Open Source Software
- Lab 1.4 See How Linux and Windows Can Be Integrated
- Lab 1.5 Investigate Linux Security

CompTIA Linux+ Exam Objectives		
Objective		**Lab**
N/A	These lab exercises do not directly address Linux+ objectives, but provide additional background information to help you master the objectives and understand the Linux operating system.	1.1, 1.2, 1.3, 1.4, 1.5

Lab 1.1 Become Familiar with Squid Proxy Server

Objectives

The goal of this lab is to become familiar with a useful Open Source software package that runs on Linux. The Squid proxy server is a great example of a high-quality software package that is free, well supported, and runs on many different hardware and software platforms.

Materials Required

This lab requires the following:

- An Internet connection and a Web browser

NOTE

This lab explores information on the World Wide Web. Because Web pages can change without notice, what you see may not exactly match the terminology described in this lab. You may have to use your judgement to find the best match for links described here. When in doubt, check with your instructor.

Activity Background

There are thousands of software packages you can run on Linux. The Squid proxy server is a particularly useful one because it can dramatically reduce the Internet bandwidth required for Web browsing, and may improve performance of FTP file transfers as well. Squid serves as a good example of the support available for Open Source software.

Estimated completion time: 30 Minutes

LAB ACTIVITY

Activity

1. Start your Web browser.
2. Type **http://www.squid-cache.org** in the Address bar of the browser, and then press **Enter**. The Squid Web Proxy Cache Web page appears.
3. Click the **FAQ** link on the left side of the screen. Spend some time reviewing the wealth of information available here. It's not important if you don't yet understand much of what you're reading. Understanding will come in time, when and if you need to use Squid in your network.
4. Click the **Back** button to go back to the home page, and then click the **Users guide** link on the left side of the screen. On the next screen, click the **Read Online (multiple smaller pages)** link. On the next screen, you see a Table of Contents that leads you to massive amounts of information about Squid. Note that all of this documentation was written by volunteers who are Squid users.

5. Click the **Choosing an Operating System** link and read the page that is displayed. You likely see one or more places where the author intended to include information but has not yet gotten around to it. In the world of Open Source software, volunteer labor sometimes means that information may be missing or incomplete. Fortunately, missing information does not usually prevent you from installing and using the software. Most often, the information you really need is there for you. Miscellaneous additional information sometimes comes later.

   On this same page, note that the author discusses how he first installed Squid on a computer running the FreeBSD operating system, but then switched to Linux. Most Open Source software, such as Squid, can run on numerous hardware and operating system platforms. With Open Source software, you're not limited to just one operating system or computer type as you are with some commercial products.

Certification Objectives

This lab does not directly map to a certification objective; however, it gives background information that can help you master the objectives and understand the Linux operating system.

Review Questions

1. Squid can cache which of the following protocols?
   a. HTTP
   b. SMTP
   c. FTP
   d. SSH
2. Squid can only run on Linux. True or False?
3. Squid performs best when you have a lot of memory in your computer. True or False?
4. Squid uses hard disk space as its secondary cache. True or False?
5. Technically, Squid is a:
   a. Web browser cache
   b. Internet object cache
   c. TCP port stretcher
   d. processor L3 cache

LAB 1.2 SEE HOW LINUX IS USED BY VENDORS

Objectives

The goal of this lab is to become familiar with how vendors use Linux in their own products. This lab focuses on two companies that have embraced Linux and Open Source software: IBM and Novell. These companies have opted to save engineering resources by using secure software that's already been written and debugged by the Open Source community. Rather than treating the Open Source community as the enemy, or claiming that Open Source software stifles innovation, IBM and Novell have recognized the win-win possibilities and have exploited them.

Materials Required

This lab requires the following:

- An Internet connection and a Web browser

NOTE

This lab explores information on the World Wide Web. Because Web pages can change without notice, what you see may not exactly match the terminology described in this lab. You may have to use your judgement to find the best match for links described here. When in doubt, check with your instructor.

Estimated completion time: 30 Minutes

LAB ACTIVITY

ACTIVITY

1. Start your Web browser.
2. Type **http://www-1.ibm.com/linux/** in the Address bar of the browser, and then press **Enter**. The Linux at IBM Web page appears.
3. Click the **IBM Software for Linux** link. On the next page, click the **WebSphere** link. The next page gives you details about IBM's WebSphere product. WebSphere can run on Linux and uses the Apache Web server—another popular Open Source software package. Because they base their for-profit products on nonprofit Open Source software, IBM can bring high-quality products to market quickly without the many security holes you find in popular commercial software.
4. Click your browser's **Back** button to go back to the previous page, or if you can't go back, close the current browser window. Now click the **White Paper Library** link. The page that appears has numerous Linux-related white papers you can read. You have to register by filling out a form.

5. Click your browser's **Back** button until you get back to the **IBM Software for Linux** page (the URL is *http://www-306.ibm.com/software/os/linux/software/*). Now click the **DB2** link and look at this page. IBM considers Linux to be one of the primary platforms for DB2. If you go to the Oracle Web site (*http://www.oracle.com*) you see that Oracle has ported its SQL database product to Linux as well. All or most high-end commercial SQL servers run on Linux, with the notable exception of Microsoft SQL Server.
6. Type **http://www.novell.com** in the Address bar of the browser, and then press **Enter**. The Novell home page appears. Click the **Search** link in the upper-right corner. Enter **Linux** and click the **Search** button. You see that there are hundreds of items found. Many Novell products either run on Linux or use Open Source software, or both. The Open Source Apache Web server is now Novell's official Web server, and a few Novell products are based on it.

Certification Objectives

This lab does not directly map to a certification objective; however, it gives background information that can help you master the objectives and understand the Linux operating system.

Review Questions

1. Many of the IBM e-commerce products are based on which of the following:
   a. Microsoft IIS Web server
   b. Apache Web server
   c. AOL Web server
   d. Microsoft Personal Web server
2. Which of the following SQL database products do not run on Linux?
   a. Oracle
   b. IBM DB2
   c. Informix
   d. Microsoft SQL Server
3. There are no enterprise-class accounting and financial applications for Linux. True or False?
4. Which of the following is Novell's official Web server for NetWare?
   a. Microsoft IIS Web server
   b. Apache Web server
   c. AOL Web server
   d. Microsoft Personal Web server
5. Explain why Open Source software may be a good thing for commercial software developers rather than a threat.

Lab 1.3 Explore Open Source Software

Objectives

The goal of this lab is to become aware of the popularity of Open Source software using a factor that is well understood in the commercial software world—market share. In this lab, you research to discover the percentage of Web servers that are running the three most popular Web server software packages: Apache, Microsoft IIS, and Sun Microsystems iPlanet.

Materials Required

This lab requires the following:

- An Internet connection and a Web browser

NOTE

This lab explores information on the World Wide Web. Because Web pages can change without notice, what you see may not exactly match the terminology described in this lab. You may have to use your judgement to find the best match for links described here. When in doubt, check with your instructor.

Estimated completion time: 20 Minutes

LAB ACTIVITY

Activity

1. Start your Web browser.
2. Type **http://news.netcraft.com/archives/web_server_survey.html** in the Address bar of the browser, and then press **Enter**. The Netcraft Web Server Survey page appears. This page has a graph that shows the market share for the most popular Web servers. Note that Apache leads the pack by a significant margin.

   One factor that significantly affects the Netcraft survey results is a Web server feature called "virtual hosting." This feature allows a single Web server to host many Internet sites or URLs. An ISP running a single Web server with 5000 virtual hosts is seen as 5000 Web servers in the Netcraft survey instead of one Web server.

3. Type **http://www.biznix.org/surveys/** in the Address bar of the browser, and then press **Enter**. The next Web page you see is the result of a Web server survey conducted by BizNix—a user group in Portland, Oregon. This survey limits itself to well-defined categories of Web server users, such as big companies, government agencies, and military departments. It minimizes the effects of virtual hosting to get a more accurate picture of Web server popularity. The results are quite a bit different than the Netcraft survey results.

Compare the results of the BizNix and Netcraft surveys. How are they similar? How do they differ? Note the BizNix survey's conclusion that Microsoft IIS popularity is a U.S. phenomenon.

Certification Objectives

This lab does not directly map to a certification objective; however, it gives background information that can help you master the objectives and understand the Linux operating system.

Review Questions

1. Why is it that the Netcraft survey may not be an accurate way of determining the number of Apache Web servers on the Internet?
   a. There's no way to know what software a Web server is using.
   b. A Web server could be using virtual hosting that allows one physical Web server to appear as numerous Web servers.
   c. Web servers can masquerade as other types or brands of software. Web server administrators may do this to improve compatibility between their servers and popular Web browsers.
2. Why are the BizNix results likely to give a more accurate picture of Apache market share?
   a. The big companies, government agencies, and military departments surveyed are less likely to use virtual hosting.
   b. The BizNix survey knows when a Web server is lying about the software it is using.
   c. The BizNix survey knows when Web servers have had their software upgraded.
3. The percentage of Apache usage by big companies in the United States is the same as big companies in other parts of the world. True or False?
4. The BizNix survey shows that the popularity of the Microsoft IIS Web server is the same in all countries. True or False?

Lab 1.4 See How Linux and Windows Can Be Integrated

Objectives

The goal of this lab is to help you become aware of the many ways that Linux and Windows computers can be integrated.

Materials Required

This lab requires the following:

- An Internet connection and a Web browser

NOTE: This lab explores information on the World Wide Web. Because Web pages can change without notice, what you see may not exactly match the terminology described in this lab. You may have to use your judgement to find the best match for links described here. When in doubt, check with your instructor.

Estimated completion time: 30 Minutes

Activity

1. Start your Web browser.
2. Type **http://www.samba.org** in the Address bar of the browser, and then press **Enter**. When the first Samba Web page appears, click a link to a Web mirror site close to you.
3. The next Web page gives you a general overview of the Samba software. Click the **documentation** link. The next page has links to a great deal of Samba-related documentation. Samba is one of the best documented Open Source software projects. Review some of this documentation. You should discover that when you run Samba on your Linux computer, it becomes a file and print server compatible with Microsoft Windows computers. A more technical way of saying this is that Samba is a SMB server or CIFS server. Samba also has a client component that allows your Linux computer to access other SMB or CIFS servers.
4. Type **http://www.winehq.org** in the Address bar of the browser, and then press **Enter**. You see a Web page for Wine, a project that allows Microsoft Windows programs to run on your Linux computer.
5. Click the **Introduction** link. This takes you to the About Wine Web page. Note that you're told that Wine is still in development. It has been for many years and its status is not likely to change soon. However, many people use Wine today with various levels of success in spite of its status as still being in development.
6. Click the **Applications** link that is along the left edge of the page. This takes you to a page that tells you which Windows applications work well in a Wine environment and which do not.
7. Type **http://www.vmware.com** in the Address bar of the browser, and then press **Enter**. You see a Web page for VMware, a commercial product that

allows you to run Windows programs on your Linux computer or vice versa. VMware takes a different approach than Wine. It requires that you install a Windows operating system inside a virtual machine running on your Linux computer (the concept of a virtual machine is explained on the Web site). When you run your Windows programs inside the virtual machine, they're running on real Windows and should, therefore, run properly. VMware is one of the best ways to run Windows applications on your Linux computer. It is also one of the most expensive ways.

8. Type **http://www.rdesktop.org** in the Address bar of the browser, and then press **Enter**. You see a Web page for rdesktop, a Windows Terminal Server client for Linux. Using rdesktop, you can run Windows programs on your Windows Terminal Server but have Linux operate your screen, keyboard, and mouse. Your Windows programs are running on a Windows computer, but you're using a Linux computer.

All of the Windows/Linux integration solutions you've seen in this lab can be used separately or in combination. There are many ways to introduce Open Source software and Linux into your company without sacrificing Windows functionality. These integration solutions allow you to run newer Linux applications on the same computers and networks that are running your legacy Windows applications.

Certification Objectives

This lab does not directly map to a certification objective; however, it gives background information that can help you master the objectives and understand the Linux operating system.

Review Questions

1. On which of the following operating systems would you *not* expect to find Samba running?
   a. Linux
   b. FreeBSD
   c. Windows
   d. NetWare
2. A Samba server is what kind of server? (Choose all that apply.)
   a. SMTP server
   b. CIFS server
   c. SMB server
   d. DNS server
3. Using Samba, a Linux computer can access files on a Windows computer. True or False?

4. Wine requires that you install a Windows operating system on your Linux computer. True or False?
5. What are some disadvantages of Wine? (Choose all that apply.)
   a. Some Windows applications may not run correctly or at all.
   b. Wine requires that you install a Windows license pack.
   c. Microsoft can alter Windows applications in the future so they will no longer run with Wine.
   d. When you run Wine, you can no longer access a Samba server.
6. When you run Windows applications in a VMware virtual machine, they may not run correctly. True or False?
7. The rdesktop program allows you to run a Windows application on a Windows Terminal Server, yet use your Linux computer's screen, keyboard, and mouse. True or False?

Lab 1.5 Investigate Linux Security

Objectives

The goal of this lab is to gain an appreciation for why typical Open Source software, including Linux, tends to be more secure than other popular operating systems.

Materials Required

This lab requires the following:

- An Internet connection and any Web browser

NOTE

This lab explores information on the World Wide Web. Because Web pages can change without notice, what you see may not exactly match the terminology described in this lab. You may have to use your judgement to find the best match for links described here. When in doubt, check with your instructor.

Estimated completion time: 30 Minutes

Activity

LAB ACTIVITY

1. Start your Web browser.
2. Type **http://www.linuxsecurity.org** in the Address bar of the browser, and then press **Enter**. You see a Web page that focuses on Linux security matters. The page contents change frequently, so you're on your own to explore as you

see fit. As you explore, note that you're cautioned about potential security holes in software, warned to use secure protocols (such as SSH) instead of insecure ones (such as Telnet), and so forth. The emphasis is on educating you about how to avoid security problems and attacks. Software updates and patches generally are available before any site on the Internet is attacked (unlike the typical scenario with commercial software, in which updates and patches become available only after sites are attacked).

3. Click the **Resources** link near the top of the page. The page that appears has a list of links along the left side of the page. Click the **Firewalls** link. The page contains a list of articles and Web sites that relate to Linux firewalls. The Linux operating system has a built-in firewall. You just need to configure it—and that can be challenging if you don't understand such protocols as IP, TCP, and UDP. The resources listed on this page help you configure your firewall by either teaching you how to do it or by supplying you with software (such as scripts) that makes it easier.

   Because Linux has a built-in firewall, you can deploy a firewall at no extra cost anywhere there is a Linux computer.

4. Type **http://www.ietf.org/rfc/rfc2137.txt** in the Address bar of the browser, and then press **Enter**. You're now looking at a document that describes an Internet standard. Formally, this is called an RFC, short for "Request for Comment," published by the Internet Engineering Task Force (IETF). The content of this document is very detailed and technical and may be beyond your comprehension, but it is not important right now. Next, you want to see how the IETF handles security concerns.

5. Scroll down until you see a section heading called Security Considerations and read the paragraphs. Most IETF RFCs have such a security section. The IETF is the caretaker of the Internet and their focus is on security issues and helping protect the Internet from attack. What do IETF RFCs have to do with Linux? Plenty. Designers of Linux and other Open Source software use open protocols and standards, such as IETF RFCs. They do this because one of the goals of Open Source software is to be compatible with other software. The only time designers use vendor-proprietary protocols is when they're designing software to integrate with a vendor product. The Samba project is a good example of that.

6. Type **http://www.nsa.gov/selinux** in the Address bar of the browser, and then press **Enter**. You're now looking at the security-enhanced Linux page. This is nicknamed SELinux and was created by the U.S. National Security Agency. SELinux adds extensions to the Linux operating system to make it far less vulnerable to break-ins. Even if a Linux computer is successfully attacked, SELinux severely limits the attacker's ability to do anything on the computer. Attacks that are common in the Windows world, such as Code Red and Nimda, are rare in the Linux world even without SELinux. With SELinux, such attacks become highly unlikely.

Certification Objectives

This lab does not directly map to a certification objective; however, it gives background information that can help you master the objectives and understand the Linux operating system.

Review Questions

1. Which of the following statements about Linux security is correct?
   a. Linux e-mail programs are easy targets for viruses, as is Microsoft Outlook.
   b. Linux has a built-in firewall that allows you to secure any Linux computer, but you must configure it.
   c. Linux Web browsers cannot use SSL to access secure Web pages.
   d. Apache Web servers are too secure. Sometimes Web browsers cannot connect to them because Apache doesn't follow open standards.
2. There are as many virus scanner programs for Linux as there are for Windows. True or False?
3. Explain why Linux is more secure than Windows, even though there are numerous software updates and patches for Windows-based software.
4. Explain why open protocols, such as those documented in IETF RFCs, tend to have fewer security issues than vendor-proprietary protocols.
5. If you use the NSA's security-enhanced Linux, in the unlikely event of a successful attack, the attacker is prevented from significantly damaging your Linux computer. True or False?

CHAPTER TWO

PREPARING FOR LINUX INSTALLATION

Labs included in this chapter

CompTIA Linux+ Exam Objectives

Objective		Lab
1.11	Select appropriate parameters for Linux installation (e.g., language, time zones, keyboard, mouse)	2.1, 2.2
6.2	Diagnose hardware issues using Linux tools (e.g., /proc, disk utilities, ifconfig, /dev, KNOPPIX, BBC, dmesg)	2.1, 2.3
1.1	Identify all system hardware required (e.g., CPU, memory, drive space, scalability) and check compatibility with the Linux distribution	2.1, 2.2, 2.4
6.3	Identify and configure removable system hardware (e.g., PCMCIA, USB, IEEE1394)	2.4

Lab 2.1 Booting from a Linux Root/Boot Disk

Objectives

The goal of this lab is to learn to create a Linux root/boot disk that you can use to discover details about your computer's hardware. This is useful if you have computers that do not reveal adequate details about their hardware.

Materials Required

This lab requires the following:

- An Internet connection and any Web browser on a computer with an operating system capable of running DOS programs, such as DOS, Windows 95, or Windows 98. Note that the following operating systems *cannot* run DOS programs: Windows 2000, Windows NT, and Windows XP.
- A program that uncompresses and unarchives .zip files such as PKUNZIP or WinZip
- A high-density 3.5-inch disk

Activity Background

In the main text, you use Windows to discover the details of the hardware in the computer on which you're going to install Linux. However, if you don't already have Windows installed, you can start the computer with a Linux root/boot disk and have Linux tell you what hardware is in your computer.

A Linux root/boot disk allows you to boot Linux from a 3.5-inch disk and run it without using your computer's hard disk. It does this by using some of your system's memory as a virtual disk. One of the more popular Linux root/boot disks is tomsrtbt, available from *www.toms.net/rb*.

Estimated completion time: 35 Minutes

LAB ACTIVITY

Activity

1. Start your Web browser.
2. Enter **www.toms.net/rb** in the Address bar of the browser, and then press **Enter**. The tomsrtbt Web page appears.
3. Click the **Download tomsrtbt** here link.
4. Click on a mirror site close to you. You should now see a list of files.

5. Click the **tomsrtbt-2.0.103.dos.zip** link to start the download. When prompted, save the file on your hard disk and note the location where you saved it.

6. Use PKUNZIP or WinZip to uncompress the file you just downloaded. Read the tomsrtbt.FAQ file and note the installation instructions. You can print the file if you think it would be helpful.

7. Following the instructions in the tomsrtbt.FAQ file, type **install** at a DOS prompt and follow the on-screen directions to create the disk.

8. Insert the 3.5-inch disk you want to use for the root/boot disk into the computer on which you will install Linux, and boot the computer. At the boot prompt, press **Enter**. The Linux operating system loads and you see a login prompt.

9. Log in as root. The on-screen instructions tell you that a password is needed and what the password is. (Yes, this seems silly to require a password, then display the password on the screen.)

   You're now logged in to a real Linux operating system running on your computer. However, the entire operating system and all the programs you're about to run are now in memory—not on your computer's hard disk.

10. Type **cd /proc** and press **Enter**.

11. Type **ls** and press **Enter**. You see many file and directory names (some of them numeric). Some of these files describe your computer's hardware.

NOTE

These are not real files. They do not actually exist on your system's hard disk. The Linux kernel simulates them. To be technically precise, the kernel allows you to view system information using file system semantics—a helpful feature found in few other operating systems.

12. Type **cat cpuinfo** and press **Enter**. You see a screen that looks similar to this:

```
processor     : 0
vendor_id     : GenuineIntel
cpu family    : 6
model         : 8
model name    : Celeron (Coppermine)
stepping      : 6
cpu MHz       : 801.834
cache size    : 128 KB
fdiv_bug      : no
hlt_bug       : no
f00f_bug      : no
coma_bug      : no
fpu           : yes
fpu_exception : yes
cpuid level   : 2
```

```
wp              : yes
flags           : fpu vme de pse tsc msr pae mce cx8 sep
                  mtrr pge mca cmov pat pse36 mmx fxsr sse
bogomips        : 1599.07
```

This tells you that the computer is a Celeron with a 128 KB cache running at 800 MHz along with other details that may not be important to you.

NOTE

The bogomips number is meant to give you an indication of your processor's effective speed, considering its clock speed, cache size, and other factors. However, it's a grossly inaccurate measure of system performance; hence, the name bogomips (bogus MIPS; MIPS stands for "millions of instructions per second," a standard measure of CPU speed). It's best to ignore this number as an indication of your system's performance.

13. Type **cat interrupts** and press **Enter**. You see a screen that looks similar to this:

```
           CPU0
  0:   38599153    XT-PIC  timer
  1:      50719    XT-PIC  keyboard
  2:          0    XT-PIC  cascade
  6:         54    XT-PIC  floppy
  8:          1    XT-PIC  rtc
 11:     216174    XT-PIC  eth0, SiS 7018 PCI Audio
 12:    2542269    XT-PIC  PS/2 Mouse
 14:     606329    XT-PIC  ide0
 15:          0    XT-PIC  ide1
NMI:          0
ERR:          0
```

This example shows you the hardware interrupts in your computer and what devices use those interrupts. This example shows that this computer has the usual hardware plus it has a LAN adapter (eth0) and audio device on interrupt 11. It also has a mouse on interrupt 12.

14. Type **cat ioports** and press **Enter**. You see a screen that looks similar to this:

```
0000-001f : dma1
0020-003f : pic1
0040-005f : timer
0060-006f : keyboard
0070-007f : rtc
0080-008f : dma page reg
00a0-00bf : pic2
00c0-00df : dma2
00f0-00ff : fpu
0170-0177 : ide1
01f0-01f7 : ide0
0376-0376 : ide1
03c0-03df : vga+
```

```
03f0-03f5 : floppy
03f6-03f6 : ide0
03f7-03f7 : floppy DIR
03f8-03ff : serial(auto)
0cf8-0cff : PCI conf1
c000-cfff : PCI Bus #01
cc80-ccff : Silicon Integrated Systems [SiS] SiS630 GUI
  Accelerator+3D
da00-daff : Silicon Integrated Systems [SiS] SiS900 10/
  100  Ethernet
da00-daff : sis900
dc00-dcff : Silicon Integrated Systems [SiS] SiS PCI
  Audio Accelerator
dc00-dcff : SiS 7018 PCI Audio
de00-deff : Adaptec AIC-7881U
ffa0-ffaf : Silicon Integrated Systems [SiS] 5513 [IDE]
ffa0-ffa7 : ide0

ffa8-ffaf : ide1
```

This example shows you I/O addresses used by the hardware in your computer. Note, for example, that here you see an Adaptec AIC-7881U SCSI card that wasn't in the list of interrupts.

15. Type **cat dma** and press **Enter**. You see a screen that looks similar to this:

```
2: floppy
4: cascade
```

This example shows that the disk drive controller uses DMA channel 2. There are no other devices in your computer that use DMA channels. Note that "cascade" is not a device. It simply indicates that your computer uses two DMA controllers connected together.

There are other files that contain hardware-related information, such as pci, devices, and meminfo. Take a look at them, but they could be a little cryptic at this point. They'll make more sense as you learn more about Linux.

16. You are finished, so shut down the computer, and remove the disk. You can shut down the computer just by using the power switch.

Certification Objectives

Objectives for the Linux+ exam:

- Select appropriate parameters for Linux installation (e.g., language, time zones, keyboard, mouse) (1.11)
- Diagnose hardware issues using Linux tools (e.g., /proc, disk utilities, ifconfig, /dev, KNOPPIX, BBC, dmesg) (6.2)

- Identify all system hardware required (e.g., CPU, memory, drive space, scalability) and check compatibility with the Linux distribution (1.1)

Review Questions

1. When you boot from a Linux root/boot disk, what disk is used after your system has booted completely?
    a. the root/boot disk
    b. the hard disk
    c. a virtual disk in your system's memory
    d. a disk in a file server
2. The files that appear in the /proc directory take up space on your hard disk. True or False?
3. What command do you use to find out information about your system's processor?
4. What command do you use to find out information about your system's interrupts?
5. Your system's bogomips rating is an accurate indicator of system performance. True or False?

Lab 2.2 Booting Linux from a CD-ROM

Objectives

Lab 2.1 had you download the tomsrtbt program and install it on a 3.5-inch disk. This may be difficult for you to do if your computer runs a version of Windows that doesn't support DOS programs. An alternative approach is to use a version of Linux that boots from a CD-ROM. If you're using a version of Windows that does not support DOS programs, such as Windows NT, Windows 2000, or Windows XP, you can burn a CD-ROM more easily than you can create a boot disk. In this lab exercise, you download and install a software package called KNOPPIX. KNOPPIX is a full-featured Linux distribution. It includes hundreds of applications including K-Office and Open Office—two popular office suites. KNOPPIX allows you to boot a full-featured Linux from a CD-ROM. It does not require that you use any of your hard disk space. You can run KNOPPIX on a computer that has Windows (or any other operating system) installed and all of its disk space already allocated.

Materials Required

This lab requires the following:

- A computer with a CD-ROM burner and software installed
- A Web browser and Internet connection

Estimated completion time: 45 minutes

Activity

LAB ACTIVITY

1. In the address bar of your Web browser, type **www.knopper.net/knoppix** and press **Enter**. Find and click the **Download** link, choose a nearby mirror site, and then download the .iso KNOPPIX file. Once it is downloaded, open the file and burn it onto a CD. Note that downloading the file may take a long time, depending on your connection speed (for example a DSL connection may take an hour and a half, or more).

   Make sure your computer supports the minimum requirements that are specified on the Web site. Your computer must use an Intel i486-compatible (or newer) processor and 16 MB of memory (RAM). If you have 96 MB or more of memory, you can run KNOPPIX in graphics mode. Note the discussion on the Web site about creating a swap partition on your hard disk so you can run graphics with less memory. However, a swap partition is not required.

2. Boot from the CD-ROM. This may require that you reconfigure your computer's BIOS to boot from a CD-ROM rather than a hard disk. Refer to your computer's documentation for how to do this. If your computer can't boot from a CD-ROM, you're better off using the tomsrtbt software described in Lab 2.1 and booting from a 3.5-inch disk.

   Because you're booting Linux from a CD-ROM, which is a relatively slow device, it takes a while for Linux to completely boot up. Eventually, depending on the amount of memory in your computer, you find yourself at either a command prompt or in a graphical KDE desktop. If you're in a KDE desktop, go to a virtual console by pressing **Ctrl+Alt+F2**. You're already logged in as the root user.

3. Go to the /proc directory by typing **cd /proc**.

4. Type **ls** and press **Enter**. You see lots of file and directory names as you did in Lab 2.1, Step 12. Again, these are not real files nor do they actually exist on your system's hard disk. The Linux kernel simulates them.

NOTE

Steps 3 through 8 here duplicate Steps 10 through 15 in Lab 2.1, so you can see that you're able to access the same functions with KNOPPIX.

5. Type **cat cpuinfo** and press **Enter** to see information about the CPU.

6. Type **cat interrupts** and press **Enter** to see information about interrupt assignments.

7. Type **cat ioports** and press **Enter** to see information about what I/O ports various devices use.

8. Type **cat dma** and press **Enter** to show devices that use DMA channels.

9. When you have finished, you can go back to the KNOPPIX graphical desktop by pressing **Alt+F5**.

Certification Objectives

Objectives for the Linux+ exam:

- Select appropriate parameters for Linux installation (e.g., language, time zones, keyboard, mouse) (1.11)
- Identify all system hardware required (e.g., CPU, memory, drive space, scalability) and check compatibility with the Linux distribution (1.1)

Review Questions

1. To run KNOPPIX, your computer *must* be capable of:
   a. booting from a 3.5-inch disk
   b. booting from a CD-ROM
   c. booting from a hard disk
   d. booting from a Web site
2. KNOPPIX requires that you create a Linux swap partition on your hard disk. True or False?
3. How much memory is required to run KNOPPIX with a graphical desktop?
   a. 32 MB
   b. 64 MB
   c. 96 MB
   d. 128 MB
4. If you have Windows installed on your computer, you cannot run KNOPPIX. True or False?
5. You can run KNOPPIX and Windows simultaneously. True or False?

Lab 2.3 Testing Your Computer's Memory

Objectives

In this exercise, you download and install a memory test program called **Memtest86**. It runs on any Intel-based computer and does not require that an operating system be installed. You typically place the program on a 3.5-inch disk and boot from that. However, you can also install the program on a hard disk or CD-ROM.

Materials Required

This lab requires the following:

- A computer running either Windows (any version) or Linux
- An Internet connection and a Web browser
- If you're using Windows, you need a program that uncompresses and unarchives .zip files such as PKUNZIP or WinZip
- A high-density 3.5-inch disk

Activity Background

Any operating system will fail to work reliably if the computer's memory is faulty. Linux is no exception. Before installing Linux, it's a good idea to check your computer's memory. The memory test that's conducted each time you start up your computer is not a comprehensive one, and some memory problems may escape detection. It's best to run a comprehensive memory testing program such as Memtest86.

Estimated completion time: 40 minutes

ACTIVITY

LAB ACTIVITY

1. Enter **www.memtest86.com** into your Web browser, and press **Enter**. Click the **Memtest86 3.1a Release** link and then click **Download - Pre-Compiled Memtest86 v3.1a installable from Windows and DOS** for Windows or **Download - Linux Memtest86 v3.1a Source and binary Package** for Linux to download the file.
2. Once the software has been downloaded to your computer, uncompress the files and view and print the readme file. Use these instructions to create the Memtest86 disk. You can do this on a computer running Linux or Windows. The disk you create is a boot disk similar to the one in Lab 2.1.
3. Place the 3.5-inch disk into your computer's 3.5-inch disk drive and reboot.
4. Once your computer starts booting from the 3.5-inch disk, the Memtest86 program should load in a few seconds and begin running immediately.
5. After running a few seconds, the screen should look similar to this:

```
Memtest-86 v 3.0            | Pass 2%   #
Pentium II     267.2 MHz | Test 70% ########
L1 Cache 32K  2620 MB/s | Test #2 [Address test, own address, no cache]
L2 Cache 512K 362 MB/s  | Testing 88K - 128M  128M
Memory 128M    113 MB/s  | Pattern: Chipset i440[bz]x
Walltime  cached  RsvdMem  MemMap   Cache  ECC  Test  Pass Errors  CC Errors
0:04:27   128M    432K     e820-Std  on     off  Std   2    0        0
```

6. Observe that the test tells you how much memory is installed in your computer. It shows you this in the fifth line ("Memory 128M" in this example).
7. Observe that the test shows you the range of memory that is being tested. This is in the fourth line ("Testing 88K – 128M" in this example).
8. Observe that the test computes and displays the speed of your processor's L1 and L2 cache in the third and fourth lines (2620 MB/s and 362 MB/s respectively). The speed of your computer's main memory is displayed in the fifth line (113 MB/s).
9. Normally, the Memtest86 program runs eight memory tests. Observe that the current test number is displayed on the third line (Test #2).

   When all eight tests are complete, this is the completion of a "pass" and the tests repeat. The number of the pass is displayed in the last line of text. In the example above, it's the "2" beneath "Pass."
10. Press **c** while the program is running. This displays the following menu that allows you to control the operation of the Memtest86 program:

```
Configuration:

(1) Cache Mode
(2) Test Selection
(3) Address Range
(4) Memory Sizing
(5) Error Summary
(6) Error Report Mode
(7) ECC Mode
(8) Restart Test
(9) Reprint Screen
(0) Cancel
```

11. Type **0** to exit this menu. Press **Esc** to exit Memtest86 and then remove the floppy from the drive. You can learn more about the configuration options in Step 10 by reading the Web page at **www.memtest86.com**.

So far, you've been running Memtest86 by booting it from a 3.5-inch disk. You can also install it on your hard disk and run it when you boot up your computer. This requires that you configure your boot loader, such as LILO, GRUB, or your Windows boot loader. You can learn how to do this from the Memtest86 readme file, as well as by reading the documentation for your boot loader.

An interesting capability of Linux is its ability to use faulty memory modules by bypassing the faulty memory locations. If you discover memory errors, you can tell Linux to avoid using that area of memory rather than replacing the memory module(s). This is called BadRAM. To use this feature, visit *rick.vanrein.org/linux/badram* and learn more.

Certification Objectives

Objectives for the Linux+ exam:

- Diagnose hardware issues using Linux tools (e.g., /proc, disk utilities, ifconfig, /dev, KNOPPIX, BBC, dmesg) (6.2)

Review Questions

1. Memtest86 requires that Linux be installed to run. True or False?
2. Memtest86 memory testing stops after how many passes?
   a. 1
   b. 2
   c. 8
   d. 16
   e. It never stops.
3. You can install Memtest86 on your hard disk and boot it quickly when you start your computer. True or False?
4. If Memtest86 discovers one or more errors with your memory and you have two memory devices (DIMM, SIMM, and so on), what do you do to determine which memory module is bad? Assume that you have no documentation for your computer's motherboard.
5. Linux can be configured to work with memory that has errors. True or False?

Lab 2.4 Research Hardware Support

Objectives

In this exercise, you research to see how well Linux supports the latest hardware, such as USB version 2.0 and IEEE 1394 (FireWire). You can find this hardware on many new computers.

Materials Required

This lab requires the following:

- A computer running either Windows (any version) or Linux
- An Internet connection and a Web browser

NOTE This lab explores information on the World Wide Web. Because Web pages can change without notice, what you see may not exactly match the terminology described in this lab. You may have to use your judgement to find the best match for links described here. When in doubt, check with you instructor.

Activity Background

Assume that you want to purchase a notebook computer and you want to choose one that works with Linux. In this lab, you look at notebook computers from Hewlett-Packard, but you can substitute any notebook computer manufacturer.

Estimated completion time: 30 minutes

LAB ACTIVITY

Activity

1. Enter **www.hp.com** into your Web browser, and press **Enter**. Follow the links on the Web site for business notebook computers. Look at the technical specifications for a few of the models.
2. Pay attention to the technical specs for interfaces or ports. Notice than most or all of these computers have one or more USB 2.0 ports. One way to see if Linux supports USB 2.0 is to do some research.

NOTE

If the computer vendor does not indicate the USB version, chances are good that it is not the latest version, which is 2.0 at the time of this book's publication.

3. Use Google to search for USB 2.0 Linux support. Enter **www.google.com** into your Web browser. Enter **linux usb** into the Google search box and click the Google Search button. Note the large number of sites found.
4. Click the listing for the Linux USB Project at **www.linux-usb.org**, which should be at or near the top of the list.
5. Click the **Linux and USB 2.0** link under **Other Helpful Links**. This page describes the differences between USB 2.0 and earlier versions—primarily USB 1.1. Notice the speed differences between the various USB versions.
6. Many HP notebook computers also have IEEE 1394 ports (also called FireWire). Learn about FireWire by visiting the 1394 Trade Association Web site. Enter **www.1394ta.org** into your Web browser. You can find introductory information by clicking the **About Technology** and **FAQ** links on the right side of the screen.
7. Use Google and search for **linux firewire**. Again, you see a large number of sites found.
8. Click the listing for the IEEE 1394 for Linux site (**www.linux1394.org**).
9. Click the **Introduction** link and notice that IEEE 1394 is called FireWire by Apple Computer, and it is called i.Link by Sony. The HP notebook computers refer to the interface as IEEE 1394. All of these terms refer to the same thing.

At the time of this book's publication, Sony uses proprietary chips for i.Link that are not yet supported by Linux. A Sony VAIO may be a poor choice if you need IEEE 1394 support from your notebook. However, as the VAIO is a popular and highly-regarded product, Linux support is likely in the future.

10. Go back to the 1394 Trade Association Web site by entering **www.1394ta.org** into your Web browser. Click the **Compliance Logo Testing Program** link. This page displays the logos that are used for FireWire and i.Link. You may see one of these logos on the computers and devices that have IEEE 1394 ports.
11. Go back to the IEEE 1394 for Linux Web site by entering **www.linux1394.org** into your Web browser. Click the **Compatibility** link. You're at the Hardware Compatibility List page. From here, you can see if your IEEE 1394 device is listed and how well it works with Linux.

Certification Objectives

Objectives for the Linux+ exam:

- Identify all system hardware required (e.g., CPU, memory, drive space, scalability) and check compatibility with Linux distribution (1.1)
- Identify and configure removable system hardware (e.g., PCMCIA, USB, IEEE 1394) (6.3)

Review Questions

1. What is the latest USB version?
2. What is the maximum speed of USB 1.1?
   a. 1 Mb/s (megabit/second)
   b. 12 Mb/s
   c. 480 Mb/s
   d. 1 Gb/s (gigabit/second)
3. What is the maximum speed of USB 2.0?
   a. 1 Mb/s
   b. 12 Mb/s
   c. 480 Mb/s
   d. 1 Gb/s
4. FireWire is a faster version of IEEE 1394. True or False?
5. FireWire and i.Link are both based on IEEE 1394 but they are different. A FireWire hard disk drive cannot be used with an i.Link computer. True or False?

CHAPTER THREE

LINUX INSTALLATION AND USAGE

Labs included in this chapter

CompTIA Linux+ Exam Objectives

Objective		Lab
1.8	Configure boot manager (e.g., LILO, ELILO, GRUB, multiple boot options)	3.1
2.9	Access and write data to a recordable media	3.2
6.2	Diagnose hardware issues using Linux tools (e.g., /proc, disk utilities, ifconfig, /dev, KNOPPIX, BBC)	3.2
N/A	These lab exercises do not directly address Linux+ objectives, but provide additional background information to help you master the objectives and understand the Linux operating system.	3.3, 3.4, 3.5

Lab 3.1 Locating the Kernel File

Objectives

The goal of this lab is to learn how to find the kernel file on your hard disk.

Materials Required

This lab requires the following:

- A working Linux system
- Access to the root account

Activity Background

The Linux kernel is typically stored on your hard disk in an ordinary file. This allows your system to boot quickly. There are a few reasons why you should know where this file is located. You might want to create a boot disk, as you'll do in Lab 3.2, or you may need to modify your boot loader (LILO or GRUB) configuration file, and knowing the kernel file's name and location is required for either task.

Estimated completion time: 10 Minutes

Activity

1. If your computer is currently displaying a graphical desktop, such as GNOME or KDE, switch to a command-line terminal (tty) by pressing **Ctrl+Alt+F2** and log in as root.
2. Most Linux distributions place the kernel file in the /boot directory but it can be located anywhere. Some distributions place the kernel in the root (/) directory. Go to the /boot directory by entering the **cd /boot** command.
3. Display the files in the directory by entering **ls -loS**. This tells the **ls** program to do a long directory listing (**-l**), to suppress printing the group (**o**) owner, and to reverse sort the files by file size (**S**). The first file displayed (the largest file) is most likely the kernel file. In this example from a Fedora Core 2 system, the kernel file is vmlinuz-2.6.5-1.358:

```
total 1659
-rw-r--r--  1 root 1199031 May  8 06:21 vmlinuz-2.6.5-1.358
-rw-r--r--  1 root  239593 May  8 06:21 System.map-2.6.5-1.358
-rw-r--r--  1 root  189785 Sep 16  1999 initrd-2.6.5-1.358.img
-rw-r--r--  1 root   46375 May  8 06:21 config-2.6.5-1.358
drwx------  2 root   12288 Sep 15  1999 lost+found
drwxr-xr-x  2 root    1024 Sep 16  1999 grub
```

4. There may be more than one kernel file on your system. If so, how can you tell which one is being used to boot your system? The answer is to look at your boot loader's configuration file. For a Fedora Core 2 system, the boot loader file is normally /etc/grub.conf. Display its contents by entering **cat /etc/grub.conf**. When the file is displayed, ignore any comments at the start of the file. Comments are lines that start with a #. Here's an example of what the file contains (minus comments):

```
default=0
timeout=10
splashimage=(hd0,0)/grub/splash.xpm.gz
title Fedora Core (2.6.5-1.358)
     root (hd0,0)
     kernel /boot/vmlinuz-2.6.5-1.358 ro root=LABEL=/
 rhgb quiet
     initrd /initrd-2.6.5-1.358.img
```

The sixth line identifies the kernel file as /boot/vmlinuz-2.6.5-1.358.

If GRUB is configured to boot from more than one kernel, you would see two title sections in the /etc/grub.conf file similar to this:

```
default=0
timeout=10
splashimage=(hd0,0)/grub/splash.xpm.gz
title Fedora Core (2.6.5-1.358)
     root (hd0,0)
     kernel /boot/vmlinuz-2.6.5-1.358 ro root=LABEL=/
 rhgb quiet
     initrd /initrd-2.6.5-1.358.img
title Slackware
     root (hd0,1)
     kernel /boot/vmlinuz root=/dev/had2
     initrd /boot initrd.img
```

5. Your system might be using the LILO boot loader rather than the GRUB boot loader. If so, the configuration file is /etc/lilo.conf. You can display its contents by typing **cat /etc/lilo.conf**. Here's an example of the file's contents:

```
boot = /dev/hda
message = /boot/boot_message.txt
prompt
timeout = 1200
vga = normal
image = /boot/vmlinuz
  root = /dev/hda1
  label = Linux
  read-only
```

The sixth line indicates that the kernel file is /boot/vmlinuz.

6. Linux kernels are not required to have certain file names. Any names can be used. You can name your kernel file mykernel or mycolonel, for example. Given that you can't tell a kernel file by its name, how can you tell if a file is a kernel file? It is simple: you use the file program. Enter **file *name***, where ***name*** is the name of the file you want to test. For example, on a Fedora Core 2 system, enter **file /boot/vmlinuz-2.6.5-1.358**. You see this:

```
/boot/vmlinuz-2.6.5-1.358: x86 boot sector
```

Certification Objectives

Objectives for the Linux+ exam:

➤ Configure boot manager (e.g., LILO, ELILO, GRUB, multiple boot options) (1.8)

Review Questions

1. Most Linux distributions place the kernel file in which directory?
   a. the root (/) directory
   b. /boot
   c. /etc
   d. /loader
2. If there is more than one kernel file on your system, how can you tell which one the system uses to boot Linux?
3. Which are the two most popular boot loader programs used with Linux?
   a. rpm and dpkg
   b. file and ls
   c. LILO and GRUB
   d. / and /boot
4. If you're using the LILO boot loader, which is its configuration file?
   a. /boot/lilo
   b. /boot/lilo.conf
   c. /etc/lilo
   d. /etc/lilo.conf
5. Which program tells you if a file is a kernel file?
   a. kernel
   b. file
   c. ls -k
   d. which

Lab 3.2 Creating a Boot Disk

Objectives

The goal of this lab is to learn another way of creating a Linux boot disk anytime after you've installed Linux.

Materials Required

This lab requires the following:

- A working Linux system
- A high-density 3.5-inch disk
- Access to the root account

Activity Background

Chapter 2 in the main text tells you that you can create a Linux boot disk while you're installing Linux. This disk can be used to boot your system should there be some problem with Linux boot-related files (such as LILO or GRUB files) on your hard disk. Other operating systems refer to this disk as an Emergency Repair Disk or some other similar name. Don't confuse this boot disk with the one you'd use if your computer can't boot from your Linux CD-ROM.

Estimated completion time: 20 Minutes

LAB ACTIVITY

Activity

1. Insert a formatted, high-density 3.5-inch disk into the appropriate drive of your computer. The disk must be a capacity greater than the 1.44 MB Microsoft format. Format the disk to a 1.722 MB format by entering:

   fdformat /dev/fd0u1722

   The format process may take a few minutes. If you see any error messages, such as sector errors, you should try a new disk.
2. Place an MS-DOS file system on the disk by entering **mformat a:**
3. Place the syslinux book loader on the disk by entering **syslinux /dev/fd0**
4. Mount the disk by entering **mount –t msdos /dev/fd0 /mnt/floppy**
5. Copy the kernel to the disk by entering:

   cp /boot/vmlinuz-2.6.5-1.358 /mnt/floppy/kernel2.6

6. Copy the initial ramdisk to the disk by entering:

   cp /boot/initrd-2.6.5-1.358.img /mnt/floppy/initrd2.6

7. You need to know which disk partition holds your root file system. Enter:

   mount | grep ' / '

   You see something similar to this:

   `/dev/hda1 on / type ext3 (rw)`

   This line tells you that your root file system is on device /dev/hda 1. You'll need this information in Step 9.

8. You must now create a configuration file for the syslinux boot loader. Use the **nano** editor for this. Enter **nano /mnt/floppy/syslinux.cfg**

9. Enter these lines, but do not press the Enter key after you enter the second line. Note that if your root file system is not /dev/hda1 (from Step 7) substitute your device name in the root= statement.

   Default kernel2.6

   Append initrd=initrd2.6 root=/dev/hda1

10. Press **Ctrl+O** to save the file. Press **Enter** to confirm.

11. Press **Ctrl+X** to exit the editor.

12. In Step 10, the file was not written to the 3.5-inch disk immediately. Force it to do so by entering **sync** and waiting for the command prompt to reappear.

13. Unmount the disk by entering **umount /dev/fd0**

14. Reboot the computer. It should now boot from the 3.5-inch disk. Once the Linux kernel loads from this disk, it begins using your hard disk.

Certification Objectives

Objectives for the Linux+ exam:

- Access and write data to a recordable media (2.9)
- Diagnose hardware issues using Linux tools (e.g., /proc, disk utilities, ifconfig, /dev, KNOPPIX, BBC) (6.2)

Review Questions

1. Which program is used to format a 3.5-inch disk to another capacity?
   a. fdisk
   b. mke2fs
   c. fdformat
   d. mformat

2. When you create a Linux boot disk, as you did in this lab, and boot from it, what disk is used when the system boots up completely?
   a. the boot disk
   b. your system's hard disk
   c. a virtual disk in system memory
   d. a ramdisk
3. It's best to use only high-density disks when you make a boot disk. True or False?
4. Which program is used to place an MS-DOS file system on a 3.5-inch disk?
   a. fdisk
   b. mke2fs
   c. fdformat
   d. mformat
5. When you save a file to a 3.5-inch disk, it is written to the disk immediately. You can remove the disk from the drive with high confidence that the file is on the disk. True or False?

Lab 3.3 Seeing Everything as a File

Objectives

The goal of this lab is to see that Linux, like UNIX, is file oriented in its behavior and treats all (or most) devices as if they were files.

Materials Required

This lab requires the following:

- A working Linux system
- Access to the root account

Activity Background

Chapter 3 in the main text introduces the concept of terminals and shows you how to move between them with Alt or Ctrl+Alt key sequences. These terminals are devices. Most or all devices in Linux can be treated as files. This activity shows you how to read from them and write to them. The practical applications for writing strings (or other data) to other terminal screens may seem elusive now, but you'll appreciate this flexibility as you gain more experience with Linux. The ability to send output to specific terminal screens is particularly useful when you write your own shell scripts and when you configure your system for logging. These topics will be covered in later chapters.

Estimated completion time: 15 Minutes

LAB ACTIVITY

Activity

1. If your computer is currently displaying a graphical desktop, press **Ctrl+Alt+F2** to go to a command prompt.
2. Log in as root.
3. Enter this command:

   echo "Hello from tty2" > /dev/tty5

   This tells Linux to send the string "Hello from tty2" to the device tty5.

NOTE

The letters "tty" are an abbreviation for teletype, an obsolete electromechanical terminal popular in the early days of computing. Linux and UNIX use this abbreviation to refer to modern-day consoles. To refer to a tty, Linux requires that you precede the name with /dev/.

4. Switch to tty5 by pressing **Alt+F5** and log in as root. You now see the string "Hello from tty2" appear on this terminal screen as in this example:

```
Fedora Core release 2 (Tettnang)
Kernel 2.6.5-1.358 on an i686

localhost login:Hello from tty2
```

NOTE

Just because you wrote a message to tty5 and it happened to appear next to a login prompt doesn't mean that you've now told the system that you want to log in as user "Hello from tty2." Any running program that happens to be using tty5 (in this case, the login program) is unaware that you just wrote to its screen.

5. From tty5, write to tty2 with this command:

   echo "Hello yourself" > /dev/tty2

6. Press **Alt+F2** to go back to tty2. Notice that the string "Hello yourself" appears here.
7. So far, you've simply sent text messages to other terminals. You can also copy one device to another. One interesting device is the random number generator, called /dev/urandom. Copy random numbers to tty5 with this command:

   cat /dev/urandom > /dev/tty5

   You'll likely hear your computer's speaker beeping. This is normal.
8. Switch to tty5 by pressing **Alt+F5**. Your screen should be rapidly filling with characters and scrolling as random characters are displayed.

NOTE The random numbers from /dev/urandom don't appear as normal decimal numbers. These are binary numbers that the tty interprets as characters.

9. Stop the random numbers from being displayed on tty5 by pressing **Ctrl+C** when you're in tty2.
10. To go back to your graphical desktop, press **Alt+F7**.

Certification Objectives

This lab does not directly map to a certification objective; however, it gives background information that will help you master the objectives and understand the Linux operating system.

Review Questions

1. Which of the following examples is the proper way of referring to terminals in Linux commands?
   a. tty5
   b. device:tty5
   c. /dev/tty5
   d. tty:5
2. If you send a string to a tty that is being used by a program, is the program aware that you wrote to its screen?
3. Suppose there was a device called /dev/dice that produced random numbers between 1 and 6 (simulating the role of a die). What command would you use to display these numbers to tty6?
   a. **cat /dev/dice > /dev/tty6**
   b. **cat /dev/dice > tty6**
   c. **cat dice > /dev/tty6**
   d. **cat dice > tty6**
4. What's the reason for not using virtual console 1 (/dev/tty1) for these lab exercises?
   a. Virtual consoles are numbered starting at 0, and there is no F0 function key.
   b. Virtual console 1 is frequently used by the graphical subsystem.

c. Old teletype machines couldn't operate as the first console, so Linux honors the same restriction.

d. The root user can't log in to virtual console 1.

Lab 3.4 Giving Shutdown Notification

Objectives

The goal of this lab is to learn how to shut down a Linux system in such a way that users are notified of the shutdown.

Materials Required

This lab requires the following:

- A working Linux system
- Access to the root account
- Access to an ordinary user account

Activity Background

When Linux computers are networked, and one computer's resources are being used by others, it's useful to notify all users when the system is being shut down. This gives users a chance to save their data and exit their applications before the shutdown. The Linux shutdown program can do this automatically when you specify a message on the command line.

Previous versions of the shutdown program that were used by Linux distributions, such as Red Hat Linux 7.3, allowed more ways of specifying relative time before a shutdown occurred. For example, you could use +5m, 5m, or 5 to mean shutdown in 5 minutes. The version of the shutdown program in Fedora Core 2 does not allow the +5m or 5m syntax. You can use +5 or 5.

Estimated completion time: 30 Minutes

LAB ACTIVITY

Activity

1. If your computer is currently displaying a graphical desktop, press **Ctrl+Alt+F2** to go to a command prompt.
2. Log in as the root user.

3. Tell Linux to shut down five minutes from now by entering this command:

   shutdown -h +5 The system is going down

   You see the following messages appear on your screen:

   ```
   The system is going down
   The system is going DOWN for system halt in 5 minutes !!
   ```

4. Wait about four minutes, and you see these additional lines displayed on your screen:

   ```
   Broadcast message from root (tty2) Mon Aug 5 08:48:36 2003...
   The system is going down
   The system is going DOWN for system halt in 1 minute !!
   ```

   The system is warning you that the system will be shutting down in one minute.

5. Press **Ctrl+C** to abort the shutdown.

6. Try this again:

   shutdown -h 5 The system is going down

   You see the familiar message:

   ```
   The system is going down
   The system is going DOWN for system halt in 5 minutes !!
   ```

7. Now go to tty5 with **Alt+F5**. Try to log in as an ordinary user. After you're prompted for your password and you enter it, you see something similar to this:

   ```
   The system is going down on Tue Aug 3 09:12:11 2004
   The system is shutting down
   Login incorrect
   login:
   ```

   The system is preventing you from logging in because it knows that it's shutting itself down soon. There's no point in allowing you to log in when a system shutdown is imminent. If you schedule a system shutdown farther in advance, are users still prevented from logging in during that time?

8. Go back to tty2 with **Alt+F2**. Press **Ctrl+C** to abort the shutdown. Schedule a shutdown for seven minutes:

   shutdown -h 7 The system is going down

9. Go to tty5 with **Alt+F5** and try to log in as the ordinary user (log out of root if necessary by using **logout**). Do this quickly—in under two minutes. You can now log in. Linux allows users to log in if the shutdown is scheduled more than five minutes away. Enter **logout**

10. Go back to tty2 with **Alt+F2** and abort the shutdown with **Ctrl+C**. Now do another shutdown for four minutes:

    shutdown -h +4 The system is going down

11. Now go back to tty5 with **Alt+F5** and try to log in as an ordinary user. The system prevents you from logging in.
12. Now log in as root. You can log in. Linux allows the root user to log in even when the shutdown is scheduled to occur in less than five minutes. The obvious reason for this is to allow a root user to cancel a system shutdown or to do something important before the shutdown occurs.
13. This is an optional step. The time required to perform this step is not included in the estimated completion time for this lab exercise. Enter the following command and note when Linux displays shutdown warning messages to your screen:

    shutdown -h +61 The system is going down

Certification Objectives

This lab does not directly map to a certification objective; however, it gives background information that will help you master the objectives and understand the Linux operating system.

Review Questions

1. When using Fedora Core 2, are these three commands equivalent?

   Shutdown -h +5m

   Shutdown -h 5m

   Shutdown -h 5

2. When you run the shutdown command, all ordinary users are prevented from logging in to the system no matter how far into the future the shutdown is scheduled. True or False?
3. Which user is always allowed to log in during a scheduled shutdown regardless of the time left before the shutdown is to occur?
4. Why is the root user allowed to log in to the system during the last five minutes of a scheduled system shutdown but ordinary users are not?
5. (Answer this question if you completed the optional Step 13.) If you use the command **shutdown –h 61m The system is going down**, when are users notified that the system is going down?

Lab 3.5 Assigning Shutdown Permissions

Objectives

Who should be allowed to shut down a Linux system? Clearly, the root user should, but should other users? This lab exercise explores this issue.

Materials Required

This lab requires the following:

- A working Linux system
- Access to the root account
- Access to two ordinary user accounts

Activity Background

Normally, Linux shuts down when the Ctrl+Alt+Del key sequence is pressed at a console, regardless of what user or users are logged in, or whose fingers are pressing the keys. Essentially, anyone can shut down Linux if they can touch the keyboard. In situations such as servers, this is not secure. You can configure Linux to only shut down if an authorized user is logged in.

Estimated completion time: 30 Minutes

Activity

1. If your computer is currently running any programs (such as a Web browser or text editor), stop them. You're going to shut down your system in the next step, and it's best for you to stop any programs so you don't lose your data or work.
2. If your computer is currently displaying a graphical desktop, press **Ctrl+Alt+F2** to go to a command prompt. Press **Ctrl+Alt+Del**. Because you're logged in as the root user, the system shuts down.
3. When the system reboots, log in as an ordinary user. If your computer is currently displaying a graphical desktop, press **Ctrl+Alt+F2** to go to a command prompt, then log in as an ordinary user.
4. Press **Ctrl+Alt+Del** to shut down the system. Notice that the system reboots even though you're not logged in as the root user.
5. When the system reboots, press **Ctrl+Alt+F2** to go to a command prompt, then log in as the root user.

6. Create a user called beth by entering **useradd beth**
7. Assign beth a password using the **passwd** program. Enter **passwd beth**. You see this:

```
Changing password for user beth.
New UNIX password:
```

8. Enter a password for user beth that you'll remember. You are prompted to enter the password a second time.
9. Create another user called tom using Steps 6, 7, and 8 as a guide.
10. Create a shutdown.allow file in the /etc directory and enter the name of a user by entering this command:

    echo "beth" > /etc/shutdown.allow

11. Edit the /etc/inittab file using your favorite text editor.
12. Locate this line:

```
Id:5:initdefault:
```

And change it to this:

```
Id:3:initdefault
```

13. Locate this line:

```
ca:ctrlaltdel:/sbin/shutdown -t3 -r now
```

And change it to this:

```
ca:ctrlaltdel:/sbin/shutdown -a -t3 -r now
```

14. Reboot the system by pressing **Ctrl+Alt+Del**.
15. When the system reboots, the graphical desktop does not load. You see a text login prompt. Log in as tom.
16. Try to shut down the system by pressing **Ctrl+Alt+Del**. You see this message:

```
Shutdown: no authorized users logged in.
```

You can't shut down the system because you're not the root user and your account name does not appear in the /etc/shutdown.allow file.

17. Switch to another console by pressing **Alt+F3**. Log in as beth.
18. Press **Ctrl+Alt+Del**. The system shuts down because beth's name appears in the /etc/shutdown.allow file.
19. Edit the /etc/inittab file using your favorite text editor.

20. Locate this line:

    `Id:3:initdefault:`

    And change it to this:

    `Id:5:initdefault`

21. Locate this line:

    `ca:ctrlaltdel:/sbin/shutdown -a -t3 -r now`

    And change it to this:

    `ca:ctrlaltdel:/sbin/shutdown -t3 -r now`

22. Reboot the system by pressing **Ctrl+Alt+Del**. It should boot into the graphical interface.

Certification Objectives

This lab does not directly map to a certification objective; however, it gives background information that will help you master the objectives and understand the Linux operating system.

Review Questions

1. Normally, Linux can be shut down by the root user. True or False?
2. Normally, Linux can be shut down by any user who is logged in to the system. True or False?
3. Normally, Linux can be shut down by anyone whose fingers can touch the keyboard. True or False?
4. It's possible to restrict who can shut down the system. True or False?
5. What command shows you who is logged in to the system?
   a. **ls**
   b. **w**
   c. **df**
   d. **dd**

CHAPTER FOUR

EXPLORING LINUX FILESYSTEMS

Labs included in this chapter

CompTIA Linux+ Exam Objectives

Objective		Lab
2.19	Create, modify, and use basic shell scripts	4.1, 4.2, 4.3, 4.4
N/A	This lab exercise does not directly address Linux+ objectives, but provides additional background information to help you master the objectives and understand the Linux operating system.	4.5

Lab 4.1 Creating Complex Functions with Simple Commands

Objectives

The goal of this lab is to create complex functions by stringing two or more simple Linux commands together. Linux commands can be connected using pipes, where the output of one command feeds the input of another. After completing this lab, you will be able to:

- Display data that pauses at each screen full
- Display text strings that are embedded in binary data
- Filter a data stream based on a word

Materials Required

This lab requires the following:

- Access as a root user on a computer running Linux

Estimated completion time:	15 Minutes

LAB ACTIVITY

Activity

1. Switch to a command-line terminal (tty2) by pressing **Ctrl+Alt+F2**, and log in to the terminal as the root user.
2. This lab uses the bash man page file. Fedora places this man page file in the /usr/share/man/man1 directory. Discover the exact filename for the man page by entering **ls –l /usr/share/man/man1/bash***. You should see something similar to this (for example, more files may be listed):

   ```
   -rw-r—r--  1 root root 64921 Mar 11 03:19 bash.1.gz
   ```

3. The bash man page file is compressed. You have to uncompress it. Enter **gunzip /usr/share/man/man1/bash.1.gz**. The file should now be uncompressed and is called bash.1. The gunzip program removes the .gz file extension after the file is uncompressed.
4. The bash.1 file is a plain text file. You can read the file with numerous text-oriented programs such as **cat**, **more**, and **less**. First, make the /usr/share/man/man1 directory your current directory by entering the following command **cd /usr/share/man/man1**.
5. Enter **cat bash.1**. Your screen scrolls for a long time because the file is large. You don't have to wait for the screen to stop scrolling. You can abort it by pressing **Ctrl+C**.

6. Because your screen is probably scrolling faster than you can read, use a program such as more to display the text a page at a time. The more program displays a page of text, and then stops and waits for you to press a key before displaying the next page. Enter **cat bash.1 | more**. You see the first page of text.

7. Press any key to see the next page of text. If you don't want to view the entire file, you can exit more and get back to the command prompt by typing **q**.
8. The more program doesn't allow you to go back in the file to see text that appeared on earlier pages. This is a feature of the less program. Enter **less bash.1** and use the Page Down and Page Up keys to move forward and backward in the file. When you have finished, press **q** to exit from the less program.
9. You can use the **grep** program to display only those lines of text that contain certain words. The grep program filters out lines that do not contain the specified string. Enter **cat bash.1 | grep input**. In this case, you're asking grep to filter out lines that do not contain the string "input." Many lines containing the word input are written to the screen, and the screen scrolls.
10. You can use the more or less programs to view all the text from the previous step. Enter **cat bash.1 | grep input | more** and notice that the screen stops after filling the page. Exit from the more or the less program by pressing **q**.
11. Leave the bash.1 file uncompressed. You'll use it in the next lab exercise.
12. Enter **logout** to log out of the system, and press **Alt+F7** to go back to your graphical screen.

Certification Objectives

Objectives for the Linux+ exam:

- Create, modify, and use basic shell scripts (2.19)

Review Questions

1. In which directory are man pages located in Fedora Linux?
   a. /etc/man
   b. /var/man
   c. /usr/sbin/man
   d. /usr/share/man
2. Man pages are normally stored in a compressed form. True or False?

3. If you want to find certain strings in a file, you filter the file's contents with which program?
   a. ls
   b. grep
   c. strings
   d. less
4. Which program would you use if you want to control when your screen scrolls?
   a. ls
   b. cat
   c. grep
   d. more
5. The less program has functionality that is similar to which other program?
   a. ls
   b. more
   c. grep
   d. cat

Lab 4.2 Performing Complex Searches

Objectives

The goal of this lab is to see how regular expressions and the grep programs may be used to do complex searches of documents. Regular expressions are useful for searching for lines in a text file or data stream that contain certain strings. Sometimes, however, there's a need to find lines based on more complex criteria. For example, if you want to extract lines from a file or data stream that contains two words that are not adjacent to one another, it may be difficult for you to create a regular expression that handles this.

A simple solution is to use two grep filters, each searching for one of the words. Any lines that pass through both filters contain both words.

Materials Required

This lab requires the following:

- Access as an ordinary user to a computer running Linux

Estimated completion time: 15 Minutes

Activity

LAB ACTIVITY

1. Switch to a command-line terminal (tty2) by pressing **Ctrl+Alt+F2**, and log in to the terminal as the root user.
2. Move to the /usr/share/man/man1 directory. To do this, enter **cd /usr/share/man/man1**.
3. Enter **cat bash.1 | grep display | less**. Notice that all the displayed lines contain the word "display" in all lowercase letters. Press **q** to quit.
4. Enter **cat bash.1 | grep Display | less**. Notice that all the displayed lines contain the word "Display" that starts with an uppercase letter. Press **q** to quit.
5. Searches using grep are normally case sensitive. You can search in a case-insensitive manner by using the **-i** option. Enter **cat bash.1 | grep -i display | less**. You see lines displayed that contain both "display" and "Display." Press **q** to quit.
6. Make the search more complex by searching for more than one word. Enter **cat bash.1 | grep –I display | grep history**. There's no need to pipe the output to the less filter because it's unlikely that there will be more than a few lines that match. You see a few lines displayed that contain the case-insensitive word "display" and the case-sensitive word "history."
7. Use grep to search for regular expressions. Enter **cat bash.1 | grep ^When | grep script**. The caret (^) indicates that grep should search for the word "When" at the start of a line. This is a simple regular expression. You see a line that contains the word "When" at the start of the line, and the word "script" elsewhere in the line.
8. You uncompressed the bash.1 file in Step 3 of the previous lab. It's fine to leave it in its uncompressed form now—the only impact is that it consumes a little more disk space. If you do want to restore it to its compressed form, enter **gzip bash.1**.
9. Enter **ls –l bash*** . You should see something similar to this:

   ```
   -rw-r—r--  1 root root 64921 Mar 11 03:19 bash.1.gz
   ```

   The file is compressed again. Notice that the file's date and time are the same as in Step 2 of the previous lab. When you use the gzip program to compress a file, the file's date and time is not changed.
10. Enter **logout** to log out of the system and press **Alt+F7** to go back to your graphical screen.

Certification Objectives

Objectives for the Linux+ exam:

- Create, modify, and use basic shell scripts (2.19)

Review Questions

1. Grep is normally case sensitive. True or False?
2. Which command allows you to search for strings regardless of the case of letters?
   a. **ls**
   b. **ls -l**
   c. **grep**
   d. **grep -i**
3. Grep can search a data stream for either literal strings or regular expressions. True or False?
4. Complex regular expressions can often be avoided by using two or more grep commands piped to one another. True or False?
5. Linux restricts you to piping only two commands together such as **ls | more**. You cannot have more than one pipe as in **ls | sort | more**. True or False?

Lab 4.3 Doing More with Less

Objectives

The goal of this lab is to see how programs, such as less, have numerous command-line options and interactive commands that allow you to move through text files.

Materials Required

This lab requires the following:

- Access as an ordinary user to a computer running Linux

Activity Background

Most Linux systems have an English word list installed that may be used by system utility programs or application programs. This word list is a plain text file, called **words**, in the /usr/share/dict directory. The file has one word per line and is alphabetized. You use this file for this lab exercise.

Estimated completion time: 15 Minutes

LAB ACTIVITY

Activity

1. Switch to a command-line terminal (tty2) by pressing **Ctrl+Alt+F2**, and log in to the terminal using any username.
2. Move to the /usr/share/dict directory. To do this, enter **cd /usr/share/dict**.
3. Display the word list file with the less command. Enter **less words**. You can see that the word list file has one word per line, and the file is alphabetized.
4. You can move forward through the file (toward the end of the file) and backward (toward the beginning of the file). Use the **spacebar** to move forward by one screen. Type **b** to move backward by one screen.
5. You can move to the beginning of the file at any time by typing **g**. You can go to the end of the file by typing **G**. Type **g** to go to the beginning of the file.
6. You can search for a word in the word list using the forward slash, followed by the search word. For example, enter **/Monday**. The screen displays the word "Monday" on the top line of the screen.
7. Normally, searching is case sensitive. That is, you won't find "**Monday**" if you search for "**monday**." You can make searching case insensitive with the **-i** command. Enter **-i**. A message about case-insensitive searching appears, and you are asked to press the **Return** key—do so. Now you can search for words regardless of case.
8. Type **g** to go to the beginning of the file. Enter **/monday** followed by the **Enter** key and the word "Monday" appears at the top of the screen.
9. Exit the less command by typing **q**.
10. Enter **logout** to log out of the system and press **Alt+F7** to go back to your graphical screen.

Certification Objectives

Objectives for the Linux+ exam:

- Create, modify, and use basic shell scripts (2.19)

Review Questions

1. Which less command allows you to move to the beginning of a file?
   a. **g**
   b. **G**
   c. **b**
   d. **B**
2. Which less command allows you to move to the end of a file?
   a. **g**
   b. **G**
   c. **b**
   d. **B**
3. What character do you enter to tell less that you want to search?
   a. **g**
   b. **/**
   c. **spacebar**
   d. **b**
4. What do you enter to tell less that you want to do a case-insensitive search?
   a. **G**
   b. **i**
   c. **-i**
   d. **z**

Lab 4.4 Displaying Binary Data

Objectives

The goal of this lab is to see how you can display binary data files in a variety of formats, such as decimal, hexadecimal, and octal.

Materials Required

This lab requires the following:

- Access as an ordinary user to a computer running Linux

Activity Background

It's sometimes necessary to search through binary files to locate text strings. The text string might tell you the version number of a program or data file. It may be easier to view the binary file directly rather than using the program with which you'd normally access the file. Whenever you need to view binary data, the tools that you use sometimes convert the data into a form that is convenient to use, but sometimes not. The **od** program is such a tool. Normally, od assumes that the binary data you want to view is a program rather than just binary data. The problem with this assumption is that it may swap bytes around so the first byte of the file appears after the second byte, the fourth byte appears before the third, and so on.

This is a reasonable thing to do if you're a programmer looking at a dump of a program running on a computer that stores a program's bytes in memory this way. It's the wrong thing to do if you just want to look at simple binary data. This lab exercise uses examples that display bytes in the same order as they appear in the file. Chances are good that this is the way you prefer to see it.

Estimated completion time: 30 Minutes

LAB ACTIVITY

Activity

1. Switch to a command-line terminal (tty2) by pressing **Ctrl+Alt+F2**, and log in to the terminal using any username.
2. Go to your home directory. You can do this from anywhere by typing **cd ~**.
3. You need a small file containing binary data. Create one by borrowing data from a program file. Enter **dd count=1 bs=65 if=/bin/sh of=bindata**. This creates a file called **bindata** in your home directory. The file contains the first 65 bytes of data from the file /bin/sh, which is usually the BASH shell on most Linux systems. Check out the man page for the **dd** command (**man dd**) if you want to see exactly how the **dd** command works.
4. By default, the od program is supposed to display data in decimal form, according to the man page. However, it seems that the od program included with Fedora Core 2 doesn't do that. Enter **od bindata**. You see something similar to this:

```
0000000 042577 043114 000401 000001 000000 000000 000000  000000
0000020 000002 000003 000001 000000 111600 004005 000064  000000
0000040 165464 000007 000000 000000 000064 000040 000006  000050
0000060 000031 000030 000006 000000 000064 000000 100064  004004
0000100 000064
0000101
```

This default format is not likely to be useful to you. The following steps produce more useful results.

5. If you prefer to view the file in hexadecimal form, enter **od -A x -t x1 bindata**. The file offsets and data are both in hexadecimal. You see something similar to this:

```
000000 7f 45 4c 46 01 01 01 00 00 00 00 00 00 00 00 00
000010 02 00 03 00 01 00 00 00 80 93 05 08 34 00 00 00
000020 34 eb 07 00 00 00 00 00 34 00 20 00 06 00 28 00
000030 19 00 18 00 06 00 00 00 34 00 00 00 34 80 04 08
000040 34
000041
```

6. If you prefer to view the file in decimal form, enter **od -A d -t u1 bindata**. The file offsets and data are both in decimal. You see something similar to this:

```
0000000 127  69  76  70   1   1   1   0   0   0   0   0   0   0   0   0
0000016   2   0   3   0   1   0   0   0 128 147   5   8  52   0   0   0
0000032  52 235   7   0   0   0   0   0  52   0  32   0   6   0  40   0
0000048  25   0  24   0   6   0   0   0  52   0   0   0  52 128   4   8
0000064  52
0000065
```

7. Sometimes the data file contains plain text, but there are nonprintable characters in the file as well. You can view these nonprintable characters in their mnemonic form. The mnemonics are abbreviations standardized by the ASCII code. Enter **od -A d -t a bindata**. You see something similar to this:

```
0000000 del   E   L   F soh soh soh nul nul nul nul nul nul nul nul nul
0000016 stx nul etx nul soh nul nul nul nul dc3 enq  bs   4 nul nul nul
0000032   4   k bel nul nul nul nul nul   4 nul  sp nul ack nul   ( nul
0000048  em nul can nul ack nul nul nul   4 nul nul nul   4 nul eot  bs
0000064   4
0000065
```

In the above example, the first byte is a DEL character also called RUB or RUBOUT in older ASCII codes. This is a mnemonic. The second character is an uppercase E. The fifth character is another mnemonic, SOH, which stands for Start Of Heading in the ASCII code.

8. Enter **logout** to log out of the system and press **Alt+F7** to go back to your graphical screen.

Certification Objectives

Objectives for the Linux+ exam:

- Create, modify, and use basic shell scripts (2.19)

Review Questions

1. Which program can be used to copy a certain number of bytes from one file into another?
   a. strings
   b. dd
   c. grep
   d. cat
2. When you use the od program, which command-line option is used to specify that you want hexadecimal offsets?
   a. **-A x**
   b. **-a x**
   c. **-a**
   d. **-t x**
3. When you use the od program, which command-line option is used to specify that you want hexadecimal data?
   a. **-A x**
   b. **-a x**
   c. **-t x**
   d. **-t o**
4. When you use the od program, which command-line option is used to specify that you want decimal data?
   a. **-A x**
   b. **-a x**
   c. **-t u**
   d. **-t o**
5. When you use the od program, which command-line option is used to specify that you want decimal offsets?
   a. **-A d**
   b. **-a x**
   c. **-t u**
   d. **-t o**

Lab 4.5 Working with Unusual File and Directory Names

Objectives

The goal of this lab is to see how Linux file systems allow file and directory names to be virtually anything you like. You can use whatever characters you like in names.

Materials Required

This lab requires the following:

- Access as an ordinary user to a computer running Linux

Activity Background

If your computing career started with DOS or early versions of Windows, you may remember that there were severe restrictions on file and directory names with these operating systems. DOS restricted file and directory names to eight characters with an option extension that could be up to three characters. Early versions of Windows had the same restriction, but Windows 95 changed this so names could be up to 256 characters, but there were limitations on the characters that were allowed.

Later versions of Windows reduced the limitations, but some still remain. Linux has few limitations. You can create names using any characters you like. You just need to realize that some characters may conflict with your system's shell. Although conflicts can result, Linux usually has a way to work around the conflicts.

Estimated completion time: 20 Minutes

LAB ACTIVITY

Activity

1. Switch to a command-line terminal (tty2) by pressing **Ctrl+Alt+F2**, and log in to the terminal using any username.
2. Change your shell prompt so you can easily see what your current directory is at all times. Enter **PS1="\w:"** and press **Enter**. Your command-line prompt now shows the current working directory.
3. Chances are good that your current directory is your home directory. If so, the command prompt should be **~:**. If your current directory is not your home directory, go to your home directory by typing **cd ~** or **cd**.
4. The tilde (~) represents your home directory. If you want to see what the actual directory is, enter **pwd**. If you're logged in as user Betty, your home directory most likely is /home/betty, though it could be different depending on how the administrator set up the system.

5. Create a directory called **test** below your home directory by typing **mkdir test**. Make this your current directory by typing **cd ~/test**. Your command prompt is now **~/test:**.
6. Linux includes a program, called **touch**, that allows you to create a file that has no contents. You'll use it to quickly and easily create files. Enter **touch abc**. Now enter **ls**. You see the abc file listed.
7. Enter **touch ABC**. Then enter the **ls** command. You see both the abc and ABC files listed. Linux distinguishes between character case.
8. Use the touch program to create a very long file name. The name must be no longer than 256 characters. Enter **ls** and see how the long name is displayed. Enter **ls -l** and see how the name is displayed.
9. Delete the file with the very long name. Rather than typing the entire file name, take advantage of the BASH tab completion feature. Enter **rm** followed by a **space**. Enter the first few characters of the file name. Press **Tab**. The command line should now display the entire file name. Press **Enter**. Enter **y** to confirm the deletion. Confirm that the file is deleted by entering **ls**.
10. Linux, like DOS and Windows, uses the name consisting of a single period (dot) to represent the current directory. The name consisting of two periods (dot dot) represents the parent directory. You can see this by entering **ls -a**. You see the dot and dot dot directory entries listed.
11. Enter **touch . . .** (that's three periods). Enter **ls -a**. You see the . . . name in the listing. This is a file, not a directory. You can see this by entering **ls -al**, and noticing that the . . . entry does not begin the line with a d (directory). Note that you can't create file or directory names that consist of only periods in any version of Windows.
12. This doesn't mean that unusual names, like . . ., are limited to files. Enter **mkdir . . . .** (that's four periods). Enter **ls -al** to see that you've created a directory. The directory entry looks like this:

    ```
    drwxr-xr-x  2   ed    users     4096  Jan 24  15:31 ....
    ```

    Make .... your current directory by typing **cd ....** and then notice your command prompt.
13. File names that begin with a dash, such as **-n**, are allowed, but are awkward because many programs assume this is a command-line option. If, for example, you want to create such a file with the touch program, you'd have a problem. Enter **touch -n** and you see this error message:

    ```
    touch: invalid option -- n
    Try 'touch —help' for more information.
    ```

4

14. To convince touch to do what you want, you need to precede the file name with -- (two dashes). This tells touch that there are no more command-line options beyond this point. Enter **touch -- -n** followed by **ls -l**. You'll see that a file was created:

```
-rw-r-r- 1  ed   users   0  Jan 24  15:31 -n
```

15. If you want to edit the file with the vi editor, you have a problem if you enter **vi -n** because vi thinks that **-n** is an option that tells it not to use a swap file, and that you didn't enter a file name. The solution is **vi -- -n**, which tells vi that no other command-line options follow the -- sequence. It now interprets the **-n** as a file name.
16. If you want to erase the **-n** file, you also have to use the -- trick. Enter **rm -- -n** followed by **y** to confirm the deletion. Then enter **ls -al** to see that the file has been erased. You can exit the editor by entering **q**.
17. If you want to restore your command prompt to what it was before you performed Step 3, log out and log in again.
18. Enter **logout** to log out of the system, and press **Alt+F7** to go back to your graphical screen.

Certification Objectives

This lab exercise does not directly address Linux+ objectives, but provides additional background information to help you master the objectives and understand the Linux operating system.

Review Questions

1. Which of the following commands immediately changes your command prompt?
    a. **prompt pg**
    b. **$PROMPT="\w\$"**
    c. **PS1="\w\$"**
    d. **echo $PS1**
2. Which of the following commands brings you to your home directory? (Choose all that apply.)
    a. **cd**
    b. **cd -**
    c. **cd ~**
    d. **cd \home**

3. Which of the following commands creates a file of zero length?
    a. **cat >> filename**
    b. **touch filename**
    c. **ls -c filename**
    d. **md filename**

4. You cannot have a file called abc as well as a file called ABC in the same directory. True or False?
5. If you create a directory called ..., this refers to:
    a. the parent directory
    b. the directory immediately above the parent directory
    c. a directory below the current directory
    d. a directory that can't be accessed
6. Which of the following commands deletes a file called -l?
    a. **rm -l**
    b. **rm --ignore -l**
    c. **rm -- -l**
    d. **rm --**

CHAPTER FIVE

LINUX FILESYSTEM MANAGEMENT

Labs included in this chapter

CompTIA Linux+ Exam Objectives

Objective		Lab
2.1	Manage local storage devices and file systems (e.g., fsck, fdisk, mkfs) using CLI commands	5.1, 5.4
2.3	Create files and directories and modify files using CLI commands	5.4, 5.5
2.6	Modify file and directory permissions and ownership (e.g., chmod, chown, sticky bit, octal permissions, chgrp) using CLI commands	5.4, 5.5
2.20	Create, modify, and delete user and group accounts (e.g., useradd, groupadd, /etc/passwd, chgrp, quota, chown, chmod, grpmod) using CLI utilities	5.4, 5.5
N/A	These lab exercises do not directly address Linux+ objectives, but provide additional background information to help you master the objectives and understand the Linux operating system.	5.2, 5.3

Lab 5.1 Exploring the Filesystem Hierarchy Standard

Objectives

The goal of this lab is to learn about the Filesystem Hierarchy Standard (FHS). When you understand FHS, you know where files should be placed in the filesystem. You will explore the Filesystem Hierarchy Standard (FHS) Web site to learn more about this important standard.

Materials Required

This lab requires the following:

- Access as an ordinary user to a computer running Linux

> **NOTE** This lab explores information on the World Wide Web. Because Web pages can change without notice, what you see may not exactly match the terminology described in this lab. You may have to use your judgement to find the best match for links described here. When in doubt, check with your instructor.

Estimated completion time: 30 Minutes

Activity

1. Log in to your Linux computer as an ordinary user.
2. Start up a Web browser, enter the following in the address line, and press **Enter**:
   http://www.pathname.com/fhs/
3. Click **FHS2.3.HTML**, then examine the Table of Contents.

FHS.2.3 → .pdf

4. Click the link to **The Filesystem** and read the text labeled "Chapter 2. The Filesystem." This section tells you that the FHS applies to any filesystem that supports the same basic security features found in most UNIX filesystems. This includes Linux but does not include non-UNIX operating systems, such as Microsoft Windows. The section also places files into four categories: shareable, unshareable, variable, and static. Use the PageUp or Home key to return to the Table of Contents.

1) space on root partition
2) evades discipline
admin may have set up for distributing standard file hierarchies

5. Click the link to **Purpose** under the heading **The Root Filesystem**. Note the caution that "Software must never create or require special files or subdirectories in the root directory" and the reasons why. Not only must software never do this, users should not do this. Of course, the only user capable of doing this is the root user if permissions are set up correctly.

/bin contains comm. that may be used both user/admin and when no filesystem is mounted

6. Go back to the Table of Contents. Click the **/bin : Essential user command binaries (for use by all users)** link. Read the Purpose section. Note that this directory is required so the system can run and be administered at a basic level even when no other filesystems are mounted. This page also tells you the files that must be present in the directory.

/etc contains config files

7. Go back to the Table of Contents. Click the **/etc : Host-specific system configuration** link. Read the Purpose and Requirements sections. This directory and any subdirectories contain files used for configuring the system, daemons, or application programs. No executable programs (binaries) may exist in this directory structure, according to the FHS.

config file – must be static and cannot be exec. binary

8. Read the Specific Options section. It tells you that certain subdirectories must exist but only "if the corresponding subsystem is installed." The best example is the X11 subdirectory that must exist only if you're running the X Windows System (the graphics system). If your Linux computer is running as a server and has no graphical system installed, the X11 directory may not exist because it's not needed. Some Linux distributions install the X11 directory anyway.

No progs must rely on home location

9. Go back to the Table of Contents. Click the **/home: User home directories (optional)** link and read the entire section. The word "optional" means that the /home directory is not required for a system to be FHS compatible. An administrator can devise an alternate method of handling user home directories.

NOTE

User home directories do not have to be in the /home directory. You can put them in any FHS-compliant place, such as /var/home. If you do this, you have to modify the home directory locations in the /etc/passwd file.

/lib contains shared library images and run commands in the root filesystem

10. Go back to the Table of Contents. Click the **/lib : Essential shared libraries and kernel modules** link. Read the Purpose and Specific Options sections. Note that you almost always have a modules subdirectory because most Linux distributions use kernel modules.

May be > /lib dir on the system contain. > 1 binary format

11. Go back to the Table of Contents. Click the **/lib<qual> : Alternate format essential shared libraries (optional)** link. Read the entire section. In the future, you're likely to run a 64-bit version of Linux on your 64-bit architecture computer. When you do, you'll likely have directories mentioned on this page: /lib32, /lib64, and a /lib symbolic link to one of them.

12. Go back to the Table of Contents. Click the **/sbin :System binaries** link. Read the entire section. Pay attention to the footnotes, which tell you that "Programs executed after /usr is known to be mounted (when there are no problems) are generally placed into /usr/sbin. Locally installed system administration programs should be placed into /usr/ local/sbin." This should be your guide when installing additional system administration-oriented software on your computer.

/sbin contains commands for booting, restoring, recovering & repairing the system in addition to binaries in /bin

/tmp is for temp files. Progs cannot assume that files in /tmp are preserved

13. Go back to the Table of Contents. Click the **/tmp : Temporary files** link. Read the entire section. The most important concept on this page is that any files placed in this directory are not expected to survive a system shutdown and startup. How this is handled is a local issue, however. Some Linux distributions erase all the files in the /tmp directory on startup and some don't.

This completes this lab exercise, but there's more FHS-related reading to do if you have the time. Optionally, you can explore links about the /usr and /var directory structures.

Certification Objectives

Objectives for the Linux+ exam:

➤ Manage local storage devices and file systems (e.g., fsck, fdisk, mkfs) using CLI commands (2.1)

Review Questions

1. The FHS is a general filesystem specification. Its guiding principles can be applied to any filesystem, such as those used by Microsoft Windows. True or False? FALSE

2. The FHS concerns itself with which of the following categories of files? (Choose all that apply.)
   a. shareable versus unshareable
   b. variable versus static
   c. read-only versus read-write
   d. those having owners versus those that are unowned

3. Which directory is used for storing variable data files?
   a. /etc
   b. /var
   c. /usr
   d. /home

4. Which directory is used for storing shareable, static files?
   a. /etc
   b. /var
   c. /usr
   d. /home

5. It's acceptable for you to create new directories in the root of the filesystem, such as /My-files. True or False?

6. Which directory is used for storing configuration files used by the system, daemons, and applications?
   a. /etc
   b. /var
   c. /usr
   d. /home
7. According to the FHS, it is permissible to place programs in the /etc directory structure as long as it is in an application-specific directory, such as /etc/apache/. True or False?
8. A /home directory does not have to exist for a filesystem to be FHS compliant. True or False?

Lab 5.2 Working with BASH Aliases

Objectives

The goal of this lab is to become familiar with BASH aliases. You'll see how to display aliases, add or delete aliases, and redefine them.

Materials Required

This lab requires the following:

- Access as an ordinary user to a computer running Linux
- The BASH shell (this is the default Linux shell)

Activity Background

This lab exercise has you create BASH aliases. These aliases are in effect while you're logged in. They disappear after you log out. If you want them to be permanent, you must add them to one of your startup scripts. If you're running Fedora, you can add them to the .bashrc file in your home directory.

Estimated completion time: 20 Minutes

Activity

1. Switch to a command-line terminal (tty2) by pressing **Ctrl+Alt+F2**, and log in to the terminal as any user.

2. Display existing aliases by entering the alias command. Enter **alias** and you see the lines below:

```
alias l.='ls -d .* --color=tty'
alias ll='ls -l --color=tty'
alias ls='ls --color=tty'
alias vi='vim'
alias which='alias | /usr/bin/which --tty-only --read-
alias --show-dot --show-tilde''
```

3. Add an alias with this simple command:

   alias lspasswd="less /etc/passwd"

4. You've added an alias to the BASH shell. You can see your creation by entering **alias**.

```
alias l.='ls -d .* --color=tty'
alias ll='ls -l --color=tty'
alias ls='ls --color=tty'
alias lspasswd='less /etc/passwd'
alias vi='vim'
alias which='alias | /usr/bin/which --tty-only --read-
alias --show-dot --show-tilde'
```

5. Run the **lspasswd** command at a BASH shell prompt. You see the contents of the /etc/passwd file displayed on your screen. As this file is being displayed by the less program, press **q** to get back to the shell prompt.

6. Suppose you don't want to have to type **q** to get back to the shell prompt. You just want to be at the shell prompt immediately after the file is displayed. There's no easy way to edit an alias. You have to redefine it. When you redefine the alias, the new alias replaces the old one. Try this:

   alias lspasswd="cat /etc/passwd"

7. Verify that the definition for the alias has changed by entering the **alias** command again:

```
alias l.='ls -d .* --color=tty'
alias ll='ls -l --color=tty'
alias ls='ls --color=tty'
alias lspasswd='cat /etc/passwd'
alias vi='vim'
alias which='alias | /usr/bin/which --tty-only --read-
alias --show-dot --show-tilde'
```

8. Run the **lspasswd** command at a BASH shell prompt and notice that you're back at the shell prompt after the file is displayed.

9. You can delete an alias with the **unalias** command. Delete the lspasswd alias like this:

   unalias lspasswd

10. Verify that the lspasswd alias is deleted by running the **alias** command.
11. Create a new alias called zzzz and assign it the string "ls -al." Here's how to do it:

    alias zzzz="ls -al"
12. Type **zzzz** and notice that the files and directories in your current directory are displayed. The shell expanded the alias and executed the ls -al command.
13. You can prevent the shell from expanding the alias. Precede the zzzz command with the shell's escape character—normally the backslash character. Enter **\zzzz** at the shell's prompt. You'll see this:

    ```
    bash: zzzz: command not found
    ```

    This is because the shell did not expand the alias and it did not find a program called zzzz to run.
14. You can have more than one alias on a command line. When the first alias value ends in a space, the shell tries to expand the next word on the command line. Create two aliases as follows (note the space after "echo"):

    alias a="echo "

    alias b="Hello World"
15. When you specify both aliases on the command line, they combine to perform the command echo Hello World. Enter **a b** and you'll see this result:

    ```
    a b
    Hello World
    ```
16. The shell tries to expand aliases recursively. To illustrate this, create these three aliases:

    alias 1="ls -l"

    alias 2="1"

    alias 3="2"
17. Enter the command **3**. You see a directory listing in the long format. The shell first expanded the **3** into **2**, then it expanded the **2** into **1**, then the **1** into **1 -l**.
18. Enter **logout**. Press **Alt+F7** to go back to your graphical screen.

Certification Objectives

This lab exercise does not directly address Linux+ objectives, but provides additional background information to help you master the objectives and understand the Linux operating system.

Review Questions

1. Which command displays all your shell aliases?
   a. **lsalias**
   b. **ls --alias**
   c. **alias**
   d. **alias --show**
2. Which command creates a shell alias?
   a. **alias zz="ls -al"**
   b. **mkalias zz "ls -al"**
   c. **alias -c ls -al**
   d. **unalias zz**
3. Which command deletes a shell alias?
   a. **alias -d zz**
   b. **delalias zz**
   c. **alias --del zz**
   d. **unalias zz**
4. You can prevent the shell from expanding an alias by:
   a. compiling the shell with the --noexpand option
   b. preceding the alias with a backslash
   c. using uppercase characters for the alias name
   d. preceding the alias with a period
5. If you want to modify an alias, you can edit it with a text editor. True or False?

Lab 5.3 Using Advanced FIND Options

Objectives

The goal of this lab is to learn how to use the more advanced options of the **find** program. These advanced options are useful to a system administrator who must care for the computer's file system.

Materials Required

This lab requires the following:

- Access as a root user to a computer running Linux

Estimated completion time: 20 Minutes

LAB ACTIVITY

Activity

1. Switch to a command-line terminal (tty2) by pressing **Ctrl+Alt+F2**, and log in to the terminal as the root user.
2. A common administration problem with filesystems is dealing with files and directories with owners that don't exist. This happens when users are removed from the system but their files are not removed. You can easily get a list of these files and directories with the **-nouser** option. Try this example of the command:

   find / -nouser

3. If you are using a fresh Fedora installation, you probably won't see any files displayed. There are no files with owners that don't exist. You can use the **chown** command to assign an invalid owner to a file. Enter the **touch me** command to create a file in the current directory. Now enter the **chown 7000 me** command to assign a nonexistent user as the file's owner. Now repeat Step 2 and you should see this displayed:

   ```
   /root/me
   ```

4. You can use the chown command to fix any files that are not owned by a valid user. Enter the **chown nobody me** command. The user nobody is now the file's owner. If you perform Step 2 again, the file will not be listed.

NOTE

When you perform these exercises, you may see a message similar to this:
find: /proc/1710/fd/4: No such file or directory.
This is normal and is not shown in the examples.

5. An administrator may wish to know which files on the system are set to SUID. These files are easily listed with the **-perm** option. You need to specify the SUID permission correctly. Here's how to do it using numeric representation of the permission (4000):

   find / -perm +4000

   The output of this command looks similar to this for a Fedora Core 2 system:

   ```
   /sbin/pwdb_chkpwd
   /sbin/unix_chkpwd
   /sbin/pam_timestamp_check
   /usr/libexec/openssh/ssh-keysign
   /usr/sbin/usernetctl
   /usr/sbin/userisdnctl
   ```

```
/usr/sbin/userhelper
/usr/X11R6/bin/Xorg
/usr/bin/gpasswd
/usr/bin/rcp
/usr/bin/chsh
/usr/bin/rlogin
/usr/bin/crontab
/usr/bin/passwd
/usr/bin/newgrp
/usr/bin/lppasswd
/usr/bin/at
/usr/bin/sudo
/usr/bin/rsh
/usr/bin/chfn
/usr/bin/chage
/bin/traceroute6
/bin/ping6
/bin/mount
/bin/su
/bin/traceroute
/bin/umount
/bin/ping
```

6. You can display all the files on your system that are larger than a specified value by using the **-size** option. For large files, you must specify kilobytes because there is no way to specify megabytes. Here's an example of how to list all the files on your system that are larger than 1 MB:

   find / -size 1024k

   For a freshly installed Fedora system, you may not have any files larger than one megabyte. You can run the command again with a smaller value until you see files displayed similar to this:

   ```
   /boot/grub/stage2
   /usr/lib/gimp/2.0/plug-ins/MapObject
   ```

7. You can list all of the symbolic links on your system with the **-type l** option. Enter this command:

   find / -type l

   You'll see output similar to this:

   ```
   /lib/libcom_err.so.2
   /lib/libNoVersion.so.1
   /lib/librt.so.1
   ```

8. Up to now, you've been searching the entire filesystem. You can search a smaller portion of your filesystem's directory tree by specifying a directory. For example, enter this command to list the symbolic links in your /sbin directory:

   find /sbin -type l

Here's the output from a freshly installed Fedora Core 2 system:

```
/sbin/restore.static
/sbin/pvscan
/sbin/pidof
/sbin/rdump.static
/sbin/poweroff
/sbin/quotaoff
/sbin/swapoff
/sbin/reboot
/sbin/vgchange
/sbin/dump.static
/sbin/modprobe
/sbin/ksyms
/sbin/vgscan
/sbin/clock
/sbin/raidhotremove
/sbin/rrestore
/sbin/lsmod
/sbin/rdump
/sbin/kallsyms
/sbin/raid0run
/sbin/lvm
/sbin/raidhotadd
/sbin/raidstop
/sbin/telinit
/sbin/rrestore.static
/sbin/rmmod
/sbin/raidsetfaulty
```

9. So far you've focused on displaying files and directories that match a criterion. The find program can also take other actions when files match criteria. In Steps 2 and 3, you used the find command to locate files that had no user owners. In Step 4, you used the chown command to assign owners to these files. You can combine these two steps into one. Here's an example of changing the group owner to the group "users" for all files and directories that have no group owner:

   find / -nogroup -exec chgrp users "{}" ";"

NOTE The -exec parameter causes the following command (chgrp) to be executed every time a file is found (by find) that has no owner. The {} contains the name of the unowned file that was found. The semicolon (;) signals the end of the command string to the find program.

10. Enter **logout**. Press **Alt+F7** to go back to your graphical screen.

Certification Objectives

This lab exercise does not directly address Linux+ objectives, but provides additional background information to help you master the objectives and understand the Linux operating system.

Review Questions

1. Which of these commands displays a list of files that have no valid user owners?
   a. **find /bin -nogroup**
   b. **find . -nouser**
   c. **find / user=""**
   d. **find nouser**
2. When you run a find command and see an error similar to "find: /proc/1710/fd/4: No such file or directory," what are you doing wrong?
   a. You don't have permission to access the find program.
   b. Nothing. This error is normal.
   c. You forgot to use the -ne option.
   d. The file(s) you're searching for can't be found.
3. You want to produce a list of all files on your hard disk that are set to SUID. Which command does this?
   a. **find / -perm +1000**
   b. **find / -perm +2000**
   c. **find / -perm +4000**
   d. **find / -perm +777**
4. You want to produce a list of all files and directories on your hard disk that have the sticky bit set. Which command does this?
   a. **find / -perm +1000**
   b. **find / -perm +2000**
   c. **find / -perm +4000**
   d. **find / -perm +777**
5. Which command produces a list of files that are equal to or greater than 2 MB?
   a. **find / -size gt 2MB**
   b. **find / -size => 2000000**
   c. **find / -size 2048k**
   d. **find / -size 2M**

6. Which command produces a list of symbolic links on your entire hard disk?
   a. **find / -type l**
   b. **find / -symlinks**
   c. **find / -type s**
   d. **find / -links**

Lab 5.4 Working with File and Directory Permissions

Objectives

The goal of this lab is to observe the details of file and directory permissions. In particular, you'll see how the sticky bit operates as a special permissions function.

Materials Required

This lab requires the following:

- Access as a root user to a computer running Linux
- Access as an ordinary user to a computer running Linux

Activity Background

In this exercise, you'll be simultaneously logged in as three users. One is the root user and the other two are ordinary users. You'll create files as one ordinary user and see the effects on the other ordinary user. You'll also be logged in as the root user because there are things to be done that the ordinary users cannot do.

Estimated completion time: 20 Minutes

LAB ACTIVITY

Activity

1. Switch to a command-line terminal (tty2) by pressing **Ctrl+Alt+F2**, and log in to the terminal as the root user.
2. Create a directory called /var/local/share by entering the command **mkdir /var/local/share**.
3. Enter the command **ls -ld /var/local/share**, and look at the output to make sure the share directory has these permissions:

```
drwxr-xr-x  2  root   root    4096 Aug 18 15:23 /var/
local/share
```

NOTE If you use the command ls -l /var/local/share instead, you'll see a list of the contents of the directory instead of the directory itself. Of course, the directory is empty because you just created it.

4. If the permissions are different, type the command **chmod 755 share**.
5. This exercise requires two ordinary user accounts. You should already have an ordinary user account set up. Assume it's called matt for this exercise. If you don't have a second user account, you need to create a new user named beth now. (If your first user is named beth, choose another name.) Add the new user beth by typing **useradd beth**. Next, type **passwd beth** and enter a password that you can remember.
6. Switch to the virtual console 3 by pressing **Alt+F3**. Log in as user beth. Type **cd /var/local/share**.
7. Switch to the virtual console 4 by pressing **Alt+F4**. Log in as user matt. Type **cd /var/local/share**.
8. Try to create a file with the command **echo "Hello from Matt" > file1**. You see this error message because you don't have write permission to this directory:

   ```
   bash: file1: Permission denied
   ```

9. Switch to virtual console 2 by pressing **Alt+F2**. You're logged in as root. Type the command **chmod o+w /var/local/share**. You've given all users write permission to the share directory.
10. Switch to virtual console 4 by pressing **Alt+F4**. You're logged in as matt. Again, try to create a file with the command **echo "Hello from Matt" > file1**. You can recall this command by using the Up arrow. This time it should succeed and no error message is displayed.
11. Type the command **ls -l file1** and notice the permissions on the file. Also note that matt is the user and group owner:

   ```
   -rw-rw-r--   1  matt   matt    16 Aug 18 15:23  file1
   ```

12. Switch to virtual console 3 by pressing **Alt+F3**. You're logged in as beth. Type **ls -l** and notice the same result as in Step 11.
13. Type **cat file1** and you see the contents of the file appear because beth has read permissions to matt's file:

   ```
   Hello from Matt
   ```

14. Try to append (write) to the file by typing **echo "Hello from Beth." >> file1**. This fails and you see an error message because beth doesn't have write permissions to matt's file.

NOTE

The >> operator tells a program to append to a file rather than to overwrite a file.

15. Switch to virtual console 2 by pressing **Alt+F2**. You're logged in as root. Enter **cd /var/local/share** to change to that directory. Try to append (write) to the file by typing **echo "Hello from root" >> file1**. This succeeds because the root user has access to all files and directories on the system regardless of permissions.

16. Switch to virtual console 3 by pressing **Alt+F3**. You're logged in as beth. Type **cat file1**, and you see the following on your screen:

```
Hello from Matt
Hello from root
```

17. Type **rm file1** and answer **Yes** if you're asked whether you want to remove the file. Type **ls -l** and notice that the file no longer exists. User beth is able to erase user matt's file. This doesn't seem right. Beth has only read access to the file. She shouldn't be able to erase it. However, beth has write access to the /var/local/ share directory and this gives her the power to delete matt's files. You can solve this security problem by setting the sticky bit on the directory as shown in the next step.

18. Switch to virtual console 2 by pressing **Alt+F2**. You're logged in as root. Type the command **chmod o+t /var/local/share**. Now type **ls –ld /var/local/share** and you see that the sticky bit (t) has been added in place of the x bit:

```
drwxr-xrwt  2  root   root    4096 Aug 18 15:23  /var/
local/share
```

19. Switch to virtual console 4 by pressing **Alt+F4**. You're logged in as matt. Again, create file1 with the command **echo "Hello from Matt" > file1**. Verify the file was created by typing **ls -l**.

20. Switch to virtual console 3 by pressing **Alt+F3**. You're logged in as beth. Again, try to delete the file by typing **rm file1**. You are prompted with:

```
rm: remove write-protected file 'file1'?
```

21. Enter **y** and you see another error message telling you that you can't erase the file:

```
rm: cannot remove 'file1': Operation not permitted
```

22. Enter **logout**. Press **Alt+F4** and enter **logout**. Press **Alt+F2** and enter **logout**. Press **Alt+F7** to go back to your graphical screen.

Certification Objectives

Objectives for the Linux+ exam:

- Manage local storage devices and file systems (e.g., fsck, fdisk, mkfs) using CLI commands (2.1)
- Create files and directories and modify files using CLI commands (2.3)
- Modify file and directory permissions and ownership (e.g., chmod, chown, sticky bit, octal permissions, chgrp) using CLI commands (2.6)
- Create, modify, and delete user and group accounts (e.g., useradd, groupadd, etc/password, chgrp, quota, chown, chmod, grpmod) using CLI utilities (2.20)

Review Questions

1. Which command appends data to a file?
   a. **echo "November 5, 2003" > /tmp/audit**
   b. **find / -nouser >> /tmp/audit**
   c. **ls -l | /tmp/audit**
   d. **cat /tmp/audit**
2. Which command saves data to a file by overwriting existing data in the file?
   a. **echo "November 5, 2003" > /tmp/audit**
   b. **find / -nouser >> /tmp/audit**
   c. **ls -l | /tmp/audit**
   d. **cat /tmp/audit**
3. Which command gives all users write access to a directory called bboard?
   a. **chmod 754 bboard**
   b. **chmod 777 bboard**
   c. **chmod 1754 bboard**
   d. **chmod 4754 bboard**
4. If users have write access to a directory but the sticky bit permission is not set, any user can erase any file in the directory regardless of ownership. True or False?
5. You want to set the sticky bit permission for directory elvis. Which two commands can do this?
   a. **chmod 4000 elvis**
   b. **chmod 1000 elvis**
   c. **chmod o+t elvis**
   d. **chmod o+s elvis**

Lab 5.5 Using the Advanced Features of SLOCATE

Objectives

The goal of this lab is for you to become familiar with the features of the **slocate** program. Slocate is an advanced version of the **GNU locate** program that has additional security features. With slocate, users cannot see that files exist in the filesystem if they don't have permissions to those files.

Materials Required

This lab requires the following:

- Access as an ordinary user to a computer running Linux
- Access as the root user to a computer running Linux

Estimated completion time: 30 Minutes

Activity

1. Switch to a command-line terminal (tty2) by pressing **Ctrl+Alt+F2**, and log in to the terminal using the root account.
2. Go to your home directory. You can do this from anywhere by typing **cd ~** or just **cd**.
3. Check to see if you have a subdirectory called test. You can do this with the command **ls test**. The subdirectory may exist from a previous lab exercise. If it does not exist, create it with the **mkdir test** command.
4. Create a file called sample99 in this directory using the command:

   echo "Hello World" > test/sample99
5. See if the locate program can find this file. Enter the command **locate sample99**. Unless you happen to have a file by that same name on your computer in some other directory, it will not find the file. This is because you just created the file and your computer only updates the update database once a day.
6. You can use the **updatedb** program to force your computer to update its database now. To do so, run this command:

   updatedb

7. The command in Step 6 may take quite a while to run because it's scanning nearly all of your hard disk. You can prevent updatedb from scanning all of your hard disk by excluding directories from the scan using the **-e** option, thus reducing the time to update the database. Here's an example of excluding most directories from the scan except the /root and /home directories:

   updatedb -e "/tmp,/etc,/usr,/var,/bin,/sbin,/boot"

8. The updatedb program uses a configuration file in the /etc directory called updatedb.conf. Type the contents of this file to the screen with the command **cat /etc/updatedb.conf**. You'll see something similar to this:

```
PRUNEFS="sysfs selinuxfs usbdevfs devpts NFS nfs afs proc
smbfs autofs auto iso9660"
PRUNEPATHS="/tmp /usr/tmp /var/tmp /afs /net"
export PRUNEFS
export PRUNEPATHS
```

9. The PRUNEFS line specifies those filesystems that the updatedb program will not scan. The PRUNEPATHS line specifies those directories that the updatedb program will not scan. You can specify additional directories that should be excluded from the scan on the command line with the -e option as you did for the updatedb command.

10. See if the locate command can find the sample99 file now. Use the command **locate sample99**. You should see the file listed as follows:

```
/root/test/sample99
```

11. Log in as an ordinary user with the su command. If your ordinary user account name is joe, you type **su joe**.

12. Try to locate the sample99 file with the command **locate sample99**. If you're running Fedora Core 2, it should not find the file. This is because you're logged in as an ordinary user but the sample99 file is in a directory that you do not have permission to access. Fedora, as well as many other Linux distributions, uses the more secure slocate program rather than the locate program.

13. Run the command **ls -l /usr/bin/locate**. You see that locate is really a symbolic link to the slocate program:

```
lrwxrwxrwx 1 root slocate 7 Mar 28 15:55 /usr/bin/locate
-> slocate
```

14. Read the man page for the slocate program by typing the command **man slocate**. Notice that slocate is a security-enhanced version of the GNU locate program. It does not display files to users who do not have access to those files. Press **q** to quit the slocate man pages.

15. Go back to the shell you were using when you were logged in as root by entering the **exit** command.

16. Temporarily allow other users to have access to the /root directory by typing this command:

    chmod -R 777 /root

17. Update the update database by typing **updatedb**.
18. Log in as an ordinary user with the **su** command. If your ordinary user account name is joe, you type **su joe**.
19. Try to locate the sample99 file with the command **locate sample99**. You should now find the file because your user account has access to the /root/test directory:

    `/root/test/sample99`

20. Go back to the shell you were using when you were logged in as root by entering the **exit** command. Restore the /root directory so other users no longer have access to it by typing **chmod –R 750 /root**.
21. Log in as an ordinary user with the **su** command. If your ordinary user account name is joe, you type **su joe**.
22. Try to locate the sample99 file with the command **locate sample99**. You should not find the file because your user account no longer has access to the /root/test directory.

NOTE

The slocate program is a well-engineered program that demonstrates the commitment to security that is typical of Open Source software.

23. Enter **exit** and then enter **logout**. Press **Alt+F7** to go back to your graphical screen.

Certification Objectives

Objectives for the Linux+ exam:

- Create files and directories and modify files using CLI commands (2.3)
- Modify file and directory permissions and ownership (e.g., chmod, chown, sticky bit, octal permissions, chgrp) using CLI commands (2.6)
- Create, modify, and delete user and group accounts (e.g., useradd, groupadd, etc/password, chgp, quota, chown, chmod, grpmod) using CLI utilities (2.20)

Review Questions

1. How often is the locate database updated?
   a. hourly
   b. daily
   c. monthly
   d. only when you run the updatedb program
2. You can force the locate database to update immediately by running the updatedb program. True or False?
3. Normally, updatedb scans all directories on your hard disk except for the /proc and /dev/pts directories. This can take a long time. How can you prevent updatedb from scanning the /var directory if you run it from the command line?
   a. **updatedb -f "/var"**
   b. **updatedb —novar**
   c. **update -e "/var"**
   d. **updatedb | grep "/var"**
4. You can exclude the /home directory from updatedb's daily scan by adding /home to the PRUNEPATHS line in the /etc/updatedb.conf file. True or False?
5. In order for an ordinary user to find a file using locate, the file must be in a directory to which the user has access permissions. This means the directory must have the Execute (x) permission set. True or False?

CHAPTER SIX

LINUX FILESYSTEM ADMINISTRATION

Labs included in this chapter

- Lab 6.1 Mounting and Ejecting CD-ROMs
- Lab 6.2 Formatting 3.5-Inch Disks
- Lab 6.3 Controlling Reserved Disk Space
- Lab 6.4 Working with USB Memory
- Lab 6.5 Using the Fuser Program

CompTIA Linux+ Exam Objectives

Objective		Lab
1.7	Configure file systems (e.g., (ext2) or (ext3) or REISER)	6.2, 6.3
2.1	Manage local storage devices and file systems (e.g., fsck, fdisk, mkfs) using CLI commands	6.2, 6.3, 6.4
2.2	Mount and unmount varied filesystems (e.g., Samba, NFS) using CLI commands	6.1, 6.2, 6.3, 6.4
2.3	Create files and directories and modify files using CLI commands	6.2, 6.4
2.9	Access and write data to recordable media	6.2, 6.4
N/A	This lab exercise does not directly address Linux+ objectives, but provides additional background information to help you master the objectives and understand the Linux operating system.	6.5

Lab 6.1 Mounting and Ejecting CD-ROMs

Objectives

The goal of this lab is to become familiar with automounting. You experiment with mounting, unmounting, and ejecting CD-ROMs. You also learn that you are unable to unmount a CD-ROM if the mount point is in any user's current directory. Most Linux distributions use **autofs** for automounting.

Materials Required

This lab requires the following:

- Access as an ordinary user to a computer running Linux. The computer must have a CD-ROM drive installed.

Activity Background

You should begin this lab without a CD-ROM in the drive.

NOTE

Most desktop computers have CD-ROM drives whose trays can be controlled by software. That is, software can open the tray and it can close the tray. Many or most notebook computers have CD-ROM trays that software can open but not close. If you're using a notebook computer for this lab, all steps may not work as written.

Estimated completion time: 10 Minutes

LAB ACTIVITY

Activity

1. Switch to a command-line terminal (tty2) by pressing **Ctrl+Alt+F2** and log in to the terminal as root.
2. Open the CD-ROM tray by pressing the button on the front panel of the CD-ROM drive. Insert a data CD-ROM, such as one of the CD-ROMs from your Linux distribution.
3. Close the tray by pressing the Eject button on the front panel of the drive. If you're using a notebook computer, manually push the tray closed.
4. Wait about ten seconds and check to see if the CD-ROM drive is mounted by entering **mount**. If a line similar to this appears in the output, your CD-ROM drive is mounted:

```
/dev/cdrom on /mnt/cdrom type iso9660 (ro,nosuid,nodev)
```

NOTE Fedora Core 2 uses autofs to automatically mount and unmount CD-ROMs.

5. Open the drive tray by entering **eject**. The drive tray opens.

NOTE If you have more than one removable media device in your computer, such as a CD-ROM drive and a Zip drive, the **eject** command may affect the wrong device. If this is the case, you must specify the device with a command such as **eject /dev/cdrom**.

eject -t Doesn't work for laptop

6. Check to see if the CD-ROM drive is mounted by entering **mount**. You should not see the line of output that appeared in Step 4. Autofs automatically unmounted the CD-ROM before ejecting it.
7. Close the drive tray, but this time have software do it. Enter **eject –t**.
8. Wait about ten seconds and check to see if the CD-ROM drive is mounted by entering **mount**. If a line similar to this appears in the output, your CD-ROM drive is mounted:

```
/dev/cdrom on /mnt/cdrom type iso9660 (ro,nosuid,nodev)
```

/dev/sr0

9. Make your current directory the mount point directory for the CD-ROM. Enter **cd /mnt/cdrom**. Enter **pwd** to verify that your current directory is /mnt/cdrom.
10. Press the Eject button on the CD-ROM drive. The tray does not open because the CD-ROM is mounted.
11. Try to unmount the CD-ROM and eject it with software. Enter **eject**. You should see an error message. You can't unmount the CD-ROM when one or more users have its mount point directory as their current directory.
12. Move out of the mount point directory by entering **cd ../**. Enter **eject**. The CD-ROM is unmounted and the drive tray opens. Enter **cd ../** again.

Certification Objectives

Objectives for the Linux+ exam:

- Mount and unmount varied filesystems (e.g., Samba, NFS) using CLI commands (2.2)

Review Questions

1. When the CD-ROM is mounted, you can eject the CD-ROM by pressing the Eject button on the drive. True or False?
2. What's wrong if you see this message when you try to unmount the CD-ROM?

   `umount: /mnt/cdrom: device is busy`
3. Which command closes the drive tray?
   a. **eject**
   b. **eject -a on**
   c. **eject -t**
   d. **eject /dev/cdrom**
4. Normally, the eject and eject /dev/cdrom commands are equivalent. Describe a condition where they may not be equivalent.
5. Which of the following commands should you use for automounting?
   a. **mkisofs**
   b. **automnt**
   c. **autofs**
   d. **ejectfs**

Lab 6.2 Formatting 3.5-Inch Disks

Objectives

The goal of this lab is to learn how to low-level format 3.5-inch disks. You need to do this when:

- You buy a box of 3.5-inch disks that are not already formatted.
- You suspect that the format of the 3.5-inch disk has been corrupted and you'd like to format it again.
- You'd like to increase the storage capacity of the 3.5-inch disk.

Materials Required

This lab requires the following:

- Access as the root user to a computer running Linux. The computer must have a 3.5-inch, high-density disk drive installed.
- One 3.5-inch, high-density disk

Activity Background

Linux doesn't restrict you to 1.44 MB (1440 KB) of space on a 3.5-inch disk as Windows does. You can low-level format your 3.5-inch disks to allow for greater capacities. Table 6-1 shows examples of the greater capacities for which you can format a 3.5-inch, high-density disk, along with the device names.

Table 6-1 Device names and capacities for 3.5-inch disks

Device Name	Capacity
/dev/fd0u1600	1600 KB
/dev/fd0u1680	1680 KB
/dev/fd0u1722	1722 KB
/dev/fd0u1743	1743 KB
/dev/fd0u1760	1760 KB
/dev/fd0u1840	1840 KB
/dev/fd0u1920	1920 KB

To format these higher-capacity disks, you use the device name with the **fdformat** program as Step 3 of the Activity shows. Note that these higher-capacity formats are not usable with Windows, which has a maximum capacity of 1440 KB for 3.5-inch, high-density disks.

Estimated completion time: 30 Minutes

Activity

1. Switch to a command-line terminal (tty2) by pressing **Ctrl+Alt+F2** and log in to the terminal using the root user account.
2. Insert a 3.5-inch, high-density disk into the disk drive. If the 3.5-inch disk has data on it, the data will be destroyed by this exercise.
3. Perform a low-level format by entering **fdformat /dev/fd0u1440**. You see this appear:

```
Double-sided, 80 tracks, 18 sec/track. Total
capacity 1440 kB.
Formatting ... done
Verifying ...done
```

NOTE

You might see an error message such as "Problem reading cylinder 27, expected 18432, read 10240." This generally means that your 3.5-inch disk is bad. Try a different or new 3.5-inch disk. Most 3.5-inch disks can't be trusted after about 10 years, and can generally be unreliable. Don't save critical data on 3.5-inch disks, and don't expect data saved on 3.5-inch disks to be readable many years later.

4. You've just low-level formatted the 3.5-inch disk to the same capacity as DOS and Microsoft Windows does. However, the disk is not yet usable. You need to place a filesystem on the disk. Place an ext2 filesystem on the 3.5-inch disk by entering **mke2fs /dev/fd0**. You see output similar to this appear on the screen:

```
Filesystem label=
OS type: Linux
Block size=1024 (log=0)
Fragment size=1024 (log=0)
184 inodes, 1440 blocks
72 blocks (5.00%) reserved for the super user
First data block=1
1 block group
8192 blocks per group, 8192 fragments per group
184 inodes per group

Writing inode tables: done
Writing superblocks and filesystem accounting information:
done

This filesystem will be automatically checked every 24
mounts or 180 days, whichever comes first.  Use tune2fs
-c or -i to override.
```

5. Mount the 3.5-inch disk by entering either:

   mount -t ext2 /dev/fd0 /mnt/floppy

   or the shorthand notation: **mount /dev/fd0**.

NOTE

You can only use the shorthand notation if you have an entry in the /etc/fstab file such as this: /dev/fd0 /mnt/floppy ext2 defaults 0 0

6. Because you just formatted the 3.5-inch disk, it should be empty. Check it now. Enter **ls -l /mnt/floppy** to get a listing of the files and directories on the 3.5-inch disk. You should see output similar to this:

```
drwxr-xr-x    2 root    root    12288 Sep  4 05:11
lost+found
```

7. The lost+found directory is created on any disk you format with the ext2 or ext3 filesystems. It's a place where Linux stores files that have become disconnected from the filesystem and are "lost." It's rare for this to happen and you might need every bit of storage on the 3.5-inch disk. Erase this directory by entering **rmdir /mnt/floppy/lost+found**.

8. Check the amount of space on the 3.5-inch disk by entering **df /dev/fd0**. You should see this:

```
Filesystem       1k-blocks    Used Available Use% Mounted on
/dev/fd0              1412       1      1339   1% /mnt/
floppy
```

9. You can now copy files to the 3.5-inch disk, create new files, and so forth. Copy the fstab file to the disk by entering **cp /etc/fstab /mnt/floppy/**.

10. Make sure the file was copied to the 3.5-inch disk by entering **ls -l /mnt/floppy**. You should see this:

```
-rw-r--r--    1 root    root         272   Sep 4 05:20 fstab
```

11. Reformat your 3.5-inch disk to a higher capacity. Format it to 1680 KB by entering:

    fdformat /dev/fd0u1680

12. You see this message, which tells you that you cannot reformat a 3.5-inch disk when it's mounted:

```
/dev/fd0u1680: Device or resource busy
```

    Unmount the 3.5-inch disk by entering **umount /dev/fd0**.

13. Try again to reformat your 3.5-inch disk to the 1680 KB capacity by entering **fdformat /dev/fd0u1680**. This time it should work and you see this:

```
Double-sided, 80 tracks, 21 sec/track. Total capacity
1680 kB.
Formatting done
Verifying  done
```

NOTE

The 1680 KB capacity is achieved by using 21 sectors per track instead of the 18 sectors per track for the 1440 KB capacity.

14. Format the 3.5-inch disk with the ext2 filesystem by entering:

    mke2fs /dev/fd0

    You see output similar to that in Step 4.

15. Mount the 3.5-inch disk by entering either:

    mount -t ext2 /dev/fd0 /mnt/floppy

    or the shorthand notation: **mount /dev/fd0**

16. Erase the lost+found directory by entering:

    rmdir /mnt/floppy/lost+found

17. Check the amount of space on the 3.5-inch disk by entering **df /dev/fd0**. You should see this:

```
Filesystem       1k-blocks    Used Available Use%
Mounted on
/dev/fd0              1648       1      1563   1% /mnt/
floppy
```

You now have 1648 blocks of disk space instead of the 1412 blocks in Step 8.

18. Try to format your 3.5-inch disk to greater capacities (listed in the Activity Background). Note that the larger capacities may give you trouble. Your media or hardware may not be able to handle it. To unmount the 3.5-inch disk, note that your current directory must not be the 3.5-inch disk's mount point. Enter **cd** to go to your home directory. Then unmount the 3.5-inch disk as in Step 12.

Certification Objectives

Objectives for the Linux+ exam:

- Configure file systems (e.g., (ext2) or (ext3) or REISER) (1.7)
- Manage local storage devices and file systems (e.g., fsck, fdisk, mkfs) using CLI commands (2.1)
- Mount and unmount varied filesystems (e.g., Samba, NFS) using CLI commands (2.2)
- Create files and directories and modify files using CLI commands (2.3)
- Access and write data to recordable media (2.9)

Review Questions

1. What command formats a 3.5-inch, high-density disk to the same capacity as used by Microsoft Windows?
   a. **fdformat /dev/fd0u1400**
   b. **fdformat /dev/fd0u1440**
   c. **fdformat /dev/fd0u1600**
   d. **fdformat /dev/fd0u1720**
2. Most 3.5-inch disks are able to store data reliably for more than 15 years. True or False?
3. When you place an ext2 filesystem on a 3.5-inch disk:
   a. It is empty of files and directories.
   b. It has a /root directory.

c. It has a lost+found directory.

d. It has a /dev/directory.

4. What command shows you the total, used, and available space on a 3.5-inch disk?

   a. **du /dev/fd0**

   b. **free /dev/fd0**

   c. **df /dev/fd0**

   d. **ls -l /dev/fd0**

5. If you see the message "/dev/fd0u1600: Device or resource busy" when you try to low-level format a 3.5-inch disk, what is the problem?

Lab 6.3 Controlling Reserved Disk Space

Objectives

The goal of this lab is to see how the ext2 filesystem reserves disk space for use by the superuser, or any user that you specify. This allows the superuser to have available disk space even if users have filled up their available disk space. In this lab exercise you set the reserved disk space on a 3.5-inch disk. (The same thing can be done on a hard disk partition.)

Materials Required

This lab requires:

- Access as a root user to a computer running Linux. The computer must have a 3.5-inch, high-density disk drive installed.
- One 3.5-inch, high-density disk

Estimated completion time: 20 Minutes

Activity

LAB ACTIVITY

1. Switch to a command-line terminal (tty2) by pressing **Ctrl+Alt+F2** and log in to the terminal as the root user.
2. Insert a 3.5-inch, high-density disk into the disk drive. If the 3.5-inch disk has data on it, the data will be destroyed by this exercise.

3. Perform a low-level format by entering **fdformat /dev/fd0u1440**. You see this appear:

```
Double-sided, 80 tracks, 18 sec/track. Total capacity
1440 kB.
Formatting ... done
Verifying ...done
```

4. Place an ext2 filesystem on the 3.5-inch disk by entering **mke2fs /dev/fd0**. You see output similar to this appear on the screen:

```
Filesystem label=
OS type: Linux
Block size=1024 (log=0)
Fragment size=1024 (log=0)
184 inodes, 1440 blocks
72 blocks (5.00%) reserved for the super user
First data block=1
1 block group
8192 blocks per group, 8192 fragments per group
184 inodes per group

Writing inode tables: done
Writing superblocks and filesystem accounting information:
done

This filesystem will be automatically checked every 24
mounts or 180 days, whichever comes first.  Use tune2fs
-c or -i to override.
```

NOTE

By default, the mke2fs program reserves 5% of disk space for the superuser.

5. Mount the 3.5-inch disk by entering either:

   mount -t ext2 /dev/fd0 /mnt/floppy

   or the shorthand notation: **mount /dev/fd0**.

NOTE

You can only use the shorthand notation if you have an entry in the /etc/fstab file such as this: /dev/fd0 /mnt/floppy ext2 defaults 0 0

6. Erase the lost+found directory by entering **rmdir /mnt/floppy/lost+found**.

7. Check the amount of space on the 3.5-inch disk by entering **df /dev/fd0**. You should see this:

```
Filesystem       1k-blocks    Used Available Use% Mounted on
/dev/fd0              1412       1      1339   1% /mnt/
floppy
```

8. Notice that Step 7 shows only 1339 blocks available. You don't have to be great at math to know that if you have 1412 blocks of space on your 3.5-inch disk but you've only used 1 block, you should have 1411 blocks available. What happened to the other 73 blocks? The answer is this line that appeared on the screen when you formatted the 3.5-inch disk:

```
72 blocks (5.00%) reserved for the super user
```

9. Unmount the 3.5-inch disk by entering **umount /dev/fd0**.
10. Place the ext2 filesystem on the 3.5-inch disk as you did in Step 4, but this time specify no reserved disk space by using the -m 0 option. Enter **mke2fs -m 0 /dev/fd0**. Notice that this time the line that appears on the screen is this:

```
0 blocks (0.00%) reserved for the super user
```

11. Mount the 3.5-inch disk by entering either:

    mount -t ext2 /dev/fd0 /mnt/floppy

    or the shorthand notation: **mount /dev/fd0**.
12. Erase the lost+found directory by entering:

    rmdir /mnt/ floppy/lost+found
13. Check the amount of space on the 3.5-inch disk by entering **df /dev/fd0**. You should now see that you have all the disk blocks (except one) available to you:

```
Filesystem       1k-blocks    Used Available Use% Mounted on
/dev/fd0              1412       1      1411   1% /mnt/
floppy
```

NOTE

You got rid of the reserved disk space in Step 10 just to observe the process. The idea of disk space that only the superuser can use is a great one, and you won't find it in many other operating systems. You may want to use this feature on your hard disk file systems—certainly the root (/) file system. However, it probably makes no sense to use it for a 3.5-inch disk or any other removable media storage device.

14. Unmount the 3.5-inch disk by entering **umount /dev/fd0**.

15. Place the ext2 file system on the 3.5-inch disk as you did in Step 4, but this time specify that half of your disk space be reserved by using the -m 50 option. Type **mke2fs -m 50 /dev/fd0**. Notice that this time the line that appears on the screen is this:

    ```
    720 blocks (50.00%) reserved for the super user
    ```

16. Mount the 3.5-inch disk by entering either:

    mount -t ext2 /dev/fd0 /mnt/floppy

    or the shorthand notation: **mount /dev/fd0**.

17. Erase the lost+found directory by entering:

    rmdir /mnt/floppy/lost+found

18. Check the amount of space on the 3.5-inch disk by entering **df /dev/fd0**. You should now see that you have about half of the disk space available to you:

    ```
    Filesystem      1k-blocks   Used Available Use% Mounted on
    /dev/fd0             1412      1       691   1% /mnt/
    floppy
    ```

NOTE

You told the mke2fs program that you wanted to reserve 50% of the disk space, so it reserved 720 blocks. This left 691 blocks available. Okay, so mke2fs can't do math very well.

Certification Objectives

Objectives for the Linux+ exam:

- Configure file systems (e.g., (ext2) or (ext3) or REISER) (1.7)
- Manage local storage devices and file systems (e.g., fsck, fdisk, mkfs) using CLI commands (2.1)
- Mount and unmount varied filesystems (e.g., Samba, NFS) using CLI commands (2.2)

Review Questions

1. How much disk space does ext2 reserve for the superuser by default?
    a. 1%
    b. 2%
    c. 5%
    d. 10%

2. Which program is used to create an ext2 file system?
   a. tune2fs
   b. dumpe2fs
   c. mke2fs
   d. create2fs
3. Which mke2fs option sets the reserved disk space to zero?
   a. **-a 0**
   b. **-m 0**
   c. **-r 0**
   d. **-t 0**
4. What directory is normally created automatically when you create an ext2 file system?
5. Which command tells you the amount of space available on your ext2-formatted 3.5-inch disk?
   a. **ls -l /dev/fd0**
   b. **du /dev/fd0**
   c. **df /dev/fd0**
   d. **dd /dev/fd0**

Lab 6.4 Working with USB Memory

Objectives

The goal of this lab is to become familiar with USB memory devices. These memory devices are often called thumb drives, flash drives, and other terms.

Materials Required

This lab requires the following:

- Access as a root user to a computer running Linux
- Your computer must have a free USB port

Estimated completion time: 20 Minutes

Activity

1. Switch to a command-line terminal (tty2) by pressing **Ctrl+Alt+F2** and log in to the terminal as the root user.
2. Monitor your messages log file by entering **tail –f /var/log/messages**. You can ignore any messages that appear on the screen now.
3. Connect a USB memory device to your computer by plugging it into a USB port. Note that the connector is polarized—it can only be plugged in one way.
4. You should see messages similar to these appear in the messages log file:

```
kernel: scsi1 : SCSI emulation for USB Mass Storage
devices
kernel:   Vendor: MicroAdv  Model: QuickiDrive64M    Rev:
2.00
kernel:   Type:   Direct-Access
ANSI SCSI revision: 02
kernel: SCSI device sda: 128000 512-byte hdwr
sectors (66 MB)
kernel: sda: assuming Write Enabled
kernel: sda: assuming drive cache: write through
kernel:  sda: sda1
kernel: Attached scsi removable disk sda at scsi1, channel
0, id 0, lun 0
```

NOTE: The most important information is "sda." This tells you that the USB memory device is seen by the system as device sda—a SCSI drive. If you see something different, such as sdb, you must modify the steps in this lab accordingly.

5. Press **Ctrl+C** to get back to the command prompt. Create a mount point for the USB memory device. Enter **mkdir /mnt/usb**.
6. Mount the device to the mount point you just created with this command:

   mount /dev/sda1 /mnt/usb

7. Make the mount point directory your current directory by entering:

   cd /mnt/usb

8. You can see the contents of your memory device by entering **ls** or **ls –l**.
9. Create a new file by entering **touch 123**. You can see the file by entering **ls**.
10. See how the USB memory device was mounted by entering **mount**. You see a line similar to this:

```
/dev/sda1 on /mnt/usb type vfat (rw)
```

This tells you that the device is formatted with the vfat filesystem. The term "vfat" is used to describe any of the Microsoft FAT-based filesystems. It also tells you that the device is mounted for read and write access.

NOTE

When you buy a USB memory device, it is formatted with a Windows FAT-based filesystem so Windows users can use it. You can reformat the device with a Linux ext2 filesystem.

11. The device looks just like a hard disk to Linux. Enter **fdisk –l /dev/sda**. You see something similar to this:

```
   Device Boot    Start    End     Blocks  Id  System
/dev/sda1   *         1    249      63728   6  FAT16
```

    This tells you that the device looks like a hard disk—it has a partition table. It uses the first partition (sda1).

12. USB memory devices require the support of the usb_storage kernel module. Enter **lsmod**. You see a line similar to this:

```
usb_storage                 55392   1
```

13. Unplug the USB memory device from the computer. Enter **ls** to again display the contents of the USB memory device. You see error messages appear, because the device was disconnected from the computer.

14. Enter **mount**. You see that Linux thinks the device is still mounted:

```
/dev/sda1 on /mnt/usb type vfat (rw)
```

15. Enter **tail –f /var/log/messages**. Plug the device back in to the same USB port and note the messages that appear. You see a line similar to this:

```
sdb: sdb1
```

    This tells you that Linux now thinks that your USB memory device is a different device—sdb. You can change this behavior, but it involves modification of hotplug configuration files and scripts—not a task for the Linux newbie.

NOTE

Linux USB support is not as highly evolved as other operating systems, such as Windows, but it's getting better.

Certification Objectives

Objectives for the Linux+ exam:

- Manage local storage devices and file systems (e.g., fsck, fdisk, mkfs) using CLI commands (2.1)
- Mount and unmount varied filesystems (e.g., Samba, NFS) using CLI commands (2.2)
- Create files and directories and modify files using CLI commands (2.3)
- Access and write data to recordable media (2.9)

Review Questions

1. USB devices are polarized. They can only be plugged in to a USB port one orientation. True or False?
2. USB memory devices appear to Linux as:
    a. 3.5-inch disk drives
    b. normal IDE hard disks
    c. SCSI hard disks
    d. ZIP drives
3. USB memory devices require the support of what kernel module?
4. When you buy a USB memory device, it is formatted with which filesystem?
    a. FAT
    b. ext2
    c. ext3
    d. ReiserFS
5. When you unplug a USB memory device, Linux may think the device is still mounted. True or False?

Lab 6.5 Using the Fuser Program

Objectives

The goal of this lab is to become familiar with the **fuser** program. This program allows you to see which users or daemons are holding files open. You might need to know this if you'd like to perform an operation on a file or files but some other user has the file(s) open. Also, as a programmer, this could tell you when you have an error in your programming.

Materials Required

This lab requires the following:

- Access as a root user to a computer running Linux

Estimated completion time: 15 Minutes

Activity

LAB ACTIVITY

1. Switch to a command-line terminal (tty2) by pressing **Ctrl+Alt+F2** and log in as the root user.
2. Switch to virtual console 3 by pressing **Alt+F3** and log in as the root user.
3. Create a zero-length file called sample by entering **touch sample**.
4. Open the file and hold it open by entering **less sample**.

> **NOTE** You cannot use the more program to hold the file open unless the file contains more than a screen of text.

5. Switch to virtual console 2 by pressing **Alt+F2**.
6. Use the fuser program to show you the process that is holding the sample file open. Enter **fuser ***. You're asking the fuser program to show you all the files in the current directory that are open. Enter the command **fuser sample**. You should see something similar to this:

```
sample:          7994
```

7. The fuser program told you that process 7994 (your process number will likely be different) is holding the file open. See what process 7994 is by entering **ps 7994** (use your process number in place of 7994). You see this:

```
  PID TTY       STAT      TIME COMMAND
 7994 tty3      S         0:00 less sample
```

8. The ps output in Step 7 tells you that process 7994 was started from virtual console 3 (tty3). If you didn't know who was logged in on tty3, you could find out by entering **w | grep tty3**. You see something similar to this:

```
root    tty3   -      23:47   1:14m  0.60s  0.60s
less sample
```

NOTE

The **w** program shows you who is logged in to the computer and what program they're running. Similar programs are **who** and **whoami**.

9. Steps 1 through 8 show how it's possible to identify a process that has a file open, and to identify the user running the process. Another use of the fuser program is to troubleshoot system problems. Type **fuser /var/log/***. You see something similar to this:

```
/var/log/cron:          57
/var/log/boot.log:      57
/var/log/maillog:       57
/var/log/messages:      57
/var/log/secure:        57
/var/log/spooler:       57
```

10. The fuser output shows you that process 57 has six log files open. Enter **ps 57** to find what the process is:

```
PID TTY      STAT     TIME COMMAND
57  ?        S        0:00 syslogd -m 0
```

It's no surprise to discover that the system logging daemon (syslogd) is holding the log files open.

11. If you are only interested in which user is holding the files open, you can use the –u option. Enter **fuser -u /var/log/***. You see that the root user has these files open:

```
/var/log/cron:          57(root)
/var/log/debug:         57(root)
/var/log/maillog:       57(root)
/var/log/messages:      57(root)
/var/log/secure:        57(root)
/var/log/syslog:        57(root)
```

12. It's particularly useful for an advanced user or programmer to use fuser to show what processes are using a shared library. Enter **cd /lib**. Enter **fuser ***. You see numerous library files displayed similar to this:

```
libcom_err.so.2:       2693m  2902m  2936m  2945m
libcrypt- 2.3.3.so:    2693m  2917m  2936m  2945m   3052m
```

NOTE

The letter m following the process numbers means that the library file is a shared library.

13. Fuser's –v option provides more information and you'll probably like the display format better. Enter **fuser –v ***. You see something similar to this:

```
                  USER      PID ACCESS COMMAND
ld-2.3.3.so       root        1 ....m  init
                  root     2497 ....m  syslogd
                  root     2501 ....m  klogd
                  root     2529 ....m  portmap
                  root     2549 ....m  rpc.statd
                  root     2577 ....m  rpc.idmapd
                  root     2671 ....m  smartd
                  root     2681 ....m  acpid
```


Certification Objectives

This lab exercise does not directly address Linux+ objectives, but provides additional background information to help you master the objectives and understand the Linux operating system.

Review Questions

1. Which program allows you to hold open a very short or zero-length file?
   a. cat
   b. more
   c. less
   d. vi
2. Which program allows you to create a zero-length file?
3. Which program allows you to find the process that's holding a file open?
   a. cat
   b. ps
   c. top
   d. fuser
4. Which of the following commands shows you all the files in a directory that are held open?
   a. **fuser sample**
   b. **fuser -u sample**
   c. **fuser -u /proc/***
   d. **fuser /var/log/messages**
5. What does it mean when fuser follows a process number by the letter m?

CHAPTER SEVEN

ADVANCED INSTALLATION

Labs included in this chapter

- 7.1 Understanding Different Types of RAID
- 7.2 Preparing Your Computer for RAID Exercises
- 7.3 Building a Linear Array
- 7.4 Building a RAID-0 Array
- 7.5 Building a RAID-5 Array

CompTIA Linux+ Exam Objectives

Objective		Lab
1.6	Partition according to pre-installation plan using fdisk (e.g., /boot, /usr, /var, /home, Swap, RAID/volume, hotfix)	7.2
6.5	Identify and configure mass storage devices and RAID (e.g., SCSI, ATAPI, tape, optical recordable)	7.1, 7.2, 7.3, 7.4, 7.5
2.2	Mount and unmount varied filesystems (e.g., Samba, NFS) using CLI commands	7.3, 7.4, 7.5
1.7	Configure file systems (e.g., ext2 or ext3 or REISER)	7.3, 7.4, 7.5
2.1	Manage local storage devices and filesystems (e.g., fsck, fdisk, mkfs) using CLI commands	7.2, 7.3, 7.4, 7.5
2.3	Create files and directories and modify files using CLI commands	7.3, 7.4, 7.5
2.10	Manage runlevels and system initialization from the CLI and configuration files (e.g., /etc/inittab and init command, /etc/rc.d, rc.local)	7.3, 7.4, 7.5

Lab 7.1 Understanding Different Types of RAID

Objectives

The goal of this lab is to demonstrate the different ways that you can build a RAID array using Linux. You can use RAID hardware that does most of the work of handling the RAID array. This is best if your goal is to unburden the CPU in your computer. You can also have the Linux kernel handle the RAID array. This places an additional load on your CPU, but allows you to use standard (inexpensive) hardware.

After completing this lab, you will be able to:

- Understand hardware-based RAID.
- Understand software-based RAID.

Materials Required

This lab requires the following:

- Access to a computer with a Web browser
- Access to the Internet

> **NOTE** This lab explores information on the World Wide Web. Because Web pages can change without notice, what you see may not exactly match the terminology described in this lab. You may have to use your judgment to find the best match for links described here. When in doubt, check with your instructor.

Estimated completion time: 45 Minutes

Activity

1. Start a Web browser and enter the following URL into the browser's Address bar: **http://www.tldp.org**. You're looking at the Linux Documentation Project Web site.
2. Select the **HOWTOs** link.
3. Scroll down until you locate the first **Alphabetical index** link. Click the link.
4. Scroll down until you locate the **ATA-RAID-HOWTO**, **Linux ATA RAID HOWTO** link. Click the link.
5. Scroll down past the Revision History and read the paragraph that describes RAID hardware for IDE drives that are built into certain motherboards. This HOWTO document covers hardware-based RAID. In hardware-based RAID, the RAID function is handled by the RAID hardware in the computer. This

document focuses on RAID hardware from Promise Technology. There are hardware RAID controllers manufactured by other companies, such as Adaptec, but this HOWTO document doesn't cover these.

6. If necessary, scroll down to the Table of Contents, and click the **Introduction** link.
7. Read Section 1. This tells you that this HOWTO document is limited to installing RAID on Red Hat Linux 7.2 systems. RAID can be used with any Linux distribution. This document just tells you about installing RAID with Red Hat Linux 7.2. Because a particular version of a Linux distribution has a lifetime of about six months before being replaced with a newer version, this document's usefulness may be limited.

NOTE

It's typical for authors and vendors to focus on Red Hat Linux even though there are many other Linux distributions available. In most cases, instructions for Red Hat Linux are similar or identical to those for other distributions.

8. Take a look through the remaining sections of this HOWTO document to get an idea of what it takes to set up hardware-based RAID on a Linux system. This is probably quite a bit more complicated than you thought it would be, but the result is a RAID array that performs well and does not burden the Linux kernel with having to perform the RAID function. Once configured, there is little maintenance required.
9. Enter the following URL into your Web browser's Address bar:

   http://www.tldp.org
10. Click the **HOWTOs** link.
11. Scroll down until you locate the first **alphabetical index** link. Click the link.
12. Scroll down until you locate the **Software-RAID-HOWTO** link. Click the link. This HOWTO document discusses software-based RAID, where the RAID functions are handled by the Linux kernel, not by RAID hardware.
13. Click the **Introduction** link. Read the entire page but focus on **The RAID levels** sections (1.4).
14. Scroll to the top or bottom of the page and click the **Next** link. You should now be viewing the **Why RAID?** link. Read the **Device and filesystem support** section. It tells you that Linux software-based RAID works with IDE or SCSI drives or a mixture of the two. You can, for example, create a RAID array using an IDE drive and a SCSI drive.
15. If necessary, scroll to the top of the page and click the **Next** link. You should now be viewing the **Devices** page. This page gives you additional information about IDE and SCSI drives. Read the whole page.

16. Scroll to the top of the page and click the **Next** link. You should now be viewing the **Hardware Issues** page. Read the entire page. Note that you're encouraged to use SCSI drives when you build a RAID array. There are significant penalties if you build an array with IDE drives without using an extra-cost, plug-in IDE controller card.
17. Scroll to the top of the page and click the **Next** link. You should now be viewing the **RAID setup** page. Read the sections (5.4 to 5.8) that describe how to implement the RAID modes such as Linear mode, RAID-0, and so forth.

Certification Objectives

Objectives for the Linux+ exam:

- Identify and configure mass storage devices and RAID (e.g., SCSI, ATAPI, tape, optical recordable) (6.5)

Review Questions

1. With hardware-based RAID, the Linux kernel performs the RAID function. True or False?
2. Hardware-based RAID can only be used with Red Hat Linux. True or False?
3. What's the main reason why people want to use IDE drives in a RAID array?
   a. IDE drives are faster.
   b. IDE drives cost less than SCSI drives.
   c. You can connect more IDE drives than SCSI drives to a bus.
   d. IDE drives work better with Linux.
4. Linux software-based RAID allows you to create a RAID array that consists of a mixture of IDE and SCSI drives. True or False?
5. Explain why it would be a poor idea to use both a master and a slave drive on the same IDE bus as part of a RAID array.

Lab 7.2 Preparing Your Computer for RAID Exercises

Objectives

The goal of this lab is to prepare your computer for completing Labs 7.4 and 7.5 on RAID. Normally, RAID arrays consist of two or more SCSI drives. Because your computer probably doesn't have SCSI drives, you'll be using partitions on ordinary IDE drives to simulate SCSI drives. In this lab exercise, you create these partitions in order to do the following lab exercises.

Materials Required

This lab requires the following:

- ➤ Root access to a computer running Linux
- ➤ Two hard disks in your computer with at least 150 MB of free space on each. If you do not have that much free space, you need to delete an existing partition, shrink an existing partition, or reinstall Linux on your computer.

Estimated completion time: 30 Minutes

Activity

LAB ACTIVITY

1. Log in to the Linux computer as root. If you're at the graphical desktop, press **Ctrl+Alt+F2** to go to a command prompt.
2. Determine what disk partitions exist on your hard disks and whether you have free disk space for creating another partition. Do this by entering **fdisk -l**. Here's an example of what you'd see if you have two IDE hard drives in your computer:

```
Disk /dev/hda: 128 heads, 63 sectors, 993 cylinders
Units = cylinders of 8064 * 512 bytes

   Device Boot     Start         End     Blocks   Id  System
/dev/hda1    *         1         960    3870688+  83  Linux
/dev/hda2            961         993     133056   82  Linux
swap

Disk /dev/hdb: 128 heads, 63 sectors, 993 cylinders
Units = cylinders of 8064 * 512 bytes

   Device Boot     Start         End     Blocks   Id  System
/dev/hdb1              1         993    4003744   83  Linux
```

In the example above, there is no free space on hard disks hda and hdb. You'd have to reinstall Linux unless you have some way of shrinking the size of these existing partitions. There are programs, such as **parted**, that allow you to shrink the size of a Linux ext2 or ext3 partition. If you have a Microsoft FAT partition, you could use the **FIPS** program, supplied with most Linux distributions, to shrink the size of the partition. Note that commercial products, such as PartitionMagic (*www.powerquest.com*), do a much better job than FIPS.

Suppose that instead of the example in Step 2, you see this:

```
Disk /dev/hda: 128 heads, 63 sectors, 993 cylinders
Units = cylinders of 8064 * 512 bytes
```

```
   Device Boot    Start       End    Blocks   Id  System
/dev/hda1   *         1       960   3870688+  83  Linux

Disk /dev/hdb: 128 heads, 63 sectors, 993 cylinders
Units = cylinders of 8064 * 512 bytes

   Device Boot    Start       End    Blocks   Id  System
/dev/hdb1             1       960   3870688+  83  Linux
```

You see that you have free space at the end of both drives. The existing partitions use the disk up to cylinder 960, but cylinders 961 to 993 are free. This means you can create two partitions of 15 cylinders each.

NOTE

It's possible that you may have free disk space that's not at the end of the drive but at the beginning or somewhere in the middle. Linux disk-partitioning programs, such as fdisk, do not force you to create partitions from the start of the hard disk's cylinders to the end.

3. Create two partitions of equal size, one on each of the two hard disks. You can use the fdisk, cfdisk, or the Disk Druid program. You use fdisk here. Assume that hard disks hda and hdb are the ones with free space. It may be different on your computer.
4. Enter **fdisk /dev/hda**. You see this prompt:

   ```
   Command (m for help):
   ```

5. To create a new partition, type **n** and press **Enter**. You see this prompt:

   ```
   Command action
      e   extended
      p   primary partition (1-4)
   ```

6. Type **p** and press **Enter** to create a primary partition. You see this prompt:

   ```
   Partition number (1-4):
   ```

7. Type **2** and press **Enter**. This is the number of the next available partition.

NOTE

The user input for Steps 7 and on is based on the output in the example in Step 2. If your partition or cylinder numbers differ, adjust the numbers in these steps to correspond to your numbers.

8. You are prompted for the starting cylinder. Enter **961** and press **Enter**.
9. You are prompted for the ending cylinder. Enter **977** and press **Enter**.

10. Create the second new partition. Type **n** and press **Enter**. You see this prompt:

```
Command action
   e   extended
   p   primary partition (1-4)
```

11. Type **p** and press **Enter** to create a primary partition. You see this prompt:

```
Partition number (1-4):
```

12. Type **3** and press **Enter**. This is the number of the next available partition.
13. You are prompted for the starting cylinder. Enter **978** and press **Enter**.
14. You are prompted for the ending cylinder. Enter **993** and press **Enter**.
15. Change the partition type for hda2. Type **t** and press **Enter**.
16. You are prompted for the partition number. Type **2** and press **Enter**.
17. You are prompted for the Hex code. Type **fd** and press **Enter**. This value sets a partition type that Linux uses to indicate RAID partitions.
18. Change the partition type for hda3. Type **t** and press **Enter**.
19. You are prompted for the partition number. Type **3** and press **Enter**.
20. You are prompted for the Hex code. Type **fd** and press **Enter**.
21. Save these changes to the hard disk by typing **w** and then pressing **Enter**. You return to the Linux command line.
22. Repeat Steps 4 through 21, except use this command in Step 4:

    fdisk /dev/hdb

    You have now created four disk partitions you can use for your RAID exercises. These partitions are hda2, hda3, hdb2, and hdb3. Your partition names may be different depending on how many existing partitions were already on your hard disk.
23. Reboot your computer for your system to recognize these changes.

Certification Objectives

Objectives for the Linux+ exam:

- Partition according to pre-installation plan using fdisk (e.g., /boot, /usr, /var, /home, Swap, RAID/volume, hotfix) (1.6)
- Identify and configure mass storage devices and RAID (e.g., SCSI, ATAPI, tape, optical recordable) (6.5)
- Manage local storage devices and file systems (e.g., fsck, fdisk, mkfs) using CLI commands (2.1)

Review Questions

1. What command can you use to list all the partitions on all your hard disks?
   a. **ls -p**
   b. **fdisk -a**
   c. **fdisk -l**
   d. **fdisk ***
2. If you have no free space on your only hard disk and the existing disk partitions are ext2, what can you do to create free space on the hard disk?
   a. Use the FIPS program.
   b. Delete one of the partitions and create a smaller one.
   c. Use the **fdisk** expert menu and select the shrink partition item in the menu.
   d. Use the **fsck -s** command.
3. If you have no free space on your only hard disk and one of the existing disk partitions is a Microsoft FAT partition, what can you do to create free space on the hard disk?
   a. Use the FIPS program.
   b. Delete one of the partitions and create a smaller one.
   c. Use the **fdisk** expert menu and select the shrink partition item in the menu.
   d. Use the **fsck -s** command.
4. What should you do if the FIPS program cannot shrink your disk partition?
5. Whenever you have free space on a hard disk, the free space is at the end of the drive (the highest cylinder numbers). True or False?

Lab 7.3 Building a Linear Array

Objectives

The goal of this lab is to build a Linear RAID array using Linux. Linear RAID has no fault tolerance. If one drive in the array fails, all data in the array is lost. Linear RAID is useful for creating filesystems that span physical drives.

Materials Required

This lab requires the following:

- A computer running Linux

- A Linux kernel with RAID support
- A hard disk with two available Linux partitions (you have this if you completed Lab 7.2)

Estimated completion time: 30 Minutes

LAB ACTIVITY

Activity

1. Log in as the root user on a computer running Linux. If you're at the graphical desktop, press **Ctrl+Alt+F2** to go to a text console. This computer should have at least two available Linux partitions with which you can experiment. (You created such partitions in Lab 7.2.) Be careful. If you make a mistake the data on these partitions will be destroyed.
2. The computer must be running a Linux kernel that has RAID functionality built in. Most Linux distributions install a kernel with RAID support. You can tell whether your running kernel has RAID support by checking to see if the /proc/mdstat file exists. If it does exist, you can continue on with this lab exercise. If it does not exist, you cannot complete this lab exercise.

NOTE

If your Linux kernel does not support RAID, you must recompile the kernel.

3. The /proc/mdstat file contains information about your computer's RAID status. Enter **cat /proc/mdstat**. You see the following if your kernel has support for RAID and no RAID arrays configured:

```
Personalities :
Unused devices: <none>
```

4. The first line in the above example shows that no RAID personalities are loaded. This means that the kernel has general RAID support built in, but does not have Linear support configured. Load the Linear personality by entering **modprobe linear**. Then enter **cat /proc/mdstat**. You should now see this:

```
Personalities :[linear]
Unused devices: <none>
```

NOTE

If you're running Fedora Core 2 and you try to load kernel modules with the **insmod** program, it will likely not work. Use the modprobe program instead, as you did in this step.

5. To configure a Linear drive array, use your favorite text editor and create a file called **/etc/raidtab**. If you have partitioned the drives as described in Lab 7.2, enter the lines below. If your available Linux partitions differ from the device names in bold italics below, then substitute the names of your partitions:

   raiddev /dev/md0

   raid-level linear

   nr-raid-disks 2

   persistent-superblock 1

   chunk-size 4

   device */dev/hda2*

   raid-disk 0

   device */dev/hda3*

   raid-disk 1

6. Initialize the drive array with this command:

   mkraid /dev/md0

7. Check on the RAID status by entering **cat /proc/mdstat**. You should see something similar to this:

```
Personalities :[linear]
md0 : active linear hda3[1] hda2[0]
      104576 blocks 4k chunks

unused devices:<none>
```

8. Now you must create a filesystem on the Linear drive array. Enter **mke2fs /dev/md0**. You see something similar to this:

```
mke 2fs 1.35 (28-Feb-2004)
Filesystem label=
OS type: Linux
Block size=1024 (log=0)
Fragment size=1024 (log=0)
26208 inodes, 104576 blocks
5228 blocks (5.00%) reserved for the super user
First data block=1
13 block groups
8192 blocks per group, 8192 fragments per group
2016 inodes per group
Superblock backups stored on blocks:
      8193, 24577, 40961, 57345, 73729

Writing inode tables: done
```

```
Writing superblocks and filesystem accounting information:
done

This filesystem will be automatically checked every 30
mounts or 180 days, whichever comes first.  Use
tune2fs -c or -i to override.
```

NOTE

You can place any filesystem on your RAID array, including ext3 and ReiserFS.

9. Next, you need a mount point for your RAID array. Enter **mkdir /mnt/linear**.
10. Mount the RAID array to the mount point. Enter **mount -t ext2 /dev/md0 /mnt/linear**.
11. Make the mount point your current directory by typing **cd /mnt/linear**.
12. Enter **ls -l** to see that your new filesystem on your newly created RAID array has a lost+found directory. Congratulations! You've created a software linear RAID drive array.

TIP

If you want to have your RAID-0 drive array automatically mounted when you start your computer in the future, add this line to your /etc/fstab file: **/dev/md0 /mnt/linear ext2 defaults 1 1**

13. Copy some files to your array. Enter **cp /etc/* ./** to copy all the files in the /etc directory to the array.
14. Enter **ls** and notice that you have numerous files in the array.
15. Enter **df –h** and notice the size of the array. Compare this to the total size of all the disk partitions that constitute the array.
16. Enter **cd** then enter **umount /mnt/linear** to unmount the RAID array.
17. Enter **raidstop /dev/md0** to disable the array.

Certification Objectives

Objectives for the Linux+ exam:

- Identify and configure mass storage devices and RAID (e.g., SCSI, ATAPI, tape, optical recordable) (6.5)
- Mount and unmount varied filesystems (e.g., Samba, NFS) using CLI commands (2.2)

- Configure filesystems (e.g., ext2 or ext3 or REISER) (1.7)
- Manage local storage devices and filesystems (e.g., fsck, fdisk, mkfs) using CLI commands (2.1)
- Create files and directories and modify files using CLI commands (2.3)
- Manage runlevels and system initialization from the CLI and configuration files (e.g., /etc/inittab and init command, /etc/rc.d, rc.local) (2.10)

Review Questions

1. How can you tell if your Linux kernel has support for basic RAID functionality?
2. Which of the following is a valid device name for a Linear drive array?
   a. /dev/linear
   b. /dev/raid-linear
   c. /dev/md0
   d. /dev/md-linear
3. Linear RAID is fault tolerant. True or False?
4. What would you do if your kernel had support for RAID (the /proc/mdstat file exists), but you had no Linear personality loaded, and you wanted to implement Linear RAID?
5. Describe how the size of the Linear array compares to the sizes of all the disk partitions that constitute the array.

Lab 7.4 Building a RAID-0 Array

Objectives

The goal of this lab is to build a RAID-0 array using Linux. The benefit over Linear RAID is that data is "striped" across all drives in the array. This tends to offer better performance than Linear RAID.

Like Linear RAID, RAID-0 has no fault tolerance. If one drive in the array fails, all data in the array is lost. RAID-0 is useful for creating filesystems that span physical drives and achieving performance that is often better than Linear RAID.

Materials Required

This lab requires the following:

- A computer running Linux
- A Linux kernel with RAID support

- A hard disk with two available Linux partitions (you have this if you completed Lab 7.2)

Estimated completion time: 30 Minutes

LAB ACTIVITY

Activity

1. Log in as the root user on a computer running Linux. If you're at the graphical desktop, press **Ctrl+Alt+F2** to go to a text console. This computer should have at least two available Linux partitions with which you can experiment. (You created such partitions in Lab 7.2.) Be careful. If you make a mistake the data on these partitions will be destroyed.

2. The computer must be running a Linux kernel that has RAID functionality built in. Most Linux distributions install a kernel with RAID support. You can tell whether your running kernel has RAID support by checking to see if the /proc/mdstat file exists. If it does exist, you can continue on with this lab exercise. If it does not exist, you cannot complete this lab exercise.

NOTE

If your Linux kernel does not support RAID, you must recompile the kernel.

3. The /proc/mdstat file contains information about your computer's RAID status. Enter **cat /proc/mdstat**. You see the following if your kernel has support for RAID and no RAID arrays configured:

```
Personalities :
Unused devices: <none>
```

4. The first line in the above example shows that no RAID personalities are loaded. This means that the kernel has general RAID support built in but does not have RAID-0 support configured. Load the RAID-0 personality by entering **modprobe raid0**. Then enter **cat /proc/mdstat**. You should now see this:

```
Personalities :[raid0]
Unused devices: <none>
```

NOTE

If you're running Fedora Core 2 and you try to load kernel modules with the insmod program, it will likely not work. Use the modprobe program instead, as you did in this step.

5. To configure a RAID-0 drive array, use your favorite text editor to modify the /etc/raidtab file. If you partitioned your drive as described in Lab 7.3, the file should be changed as follows:

   raiddev /dev/md0

   raid-level 0

   nr-raid-disks 2

   persistent-superblock 1

   chunk-size 4

   device ***/dev/hda2***

   raid-disk 0

   device ***/dev/hda3***

   raid-disk 1

6. Initialize the drive array with **mkraid/dev/md0**. If you get an error message similar to the following:

   ```
   /dev/hda2 appears to contain an ext2 filesystem-- use f
   to override mkraid aborted
   ```

   enter the command **mkraid -R /dev/md0**.

7. Check on the RAID status by entering **cat /proc/mdstat**. You should see something similar to this:

   ```
   Personalities :[linear][raid0]
   Read_ahead 1024 sectors
   md0 : active raid0 hda3[1] hda2[0]
         104576 blocks 4k chunks

   unused devices:<none>
   ```

8. Now you must create a filesystem on the RAID-0 drive array. Enter **mke2fs /dev/md0**. You see something similar to this:

   ```
   mke 2fs 1.35 (28-Feb-2004)
   Filesystem label=
   OS type: Linux
   Block size=1024 (log=0)
   Fragment size=1024 (log=0)
   26208 inodes, 104576 blocks
   5228 blocks (5.00%) reserved for the super user
   First data block=1
   13 block groups
   8192 blocks per group, 8192 fragments per group
   2016 inodes per group
   ```

```
Superblock backups stored on blocks:
      8193, 24577, 40961, 57345, 73729

Writing inode tables: done
Writing superblocks and filesystem accounting information:
done

This filesystem will be automatically checked every 30
mounts or
180 days, whichever comes first. Use tune2fs -c or
-i to override.
```


NOTE

You can place any filesystem on your RAID array, including ext3 and ReiserFS.

9. Next, you need a mount point for your RAID array. Enter **mkdir /mnt/raid0**.
10. Mount the RAID array to the mount point. Enter **mount -t ext2 /dev/md0 /mnt/raid0**.
11. Make the mount point your current directory by typing **cd /mnt/raid0**.
12. Enter **ls -l** to see that your new filesystem on your newly created RAID array has a lost+found directory. Congratulations! You've created a software RAID-0 drive array.

TIP

If you want to have your RAID-0 drive array automatically mounted when you start your computer in the future, add this line to your /etc/fstab file: **/dev/md0 /mnt/raid0 ext2 defaults 1 1**

13. Copy some files to your array. Enter **cp /etc/* ./** to copy all the files in the /etc directory to the array.
14. Enter **ls** and notice that you have numerous files in the array.
15. Enter **cd** then enter **umount /mnt/raid0** to unmount the RAID array.
16. Enter **raidstop /dev/md0** to disable the array.

Certification Objectives

Objectives for the Linux+ exam:

- Identify and configure mass storage devices and RAID (e.g., SCSI, ATAPI, tape, optical recordable) (6.5)

- Mount and unmount varied filesystems (e.g., Samba, NFS) using CLI commands (2.2)
- Configure filesystems (e.g., ext2 or ext3 or REISER) (1.7)
- Manage local storage devices and filesystems (e.g., fsck, fdisk, mkfs) using CLI commands (2.1)
- Create files and directories and modify files using CLI commands (2.3)
- Manage runlevels and system initialization from the CLI and configuration files (e.g., /etc/inittab and init command, /etc/rc.d, rc.local) (2.10)

Review Questions

1. Which of the following is a valid device name for a RAID-0 drive array?
   a. /dev/raid0
   b. /dev/raid-0
   c. /dev/md0
   d. /dev/md-raid0
2. How can you tell if your Linux kernel has support for RAID-0?
3. What would you do if your kernel had support for RAID (the /proc/mdstat file exists), but you had no RAID-0 personality loaded, and you wanted to implement RAID-0?
4. Which file do you edit in order to define the name of the RAID device, and the disk partitions that are part of the RAID array?
   a. /etc/raidtab
   b. /proc/mdstat
   c. /etc/mdstst
   d. /proc/raidtab
5. Before you can use a RAID array, you must initialize it. Which command does this?
   a. **startraid /dev/md0**
   b. **mkraid /dev/md0**
   c. **initraid /dev/md0**
   d. **cat /proc/mdstat**

Lab 7.5 Building a RAID-5 Array

Objectives

The goal of this lab is to build a RAID-5 array using Linux. The benefit over Linear RAID and RAID-0 is fault tolerance. If one drive in the array fails, no data in the array is lost.

Materials Required

This lab requires the following:

- A computer running Linux
- A Linux kernel with RAID support
- One or two hard disks with four available Linux partitions (you have this if you completed Lab 7.2)

Activity Background

A RAID-5 drive array consists of at least three hard drives. You are free to use more than three hard drives in a RAID-5 drive array. There's no specified maximum number of drives. You're limited to the number of physical drives you can connect to your computer, but there are reasons why you'd want to restrict the number. For example, you risk overloading a SCSI bus and thus creating a performance problem.

If you use hard drives of unequal sizes, the RAID-5 drive array uses the smallest size for all drives. For example, if you build a RAID-5 drive array with three drives that have capacities of 4, 6, and 8GB, only 4GB of space are used on all three drives. It's best that you use the same size drives in a RAID-5 drive array, but the only downside to using unequally sized drives is wasted disk space.

The size of a RAID-5 drive array is $(n-1)*s$, where n is the number of drives in the array and s is the size of each drive. For example, if you use four drives and each is 8GB, the capacity of the array is 24GB ((4-1)*8). The missing 8GB is used to store parity information, which is used to keep the array operating if one drive fails.

Estimated completion time: 30 Minutes

Activity

1. Log in as the root user on a computer running Linux. If you're at the graphical desktop, press **Ctrl+Alt+F2** to go to a text console. This computer should have at least four available Linux partitions with which you can experiment. The data on these partitions will be destroyed. You have these partitions if you completed Lab 7.2.

2. Enter **cat /proc/mdstat**. Assuming that you completed the previous lab, you see that you already have RAID-0 support loaded:

   ```
   Personalities : [linear] [raid0]
   Unused devices: <none>
   ```

3. Now load the RAID-5 personality. Enter **modprobe raid5**. Enter **cat /proc/mdstat**. You should now see this:

   ```
   Personalities : [linear] [raid0] [raid5]
   Unused devices: <none>
   ```

4. Edit the **/etc/raidtab** file for RAID-5 so it looks similar to this:

   ```
   raiddev /dev/md0
           raid-level       5
           nr-raid-disks    4
           nr-spare-disks   0
           parity-algorithm  left-symmetric
           persistent-superblock 1
           chunk-size      32
           device           /dev/hda2
           raid-disk        0
           device           /dev/hda3
           raid-disk        1
           device           /dev/hdb2
           raid-disk        2
           device           /dev/hdb3
           raid-disk        3
   ```

NOTE You should use your partitions if they differ from the previous example.

5. If you're using the same disk partitions as you did for the previous lab, these partitions contain filesystems. The **mkraid** program does not normally allow you to use these partitions in a new array. It doesn't want you to lose your data. You must override this using the –R command-line option. Enter **mkraid -R /dev/md0**.

6. Check on the RAID status by entering **cat /proc/mdstat**. You should see something similar to this:

   ```
   Personalities : [linear] [raid0] [raid5]
   md0 : active raid5 hdb3[3] hdb2[2] hda3[1] hda2[0]
         156864 blocks level 5, 32k chunk, algorithm 2 [4/
   4] [UUUU]

   unused devices: <none>
   ```

7. Now you must create a filesystem on the RAID-5 drive array. Enter **mke2fs /dev/md0**. You see something similar to this:

```
mke 2fs 1.35 (28-Feb-2004)
Filesystem label=
OS type: Linux
Block size=1024 (log=0)
Fragment size=1024 (log=0)
26208 inodes, 104576 blocks
5228 blocks (5.00%) reserved for the super user
First data block=1
13 block groups
8192 blocks per group, 8192 fragments per group
2016 inodes per group
Superblock backups stored on blocks:
      8193, 24577, 40961, 57345, 73729

Writing inode tables: done
Writing superblocks and filesystem accounting information:
done

This filesystem will be automatically checked every 30
mounts or
180 days, whichever comes first.  Use tune2fs -c or
-i to override.
```


8. Next, you need a mount point for your RAID array. Enter **mkdir /mnt/raid5**.
9. Mount the RAID array to the mount point. Enter **mount -t ext2 /dev/md0 /mnt/raid5**.
10. Make the mount point your current directory by typing **cd /mnt/raid5**.
11. Enter **ls -l** to see that your new filesystem on your newly created RAID array has a lost+found directory. Congratulations! You've created a software RAID-5 drive array.

TIP

If you want to have your RAID-5 drive array automatically mounted when you start your computer in the future, add this line to your /etc/fstab file: **/dev/md0 /mnt/raid5 ext2 defaults 1 1**

12. Copy some files to your array. Enter **cp /etc/* ./** to copy all the files in the /etc directory to the array.
13. Enter **ls** and notice that you have numerous files in the array.
14. Enter **cd** then enter **umount /mnt/raid5** to unmount the RAID array.
15. Enter **cd**, then enter **umount /mnt/raid0** to unmount the RAID array.

Certification Objectives

Objectives for the Linux+ exam:

- Identify and configure mass storage devices and RAID (e.g., SCSI, ATAPI, tape, optical recordable) (6.5)
- Mount and unmount varied filesystems (e.g., Samba, NFS) using CLI commands (2.2)
- Configure filesystems (e.g., ext2 or ext3 or REISER) (1.7)
- Manage local storage devices and filesystems (e.g., fsck, fdisk, mkfs) using CLI commands (2.1)
- Create files and directories and modify files using CLI commands (2.3)
- Manage runlevels and system initialization from the CLI and configuration files (e.g., /etc/inittab and init command, /etc/rc.d, rc.local) (2.10)

Review Questions

1. What is the minimum number of drives in a RAID-5 drive array?
   a. 1
   b. 2
   c. 3
   d. 4
2. What is the maximum number of drives in a RAID-5 drive array?
3. What happens if the drives in a RAID-5 drive array are of unequal sizes?
4. If you have a RAID-5 drive array that consists of four drives, and each is a 20GB drive, what is the resulting capacity of the array?
   a. 20
   b. 40
   c. 60
   d. 80
5. What would you do if your kernel had support for RAID (the /proc/mdstat file exists), but you had no RAID-5 personality loaded?

CHAPTER EIGHT

WORKING WITH THE BASH SHELL

Labs included in this chapter

- Lab 8.1 Using the BASH History Feature
- Lab 8.2 Customizing the BASH History Feature
- Lab 8.3 Customizing Your Shell Prompts
- Lab 8.4 Adding Automation to the BASH Prompt
- Lab 8.5 Setting CDPATH

CompTIA Linux+ Exam Objectives

Objective		Lab
2.3	Create files and directories and modify files using CLI commands	8.2, 8.4
2.19	Create, modify, and use basic shell scripts	8.4
2.23	Redirect output (e.g., piping, redirection)	8.1, 8.2, 8.4
3.12	Set up environment variables (e.g., $PATH, $DISPLAY, $TERM)	8.2, 8.3, 8.4, 8.5

Lab 8.1 Using the BASH History Feature

Objectives

The goal of this lab is to acquaint you with the BASH command history. The goal of the history feature is to reduce the number of keystrokes you need to type to get something done.

After completing this lab, you will be able to:

- Use the BASH command history feature to recall previous commands with the Up arrow key; by specifying historic command numbers; by searching for historic commands that contain a certain string; and by replacing words in the most recent command.

Materials Required

This lab requires the following:

- Access as an ordinary user to a computer running Linux

Estimated completion time: 15 Minutes

Activity

1. Switch to a command-line terminal (tty2) by pressing **Ctrl+Alt+F2**, and log in to the terminal using any username.
2. The BASH shell keeps a history of the commands you've entered in the past. You can access this history in a few ways. The easiest way is to use the **Up arrow** key. Press the **Up arrow** key now. Your most recent command appears. Press the **Up arrow** key again to see the next most recent command.
3. Clear the command line of characters using the **Backspace** key.
4. Next, give BASH some commands to remember. Enter the following lines, pressing **Enter** after each line:

   cd

   ls -l /etc

   ls -l

   whoami

   who

5. Next, check to see if these commands were added to the history. You can get a list of all historic commands with the **history** command. Type **history** and press **Enter**. The screen scrolls, but the commands you entered in Step 4 are now visible. You can see that each historic command is numbered, like this:

```
779 cd
780 ls -l /etc
781 ls -l
782 whoami
783 who
784 history
```

6. You can select any of the historic commands by stepping back through history with the Up arrow key, but this is more and more troublesome as the age of the command increases (it's further back in history). An easier way is to either specify the number of the historic command, or search for it. To select and execute a command by number, you enter an exclamation point (!) followed by the number of the command. Enter **!** followed by the number of your ls –l /etc command. You see a long listing of the /etc directory.

7. Referring to a historic command by number requires that you first list the history to get the number. This is inefficient. You can search for the command you want instead. Enter **!?etc?** Once again, you see the long listing of the /etc directory. BASH searched for the most recent command that contained the string "etc" and then executed it.
8. Type **history** and press **Enter**. You see that the second-to-last historic command is **ls -l /etc**, not **!?etc?**. BASH only saves historic commands, not the strings that are used to search for commands.
9. Enter **!?wombat99?** Because the string "wombat99" is not likely to be in your command history, BASH can't find it. It produces the error message:

```
-bash: !?wombat99?: event not found
```

10. If you want to search for commands in which the string you're searching for is at the start of the command line, you can eliminate the question marks around the string. Enter **!who**. BASH finds and executes the **who** command.

whoami – logged user
who – start the terminal

11. Suppose you wanted the **whoami** command to run instead. You'd have to enter just one more keystroke, because the **who** command is a more recent historic command than the **whoami** command. Enter **!whoa**. The **whoami** command runs.
12. The BASH history feature also allows substitution of strings in the most recent historic command. Experiment with this by entering **cat /bin/bash | strings | grep shell | less**. This lengthy command displays all the strings in the /bin/bash file that contain the word "shell." Because there are likely to be a lot of them, the output is piped through the less filter. Press **q** to exit **less**.

13. If you now want to display the strings that contain the word "alias," you don't have to type another lengthy command. Type **^shell^alias^** and press **Enter**. This replaces the word "shell" with the word "alias" in the most recent historic command and executes the **alias** command.
14. Press **Alt+F7** to return to your graphical desktop.

Many of the examples in this lab are simple and short. Clearly, the BASH history feature is more useful as the length of the commands increase.

Certification Objectives

Objectives for the Linux+ exam:

- Redirect output (e.g., piping, redirection) (2.23)

Review Questions

1. Which command displays all your historic commands?
   a. **ls --history**
   b. **ls --h**
   c. **history**
   d. **histfile**
2. Which command executes historic command number 213?
   a. **history 213**
   b. **!history 213**
   c. **!?213?**
   d. **!213**
3. Which command executes the most recent historic command that contains the string **/usr/sbin**?
   a. **history "/usr/sbin"**
   b. **!hist "/usr/sbin"**
   c. **!?/usr/sbin?**
   d. **!"/usr/sbin"**
4. Which command executes the most recent historic command that starts with the string "touch"?
   a. **!touch**
   b. **!?touch?**
   c. **history "touch"**
   d. **hist ?touch?**

5. You want to execute the same command as the last one you executed, except that you want the word "report" to be replaced by "summary." Which command does this?
   a. **s/summary/report/**
   b. **?report?summary?**
   c. **^report^summary^**
   d. **| summary | report|**

Lab 8.2 Customizing the BASH History Feature

Objectives

The goal of this lab is to familiarize you with the various ways that you can customize the BASH command history feature.

After completing this lab, you will be able to:

- Understand when the BASH history file is updated.
- Specify the number of historic commands that are remembered.
- Set the HISTSIZE environment variable.

Materials Required

This lab requires the following:

- Access as an ordinary user to a computer running Linux

Estimated completion time: 20 Minutes

Activity

1. Switch to a command-line terminal (tty2) by pressing **Ctrl+Alt+F2**, and log in to the terminal using an ordinary username. Do not log in as root.
2. Historic commands are remembered even if you log out and log in again. This is achieved with the help of a history file stored in your home directory. The file is called .bash_history. Ensure that you're in your home directory by entering the command **cd**.

3. Look at the last several lines in the .bash_history file by typing **tail .bash_history**. Notice that the last line of the file is not **tail .bash_history** and the previous command is not **cd**. This means that the .bash_history file is not up to date.
4. Enter **history**. You see that the last line that appears is the command **history**. The previous line is **tail .bash_history**. The history command seems to be up to date even though the .bash_history file is not. This is because command history is kept in system memory. In the next steps, you see when the .bash_history file is updated.
5. Enter **echo 'This is my command'**.

NOTE

When you use the echo command, it's best to use single quotes rather than double quotes around the string. Single quotes prevent the shell from trying to interpret special characters.

6. Enter **logout**. After you're logged out, you are at a login prompt.
7. Log in again as the same ordinary user.
8. Enter **history**. You see the command **echo 'This is my command'** near the end of the list.
9. Enter **tail .bash_history**. You see the command **echo 'This is my command'** near the end of the list. This means that the .bash_history file was updated when you logged out.
10. Your history file can be quite large if you've used your computer a lot, and most of it quickly scrolls by the screen. You can use the **more** or **less** commands to prevent the scrolling. Enter **history | less**. You see the oldest history commands on your screen. Press the **spacebar** to see more of the file. You can exit at any time by pressing **q**.
11. You can use the **wc** (word count) program to see exactly how many historic commands are in the file. You can ask it to count lines rather than count words. Enter **wc -l .bash_history**. You see something similar to this:

```
1000  .bash_history.
```

12. The above output shows you that there are 1000 historic commands stored in the history file. This is normally the limit set by Fedora Core 2. The value may be different with other Linux distributions. This limit is imposed by an environment variable called HISTSIZE. You can see the value of HISTSIZE on your system. Enter **set | grep HISTSIZE**. You see this:

```
HISTSIZE=1000
```

13. Suppose you don't want to be limited to 1000 historic commands. You want 5000. You have to change the HISTSIZE variable in your startup script. This script is called .bashrc and is in your home directory. If the HISTSIZE variable is defined in this file, you can use your favorite text editor to change the value. However, with Fedora Core 2, the HISTFILE variable is not set in the .bashrc file. Let's add the statement without using a text editor. Enter **echo 'HISTSIZE=5000' >> .bashrc**. This new value is honored the next time the BASH shell rereads the .bashrc file—typically when you log in again.

NOTE

If your system does not set the HISTSIZE variable in any of the startup or login scripts, BASH typically defaults to 500 commands.

NOTE

With Fedora Core 2, the HISTSIZE variable is set in the /etc/profile file. If you change it there, it affects every user that logs in to the system.

14. Enter **logout**.
15. Log in again as the same user.
16. Enter **set | grep HISTSIZE**. You should now see that the HISTSIZE has changed:

    ```
    HISTSIZE=5000
    ```

17. Enter the **history** command several times. Notice that each time you do this, a **history** command is added to the history. This is okay if you want the BASH history to be a faithful record of every command you type, but it's a waste if you just use the BASH history as a way to save keystrokes.
18. You can configure BASH to not add a command to history if the same command is the previous command. You do this by adding an environment variable called HISTCONTROL and assigning it a value of **ignoredups**. You can add this to your .bashrc file, similarly to what you did in Step 13. Enter **echo 'HISTCONTROL=ignoredups' >> .bashrc**. This new value is honored the next time the BASH shell rereads the .bashrc file, usually when you log in again.
19. Enter **logout** to return to the login prompt.
20. Log in as the same user again.
21. Enter the **history** command several times. Notice that even though you're entering the same command over and over, only one **history** command is added to history.

Certification Objectives

Objectives for the Linux+ exam:

- ➤ Create files and directories and modify files using CLI commands (2.3)
- ➤ Redirect output (e.g., piping, redirection) (2.23)
- ➤ Set up environment variables (e.g., $PATH, $DISPLAY, $TERM) (3.12)

Review Questions

1. In which file are your historic commands saved?
   a. .bashrc
   b. profile
   c. .bash_history
   d. .history
2. Your BASH history file is updated:
   a. when you log in
   b. when you log out
   c. when you execute any BASH command
   d. when the filesystem cache is flushed to disk
3. Which command lets you easily see how many lines are in your .bash_history file?
   a. **grep "*" .bash_history**
   b. **wc -l .bash_history**
   c. **ls -l .bash_history**
   d. **history --lines**
4. How many commands does BASH typically save to the history file if you have no HISTSIZE variable?
   a. 500
   b. 650
   c. 800
   d. 1000
5. How do you eliminate adjacent duplicate commands from being saved to the BASH history?
   a. You must recompile BASH with the --suppressdups switch.
   b. Set the value of the HISTCONTROL environment variable to ignoredups.

c. Hold the Control key down when you type a command.

d. Type this command: **echo "1" > /proc/sys/kernel/bash/duplicates**.

Lab 8.3 Customizing Your Shell Prompts

Objectives

The goal of this lab is to see how you can control the two most often used shell prompts: PS1 and PS2.

After completing this lab, you will be able to:

- Set the BASH PS1 and PS2 prompts to display system information.
- Configure any of the BASH prompts to use color.

Materials Required

This lab requires the following:

- Access as an ordinary user to a computer running Linux

Estimated completion time: 20 Minutes

LAB ACTIVITY

Activity

1. Switch to a command-line terminal (tty2) by pressing **Ctrl+Alt+F2**, and log in to the terminal using any username.
2. The main BASH prompt is configured by setting the value of the PS1 environment variable. Instead of displaying a static string as a prompt, you might want the string to be dynamic. That is, you might want it to show the current directory or current time, for example. Enter **PS1='\t:'** to display the current system time in 24-hour format as the BASH prompt. You see the current time in HH:MM:SS format such as 18:31:00:.
3. You can see the time in the 12-hour format with AM and PM indicators by entering **PS1='\@:'** . You see the current time in HH:MM:SS format such as 06:31pm:. Note the AM or PM indicator replaced the seconds display.
4. Most people want the BASH prompt to display the current working directory. The directory can be displayed with the entire path or just the directory name. The **\W** special character displays just the directory name. The **\w** special character displays the entire path. Enter **PS1='\w:'**. If your current directory is your home directory, you see this prompt: **~:**

5. Enter **cd /usr/sbin**. You now see /usr/sbin: as your prompt.
6. Enter **PS1='\W:'**. You now see the sbin: prompt.
7. There are other BASH prompts that you can customize. These are PS2, PS3, and PS4. The PS2 prompt is used as the secondary prompt. To see how it's used, type **echo 'Hello** (do not enter the closing quote) and press **Enter**. The greater-than symbol (>) appears. This tells you that BASH is waiting for you to complete your command.

NOTE

The PS3 and PS4 prompts won't be covered in this exercise.

8. Type the closing quote (') and press **Enter**. The command is now complete and the PS2 prompt, the word **Hello**, appears followed by the PS1 prompt on a new line.
9. You can change the PS2 prompt just as you changed the PS1 prompt. Enter **PS2='Finish entering your command:'**.
10. Type **echo 'Hello** (do not enter the closing quote), and press **Enter**. You are prompted on the next line with `Finish entering your command:`
11. Type the closing quote (') and press **Enter**. The command is now complete, and the word **Hello** appears followed by the PS1 prompt on a new line.

NOTE

A useful addition to the PS2 prompt is to have it produce a beep along with the greater-than (**>**) prompt. You can do this by using the \a special character as in this example: PS2='> \a'.

12. You can have your BASH prompts be displayed in color by surrounding the prompt string with color-setting strings. In the following examples, the BASH prompt is set to **\w\$**, which simply displays the current working directory followed by a **$** (or **#** if you're logged in as root). To set the prompt to blue, enter:

    PS1='\033[0;34m\w\$ \033[0;37m'

NOTE

It's important that you use single quotes rather than double quotes in these exercises.

13. You should now see a blue prompt. The color is controlled by the number 34 used in the previous step. If you change the number, you get a different color. Enter the following command to get a red prompt:

    PS1='\033[0;31m\w\$ \033[0;37m'

TIP

Here are some color values that you can experiment with: 30=black, 31=red, 32=green, 34=blue, 35=purple, 36=cyan, 37=white. Rather than typing these commands again and again, use the BASH history feature. Recall these commands with the Up arrow key and modify them.

14. You can have multiple colors within the prompt. You can display the current working directory in red and the $ character in green. Enter the following to do this:

    PS1='\033[0;31m\w\033[0;32m\$ \033[0;37m'

15. You can control other visual attributes of shell prompts such as brightness, blinking, and reverse. The most useful is the bright attribute. Enter the following to make the prompt brighter (though your display hardware may make it difficult to see a significant change in brightness):

    PS1='\033[1;31m\w\033[1;32m\$ \033[0;37m'

16. The bright attribute is controlled by the number 1. If you change the number, you get a different visual attribute. Enter the following command to get reverse video:

    PS1='\033[7;31m\w\033[7;32m\$ \033[0;37m'

17. As you can see, reverse is where the character cell background is displayed in the selected color and the character is black within the cell. Enter the following for a blinking prompt:

    PS1='\033[5;31m\w\033[5;32m\$ \033[0;37m'

Certification Objectives

Objectives for the Linux+ exam:

- Set up environment variables (e.g., $PATH, $DISPLAY, $TERM) (3.12)

Review Questions

1. Which special character displays the system time in a 24-hour format (HH:MM:SS)?

    a. **\T**

    b. **\t**

    c. **\r**

    d. **\R**

2. Which special character displays the complete path?
   a. **\w**
   b. **\W**
   c. **/p**
   d. **/P**
3. The PS2 prompt is displayed when:
   a. You're in a subshell.
   b. You're using a shell other than BASH.
   c. You have not completed typing a command but you press the Enter key.
   d. You press the Tab key.
4. Which command causes a beep?
   a. **PS1='\w\$'**
   b. **PS2='> \a'**
   c. **PS1='\u.\h.\w'**
   d. **PS2='> ' --beep**
5. Which of these commands produces a green prompt string?
   a. **PS1='\033[0;31m\w\$ \033[0;37m'**
   b. **PS1='\033[0;32m\w\$ \033[0;37m'**
   c. **PS1='\033[0;33m\w\$ \033[0;37m'**
   d. **PS1='\033[0;34m\w\$ \033[0;37m'**

Lab 8.4 Adding Automation to the BASH Prompt

Objectives

The goal of this lab is to show you how you can configure BASH to automatically run shell scripts.

After completing this lab, you will be able to:

- Run a program automatically when the PS1 prompt is displayed.

Materials Required

This lab requires the following:

- Access as an ordinary user to a computer running Linux

Activity Background

In this exercise, you build a list of names of people. The list is stored in a file called list. Each name is followed by a simple number that has some significance to you. Perhaps it's an index into another file or database. Also, each time you add a new name to the list you want to be sure the list is sorted in alphabetical order. There are many ways to do this, of course.

In this exercise, you use a feature of BASH that allows you to automatically run a program whenever the BASH PS1 prompt is displayed. The PS1 prompt is the main prompt that appears whenever control is returned to the BASH shell. Note that this feature does not exist in some other shells.

Estimated completion time: 15 Minutes

LAB ACTIVITY

Activity

1. Switch to a command-line terminal (tty2) by pressing **Ctrl+Alt+F2**, and log in to the terminal using any username.
2. Go to your home directory by entering **cd ~** or **cd**.
3. Create the file called list. Enter **touch list**.
4. First you create a simple shell script program to sort the list file using a simple shell script. You could use a text editor to create the file, but because it's only one line, use the **echo** command to create the file. Enter the following:

   echo 'sort ~/list > ~/r13; mv ~/r13 ~/list' > ~/sorter

5. You just created a script file called **sorter** in your home directory. Now, to make it executable, enter **chmod +x sorter**.

NOTE

Normally, programs of any type should be located in an appropriate directory, not your home directory. You studied the Filesystem Hierarchy Standard in a previous chapter, so you should have some idea which directories to use. For simplicity in this exercise, you put the script in your home directory. For simplicity, the hashpling is also not being used (the first line in shell script files that defines which shell is used; also referred to as the shebang line).

6. The next thing to do is to tell BASH that you want to run the sorter program every time BASH displays the PS1 prompt. To do this, create an environment variable called PROMPT_COMMAND whose value is the name of the sorter program by entering **PROMPT_COMMAND=~/sorter**.
7. Enter **echo 'Smith, John:13001'>>list**. The string 'Smith, John:13001' is appended to the end of the file.

8. Enter **cat list**. You see the contents of the list file. At this point, the file has only one line so you can't determine if it's sorted.
9. Enter several commands similar to the one in Step 7 but with different names and numbers. Do not enter the names in alphabetical order. Now enter **cat list**. You see that the file is alphabetized even though you did not enter the names in alphabetical order. The file was sorted each time BASH displayed the PS1 prompt.
10. It's unlikely that you'll want BASH to alphabetize files all the time, so you probably don't want to put the **PROMPT_COMMAND=~/sorter** statement in a shell configuration file such as .bashrc. When you want BASH to stop running the sorter program, you can either enter **PROMPT_COMMAND=** or log out and log in again.

Certification Objectives

Objectives for the Linux+ exam:

- Create files and directories and modify files using CLI commands (2.3)
- Create, modify, and use basic shell scripts (2.19)
- Redirect output (e.g., piping, redirection) (2.23)
- Setup environment variables (e.g., $PATH, $DISPLAY, $TERM) (3.12)

Review Questions

1. What must you do to ensure that a shell script can execute?
   a. After creating the shell script, log out and log in again.
   b. Make sure that the /bin/bash file has the execute permission.
   c. Make sure that the shell script file has the execute permission.
   d. You must be logged in as the root user.
2. What is the name of the main BASH prompt?
   a. PS1
   b. PS2
   c. prompt
   d. prompt1
3. How do you configure BASH to execute a program or command whenever the main prompt is displayed?
   a. Put a PROMPT_COMMAND statement in one of the BASH configuration files.
   b. Create the PROMPT_COMMAND environment variable and set its value to the name of the program or command you want executed.

c. You must run another copy of the BASH shell using the **--run** command-line option.

d. You must include the name of the program or command in the PS1 environment variable value.

4. If you want BASH to stop automatically executing a program or command when the prompt is displayed, you can type **PROMPT_COMMAND=** and press **Enter**. True or False?

5. The ability to execute a program or command automatically when the shell prompt is displayed is a feature of all shells, not just BASH. True or False?

Lab 8.5 Setting CDPATH

Objectives

The goal of this lab is to explore the use of the BASH feature called CDPATH. This feature does for the cd command what the shell's PATH feature does for running programs: it searches for the correct directory.

After completing this lab, you will be able to:

- Understand and use the CDPATH feature of BASH.

Materials Required

This lab requires the following:

- Access as an ordinary user to a computer running Linux

Estimated completion time: 15 Minutes

Activity

1. Switch to a command-line terminal (tty2) by pressing **Ctrl+Alt+F2**, and log in to the terminal using any username.

2. Ensure that your current working directory is your home directory. If necessary, enter **cd** to go to your home directory.

3. Set your BASH PS1 prompt to display the current directory. Enter **PS1='\w:'**.

4. Enter **cd bin**. You see the following error message because there is no bin directory below your home directory:

```
bash: cd: bin: No such file or directory
```

5. Enter **CDPATH=:/usr**. You've told BASH that if it can't find a bin directory below the current directory, it should look for one below the /usr directory.
6. Enter **cd bin**. This time, there is no error message. Instead, your current working directory is changed to /usr/bin. The BASH prompt shows you this.
7. Enter **cd** to go back to your home directory.
8. Enter **mkdir ~/bin**. This creates a bin directory below your home directory.
9. Enter **cd bin**. This time, the current working directory is set to ~/bin, the bin directory below your home directory.
10. Enter **CDPATH=/usr**. Note that you eliminated the colon that was present in the similar command you typed in Step 5. Steps 11 and 12 show the results of this.
11. Enter **cd** to go back to your home directory.
12. Enter **cd bin**. The current working directory is set to /usr/bin—the bin directory below the /usr directory—not the bin directory below your home directory. What happened? By eliminating the colon, you told BASH not to search for directories below your current working directory, in this case, your home directory.

NOTE The CDPATH feature does not search for directories if you use a cd command that specifies a directory that begins with a slash (/), dot (.) or dot-dot (..) characters.

13. Go back to your home directory by entering **cd**.
14. Enter **cd ~/bin**. This time, BASH set the current working directory to the ~/bin directory because you explicitly specified it. BASH didn't have to search for it.
15. Next, make it more complex. Enter **CDPATH=:/usr:/var**. You've told BASH to search your current working directory first, followed by the /usr directory, and then the /var directory.
16. Go back to your home directory by entering **cd**.
17. Enter **cd log**. The current working directory is set to /var/log. BASH could not find a log directory below the current working directory or the /usr directory, but did find a log directory below /var.

Certification Objectives

Objectives for the Linux+ exam:

- Set up environment variables (e.g., $PATH, $DISPLAY, $TERM) (3.12)

Review Questions

1. You've entered the command **CDPATH=:/usr:/var**. In what order does BASH search for directories?
   a. It searches the /usr directory followed by the /var directory.
   b. It searches the /var directory followed by the /usr directory.
   c. It searches the current working directory followed by the /usr directory followed by the /var directory.
   d. It searches the /var directory followed by the /usr directory followed by the current working directory.
2. What's the problem with the command **CDPATH=/usr** ?
   a. It conflicts with the PATH.
   b. It doesn't find directories below your current working directory.
   c. It doesn't allow you to make the /usr directory the current working directory.
   d. It doesn't allow you to go to directories to which you've mounted your CD-ROM.
3. If you've executed the command **CDPATH=/usr** and your current working directory is your home directory, you can go to the /bin directory by entering **cd /bin**. True or False?
4. If you're logged in as root, if your current working directory is your home directory, and you've executed the command **CDPATH=/usr**, you can go to the /bin directory by entering **cd ../bin**. True or False?
5. If you've executed the command **CDPATH=/usr** and your current working directory is your home directory, you can go to the bin directory below your home directory by entering **cd ~/bin**. True or False?

CHAPTER NINE

SYSTEM INITIALIZATION

Labs included in this chapter

CompTIA Linux+ Exam Objectives

Objective		Lab
2.3	Create files and directories and modify files using CLI commands	9.1, 9.2, 9.3
2.10	Manage runlevels and system initialization from the CLI and configuration files (e.g., /etc/inittab and init command, /etc/rc.d, rc.local)	9.1, 9.2, 9.3
2.11	Identify, execute, manage and kill processes (e.g., ps, kill, killall, bg, fg, jobs, nice, renice, rc)	9.1, 9.2, 9.3
2.15	Perform text manipulation (e.g., sed, awk, vi)	9.1, 9.2, 9.3
N/A	This lab does not directly map to a certification objective; however, it gives background information that will help you master the objectives and understand the Linux operating system.	9.4, 9.5

Lab 9.1 Setting the Initial Runlevel

Objectives

The purpose of this lab is to learn how to change the default runlevel at startup. Many Linux distributions, including Fedora Core 2, set the initial runlevel to 5, which automatically starts the graphical user interface. Some Linux users don't want this and prefer that the system boot up to a command prompt. Runlevel 3 provides this. You can easily configure this by modifying the /etc/inittab file. In this lab, you experiment with initial runlevels, including not specifying a runlevel at all.

Activity Background

The common runlevels and their meanings are:

0—Halt the system.

1—Use single user mode.

2—Use multi-user mode but no networking support.

3—Use multi-user mode with full networking support.

5—Use multi-user mode with full networking support and start the graphical user interface.

6—Reboot the system.

Materials Required

This lab requires the following:

- Access as a root user to a computer running Linux

Estimated completion time: 15 Minutes

Activity

LAB ACTIVITY

1. Switch to a command-line terminal (tty2) by pressing **Ctrl+Alt+F2**, and log in to the terminal as root.
2. Using your favorite text editor, edit the /etc/inittab file.
3. Locate the statement that looks similar or identical to this:

   ```
   id:5:initdefault:
   ```

   This statement tells the **init** program that it should start Linux in runlevel 5 when you boot your computer. This loads the graphical subsystem before you're prompted to log in.

4. Change this so your computer boots to runlevel 3. Modify the line so it looks like this:

   ```
   id:3:initdefault:
   ```

5. Save the file and exit the editor.

6. Reboot the computer by pressing **Ctrl+Alt+Del**. When the kernel is finished loading itself, it begins running the init program. The init program reads the /etc/inittab file and begins performing the actions it finds there. The statement you modified tells it to start in runlevel 3. It does not start the graphical user interface. You see a text-mode login prompt. Log in as root.

7. Edit the /etc/inittab file again. See what happens if you do not tell the init program what runlevel to use. You can do this by commenting the line. Add a number sign (#) at the start of the line. The line should look like this:

   ```
   #id:3:initdefault:
   ```

8. Save the file and exit the text editor.

9. Reboot the computer by pressing **Ctrl+Alt+Del**. When the kernel is finished loading, the init program reads the /etc/inittab file and begins performing the actions it finds there. Because you removed the line that tells init the initial runlevel, init doesn't know what to do. It prompts you for the runlevel, as shown here:

   ```
   Enter runlevel:
   ```

10. To start the system in runlevel 3, enter **3**. The system finishes booting in runlevel 3. You see a text-mode login prompt. Log in as root.

11. If you don't want to be prompted for the runlevel every time you boot Linux, restore the /etc/inittab file by editing it to remove the number sign at the start of the line that specifies the initial runlevel. If you're running your computer as a desktop, it probably makes sense to set the initial runlevel to 5. If you're running your computer as a server, it probably makes sense to set the initial runlevel to 3. If you want to choose the runlevel every time you boot the computer, remove the line from the /etc/inittab file or comment it out.

9

Certification Objectives

Objectives for the Linux+ exam:

- Create files and directories and modify files using CLI commands (2.3)
- Manage runlevels and system initialization from the CLI and configuration files (e.g., /etc/inittab and init command, /etc/rc.d, rc.local) (2.10)
- Identify, execute, manage and kill processes (e.g., ps, kill, killall, bg, fg, jobs, nice, renice, rc) (2.11)
- Perform text manipulation (e.g., sed, awk, vi) (2.15)

Review Questions

1. The initial runlevel is determined by which file?
   a. /etc/lilo.conf or /etc/grub.conf
   b. /etc/inittab
   c. /etc/runlevel
   d. /etc/boot.conf
2. What happens if there is no initial runlevel statement in the configuration file?
   a. The operating system refuses to load, and the system hangs.
   b. The operating system loads, but the init program hangs.
   c. The operating system loads, and the init program prompts you for the runlevel.
   d. Runlevel 1 is assumed.
3. Runlevel ________________ starts the system in multi-user mode, but has no networking support.
4. Runlevel ________________ halts the system.
5. Under what conditions does it make most sense to always start the computer in runlevel 3?

Lab 9.2 Modifying Keys

Objectives

In this lab exercise, you learn to reconfigure the "shutdown" key sequence (Ctrl+Alt+Del) to halt the computer rather than reboot it (the usual configuration). Rebooting your computer may be a common thing to do in Windows, but it's rare to have to reboot in Linux. Rebooting is not required after most configuration changes in Linux. After you redefine the Ctrl+Alt+Del key sequence to halt the computer rather than reboot it, you change the key combination that causes the shutdown process to occur. To do this, you modify the keyboard map file.

Activity Background

The keyboard map is a text file that has a standard format, but the location of the file is not the same for all Linux distributions. Red Hat Linux and Fedora Core 2 place the file in the /lib/kbd/keymaps/i386/qwerty/ directory if you're using a PC. Slackware places it in the /usr/share/kbd/keymaps/i386/qwerty/ directory. Other distributions may place it in still other directories. The program that reads the keyboard map file, **loadkeys**, has this directory compiled into it so you don't have to specify the directory, though you could do so.

There are many keyboard map files in the directory. Each file is for a different physical keyboard layout, usually for different countries and languages. The names of the files give you a clue about the language or country. The keyboard map you use in the United States is us.map and the Finnish keyboard map file is fi.map in Fedora Core 2. Other Linux distributions might use different names. Regardless of the file names, most distributions compress these files. You'll likely find us.map.gz instead of us.map and fi.map.gz instead of fi.map. The **loadkeys** program can read the file whether it's compressed or not.

Materials Required

This lab requires the following:

- Access as the root user to a computer running Linux

Estimated completion time: 45 Minutes

Activity

/etc/init/control-alt-delete.conf

1. Switch to a command-line terminal (tty2) by pressing **Ctrl+Alt+F2**, and log in to the terminal as root.
2. Using your favorite text editor, edit the /etc/inittab file.
3. Locate the line that looks similar to this:

   ```
   ca::ctrlaltdel:/sbin/shutdown -t3 -r now
   ```

4. The shutdown program -r option tells it to reboot your system. Change this line so your computer halts, and does not reboot on shutdown. To make this change, edit the line to use the **-h** (halt) option, like this:

   ```
   ca::ctrlaltdel:/sbin/shutdown -t3 -h now
   ```

5. Save the file and exit the editor.
6. The init program does not automatically recognize the change. You can reboot the computer to get it to reread the inittab file, but there's a quicker way. Enter **kill -HUP 1**. The init program rereads the inittab file and is now reconfigured to halt instead of reboot on shutdown.
7. Press **Ctrl+Alt+Del**. Your computer shuts down and halts, instead of restarting. If your computer has power management and your Linux supports it, your computer shuts itself off. If not, you have to power off your computer manually.
8. Power on your computer and start it up again.
9. Switch to a command-line terminal (tty2) by pressing **Ctrl+Alt+F2**, and log in to the terminal as root.

10. Change the key combination that shuts down your computer. Instead of Ctrl+Alt+Del, use Ctrl+Alt+Page Up. To do this, you have to modify the keyboard map file. You need to know the key code for the Ctrl+Alt+Page Up key combination. You can easily find the key code by running the **showkey** program. Enter **showkey**. You see a prompt that tells you to press any key and that the program terminates after 10 seconds of the last key press.

NOTE

It's important that you do this at a virtual console. Don't do this in an xterm.

11. Press the **Page Up** key. You see this:

```
press any key (program terminates after 10s after last
keypress)...
keycode 104 press
keycode 104 release
```

    Note that your keyboard may have two Page Up keys — typically 73 and 104. Choose 104.This output from the showkey program tells you that the key code for the Page Up key is 104. In about ten seconds, the shell prompt returns.

12. This step assumes that you're running Fedora Core 2 and the keyboard map file is /lib/kbd/keymaps/i386/qwerty/us.map.gz. Before you can edit the file, you have to uncompress it. Enter the following:

    gunzip /lib/kbd/keymaps/i386/qwerty/us.map.gz

13. Using your favorite text editor, edit the file that is now called:

    /lib/kbd/keymaps/i386/qwerty/us.map.

14. Add this line to the end of the file:

    control alt keycode 104 = Boot

15. Save the file and exit the editor.
16. You must reload the keyboard map for the change to take effect. Enter **loadkeys us**.
17. Shut down your computer by pressing **Ctrl+Alt+Page Up**. Notice that it works.
18. Start up your computer.
19. Switch to a command-line terminal (tty2) by pressing **Ctrl+Alt+F2**, and log in to the terminal as root.
20. By modifying the keyboard map, you made the Ctrl+Alt+Page Up key combination shut down your computer. Did this disable the Ctrl+Alt+Del key combination from also shutting down your computer? Press **Ctrl+Alt+Del**.

Your computer shuts down. The Ctrl+Alt+Del key combination still shuts down your computer.

21. Power on your computer, and start it up again.
22. Switch to a command-line terminal (tty2) by pressing **Ctrl+Alt+F2**, and log in to the terminal as root.
23. You can prevent the Ctrl+Alt+Del key combination from shutting down the computer by modifying your keyboard map. The key code for the Delete key is 111. You would use the showkey program if you didn't know the key code. Using your favorite text editor, edit the file called:

    /lib/kbd/keymaps/i386/qwerty/us.map.

24. Set the key combination to do nothing at all by adding this line to the end of the file:

    ```
    control alt keycode 111 = nul
    ```

    use /etc/init/control-alt-delete.conf instead

25. Save the file and exit the editor.
26. You must reload the keyboard map for the change to take effect. Enter **loadkeys us**.
27. Press **Ctrl+Alt+Del**. Your computer does not shut down. You've disabled Ctrl+Alt+Del.
28. To restore your computer to the way it was before this lab exercise, edit the keyboard map file to remove the lines that you added during the lab. Then reload the keyboard map by entering **loadkeys us**. Test the Ctrl+Alt+Del sequence to be sure it functions as it did originally.

Certification Objectives

Objectives for the Linux+ exam:

- Create files and directories and modify files using CLI commands (2.3)
- Manage runlevels and system initialization from the CLI and configuration files (e.g., /etc/inittab and init command, /etc/rc.d, rc.local) (2.10)
- Identify, execute, manage and kill processes (e.g., ps, kill, killall, bg, fg, jobs, nice, renice, rc) (2.11)
- Perform text manipulation (e.g., sed, awk, vi) (2.15)

Review Questions

1. What happens normally when you press the Ctrl+Alt+Del key combination?
   a. Your computer reboots.
   b. Your computer shuts down and halts.
   c. You are logged out of the terminal or virtual console.
   d. Your X server is terminated.
2. If you want the Ctrl+Alt+Del key combination to have a different action, what file must you modify?
   a. /etc/lilo.conf or /etc/grub.conf
   b. /etc/fstab
   c. /etc/inittab
   d. /etc/loadkeys
3. If you modify the /etc/inittab file, what is the quickest way to have the changes take effect?
   a. Press **Ctrl+Alt+Del**.
   b. Press **Ctrl+Alt+Backspace**.
   c. Enter **shutdown -r now**.
   d. Enter **kill -HUP 1**.
4. If your computer supports power management, it automatically powers off when you halt the system only if the Linux kernel has power management support. True or False?
5. Which program tells you the code of a keyboard key?
   a. scankey
   b. showkey
   c. showcode
   d. reveal_codes
6. Whenever you make changes to the keyboard map, what command must you enter?
   a. **loadkeys us**
   b. **kill -HUP init**
   c. **kill -HUP loadkeys**
   d. Reboot your computer.

Lab 9.3 Defining and Redefining Keys

Objectives

The purpose of this lab is to give you additional practice in defining and redefining keys. In the previous lab exercise, you saw how you can control the Ctrl+Alt+Del key combination that normally shuts down your computer. There is another special key combination defined in the /etc/inittab file called the KeyboardSignal, usually assigned to the Alt+Up arrow key combination, which can also be customized. To do this, you must modify the /etc/inittab file and the keyboard map file as you did in the previous lab. In fact, Linux allows you to redefine the actions of any key or keyboard combination by modifying the keyboard map file. In this lab exercise, you define and redefine several keys and key combinations.

Materials Required

This lab requires the following:

- Access as the root user to a computer running Linux

Estimated completion time: 30 Minutes

LAB ACTIVITY

Activity

1. Switch to a command-line terminal (tty2) by pressing **Ctrl+Alt+F2**, and log in to the terminal as root.
2. Using your favorite text editor, edit the /etc/inittab file.
3. See if there is a line that begins with this:

   ```
   kb::kbrequest:
   ```

4. If you're running Red Hat Linux or Fedora Core 2, this line probably won't be in the file. Other distributions may have this line. If you have this line, add **cal** to the end of it as shown below.

   ```
   kb::kbrequest:cal
   ```

   If you don't have this line, you must add the whole line shown above to the file. This line runs the **cal** (calendar) program when you press the Alt+Up arrow key combination. Save the file and exit the editor.
5. Enter **kill -HUP 1** so the init program rereads the inittab file.
6. If you have already performed Lab 9.2, you can skip this step (though you should read it). Enter **gunzip /lib/kbd/ keymaps/i386/qwerty/ us.map.gz**

This command uncompresses the keyboard map file. With most Linux distributions, you can press the **Alt+Up arrow** key combination and see a calendar appear. With Red Hat Linux and Fedora Core 2, it does not appear, because the keyboard map does not define Alt+Up arrow as a special key combination (called the KeyboardSignal). You have to modify the keyboard map file to make this assignment.

7. Rather than using the awkward Alt+Up arrow key as the KeyboardSignal, use the Windows key (the key with the Windows logo on it). This key is not normally used in Linux. To find the key code for this key, enter **showkey**. You see a prompt that tells you to press any key and that the program terminates after 10 seconds of the last key press. If your keyboard does not have a Windows key, choose a different key. Find its key code as described in this step and Step 8, and use that key code when you edit the key map file in Step 16.
8. Press the **Windows** key. You see this:

```
press any key (program terminates after 10s after last
keypress)...
keycode 125 press
keycode 125 release
```

9. The above output from the showkey program tells you that the key code for the Windows key is 125. In about 10 seconds, the shell prompt returns.
10. Using your favorite text editor, edit the file that is now called:

    /lib/kbd/keymaps/i386/qwerty/us.map.
11. Add this line to the end of the us.map file:

    keycode 125 = KeyboardSignal
12. Save the file and exit the editor.
13. You must reload the keyboard map for the change to take effect. Enter **loadkeys us**.
14. Press the **Windows** key or whichever key you mapped in Step 11. A calendar should appear for the current month.
15. When the calendar appears, note that the shell prompt does not appear below it. This is because the init program runs the cal program, not your shell. Your shell is not aware that its screen is being used. Press **Enter** and the shell prompt appears.

NOTE

There is only one KeyboardSignal. You cannot define more than one key or key combination to have a special action in /etc/inittab.

16. You can redefine any key on the keyboard. Using your favorite text editor, edit your keyboard map file.

17. Define some keys that, when pressed, produce strings of characters rather than a single character. To have the Alt+A key combination produce the string "Batteries not included," add these lines to the end of your keyboard map file:

    alt keycode 30 = F100

    string F100 = "Batteries not included"

18. To have the Alt+B key combination produce the string "Close cover before striking" followed by a new line (carriage return and line feed), add these lines to your keyboard map file:

    alt keycode 48 = F101

    string F101 = "Close cover before striking\n"

19. Instead of using a shell alias to reduce your typing when you want to run a program with a long string of command-line options, you can define a key to enter all those options in one keystroke or key combination. Add the following to your keyboard map to have the Alt+P key combination ping your computer's network interface. (Ping simply sends a packet to your computer and your computer responds, so you know the two computers are communicating over the network):

    alt keycode 25 = F102

    string F102 = "ping 127.0.0.1\n"

NOTE Whenever you define a key to produce a string that is to be executed by the shell, you must end the string with a new line, represented by \n.

20. Save the file and exit the editor.
21. Reload the keyboard map for these changes to take effect. Enter **loadkeys us**.
22. Press **Alt+P**. The ping program should run and ping your local network interface. Note that you didn't have to press the Enter key to run the program. Stop ping by pressing **Ctrl+C**.
23. Run your favorite text editor and open a new file.
24. Press **Alt+A**. The string "Batteries not included" appears on your editor screen. The cursor should remain on the same line.
25. Press **Alt+B**. The string "Close cover before striking" appears on your editor screen. The cursor should be on the next line because the Alt+B key definition has a \n at the end of its string.
26. To restore your computer to the way it was before this lab exercise, edit the keyboard map file to remove the lines that you added during the lab. Then reload the keyboard map with the **loadkeys us** command.

27. Once you've returned the keyboard map file to its original state, or have included the modifications you want, you can compress it with the **gzip** program by entering **gzip /lib/kbd/keymaps/i386/qwerty/us.map**.

Certification Objectives

Objectives for the Linux+ exam:

- Create files and directories and modify files using CLI commands (2.3)
- Manage runlevels and system initialization from the CLI and configuration files (e.g., /etc/inittab and init command, /etc/rc.d, rc.local) (2.10)
- Identify, execute, manage and kill processes (e.g., ps, kill, killall, bg, fg, jobs, nice, renice, rc) (2.11)
- Perform text manipulation (e.g., sed, awk, vi) (2.15)

Review Questions

1. You can define as many special keys or key combinations in /etc/inittab as you like. True or False?
2. When you change the keyboard map file, you must reboot for it to take affect. True or False?
3. Any key on the keyboard can be redefined in the keyboard map file. True or False?
4. Once you've made all your modifications to the keyboard map file, you can compress it with the gzip program. True or False?
5. When you define keys to produce strings, you can embed control characters, such as tab (the character is \t) and new line (the character is \n) in the string. True or False?

Lab 9.4 Running an X Server

Objectives

Gnome and KDE are Linux graphical desktop environments that have rich features similar to those found in the Macintosh OS and in Windows. These environments are complex. There are layers of software, and configurations for each layer. In this lab you run only one of these layers—the X server. You see what functionality an X server provides and how you interact with the X server to run application programs.

In case you think that this is not a practical exercise, running an X server without the other layers of a graphical desktop environment can be used to reduce system resource requirements and lock down a desktop so users can only run authorized applications. You might use this technique for building a kiosk.

After completing this lab, you will be able to:

- Start and stop an X Server.
- Run X application programs from a command line.
- Specify command-line options to set the window properties.

Materials Required

This lab requires the following:

- Access as a root user to a computer running Fedora Core 2 on a PC. These labs should work on any Intel-based PC running any Linux distribution.

Estimated completion time: 45 Minutes

Activity

1. This lab exercise is best conducted with your computer configured for run-level 3. Using a text editor, modify the /etc/inittab file so the initdefault line is set to **3**. Here's what the line should look like:

```
id:3:initdefault:
```

2. Save the file to disk and exit the editor.
3. Reboot your computer. When the computer reboots, you eventually see a text-mode login prompt. Log in as root.
4. You're going to start the X server. The X server program is located in the /usr/X11R6/bin directory. It's a file called Xorg, but there's also a symbolic link to it called X. Enter **X**. The screen should flash some text, turn blank, and then in a few second the screen should have a mouse cursor displayed.

NOTE: Linux distributions use either the Xorg or XFree86 X servers. You can choose to use a commercial X server instead.

5. Move the mouse. The cursor moves!
6. Click the left mouse button. Nothing happens.
7. Click the right mouse button. Nothing happens.
8. Click both mouse buttons. Nothing happens.
9. Press **Ctrl+Alt+Backspace**. This stops the X server and brings you back to the virtual console, which now displays text similar to the following:

```
Release Date: 18 December 2003
X Protocol Version 11, Revision 0, Release 6.7
Build Operating System: Linux 2.4.21-14.ELsmp i686 [ELF]
Current Operating System: Linux ed.alcpress.com 2.6.5-
1.358 #1 Sat May 8 09:04:50 EDT 2004 i686
Build Date: 26 June 2004
Build Host: tweety.build.redhat.com

Before reporting problems, check http://wiki.X.Org
to make sure that you have the latest version.
Module Loader present
OS Kernel: Linux version 2.6.5-1.358 (bhcompile@bugs.
build.redhat.com) (gcc version 3.3.3
20040412 (Red Hat Linux 3.3.3-
7)) #1 Sat May 8 09:04:50 EDT 2004
Markers: (--) probed, (**) from config file, (==)
default setting,
(++) from command line, (!!) notice, (II) informational,
(WW) warning, (EE) error, (NI) not implemented, (??)
unknown.
(==) Log file: "/var/log/Xorg.0.log", Time: Sun Aug 15
18:53:18 2004
(==) Using config file: "/etc/X11/xorg.conf"
(WW) VESA(0): Failed to set up write-combining range
(0xd8000000,0x2000000)
```

This text gives you useful information such as the identity and version of the server. The information looks different with other Linux distributions. It also tells you that the X server is logging errors and messages to the /var/log/Xorg.0.log file and that it's using the /etc/X11/Xorg.conf file for its configuration information.

NOTE

The above text was displayed when the X server was started, not when you stopped the X server. Because the X server immediately brought you to its graphical screen, you didn't have an opportunity to see it when the X server first started.

10. Enter **X**. This starts the X server. The X server screen appears.
11. Go to virtual console 1 by pressing **Ctrl+Alt+F1**. You see the same text as you did in Step 9. You do not see the command prompt. That's because the X server is running as a foreground process in this virtual console.
12. Stop the X server by pressing **Ctrl+C**. The X server stops and the command prompt appears.
13. If you want to start the X server from a virtual console but run it as a background process, enter **X &**. The X server screen appears.
14. Go to virtual console 1 by pressing **Ctrl+Alt+F1**. Press **Enter** once. You should see a command prompt. This tells you that the X server is running in

the background. To confirm that it is running, type **ps ax | grep X** and press **Enter**. You should see something similar to this if the X server is running:

```
2333 ?          S       0:02   X
```

15. You can further confirm that the X server is running by pressing **Alt+F7** to go to the X server screen.

NOTE

You may have to press another key sequence to get back to the X screen if you added virtual consoles in a previous lab.

16. It's time to see how to run graphical programs when you only have an X server running. Recall from Steps 6, 7, and 8 that using the mouse buttons did not bring up a menu or any other way of choosing programs. When you only have an X server running, you must start programs from a virtual console. Press **Ctrl+Alt+F1** to go to the first virtual console.
17. Run the graphical clock program by entering **xclock -display :0 &**. Something similar to `[2] 2408` appears on the screen and the command prompt appears.

NOTE

You must specify the -display option because the DISPLAY environment variable does not exist (yet). The DISPLAY variable determines which X server and on which computer the program's window should appear. The DISPLAY variable will be covered in more detail in following lab exercises.

18. Switch to the X server screen by pressing **Alt+F7**. You see the clock displayed in the upper-left corner of the screen. Note that there's no title bar. Nothing happens if you position the mouse cursor over the clock and click the left or right mouse buttons. You have no control of it here. The control is back at the virtual console.
19. Suppose you want the clock to appear somewhere else on the X server screen. How do you do this? You can use the **-geometry** command-line option. Go back to virtual console 1 by pressing **Ctrl+Alt+F1**. Start another copy of the xclock program with the -geometry option to set its size and screen position. Enter **xclock -display :0 -geometry 96x96-0-0 &**. This says that the clock should be 96 pixels wide by 96 pixels high and should be in the lower-right corner (-0-0) of the screen.
20. Go to the X server screen by pressing **Ctrl+Alt+F7**. You see the X server screen with the clock in the lower-right corner.
21. Go back to virtual console 1 by pressing **Ctrl+Alt+F1**. To stop both of the xclock processes with one command, enter **killall xclock**. Go back to the X server screen by pressing **Alt+F7** and notice that the clocks are gone.

22. To avoid having to switch frequently between the X server screen and virtual consoles using an Alt-key sequence, you can make a command prompt available to you in the X server screen. Return to the virtual console by pressing **Ctrl+Alt+F1**. To do this, you run a graphics terminal program (an xterm), using the -geometry option to position it at the bottom of the X server screen and set its size so that it can display 80 columns and 20 lines. Enter **xterm -display :0 -geometry 80x20-0-0 &**.

NOTE When you use a graphical terminal program such as xterm, the WIDTH and HEIGHT -geometry parameters are expressed in characters rather than pixels.

23. Go to the X server screen by pressing **Alt+F7**. You see the X server screen with the xterm window in the lower-right corner, as shown in Figure 9-1.

Figure 9-1 Showing a command prompt in an xterm window on an X server screen

24. You now have a command prompt that you can use to run programs. Move the mouse cursor over the xterm window and enter **ls**. You see a listing of the current directory.

25. Start another xterm program by entering **xterm -geometry 40x10+0-0 &**. Another xterm window appears in the lower left of the screen, as shown in Figure 9-2.

NOTE When you start an application from an xterm, you don't have to specify the -display option. This is because the xterm sets the DISPLAY environment variable when it loads.

26. Whenever multiple windows occupy the same screen, there must be some way to select one window as the active window (the one to which the keyboard

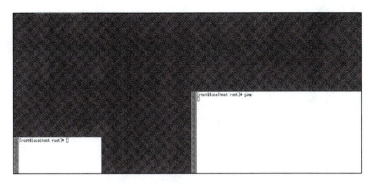

Figure 9-2 Adding another xterm window

sends keystrokes). When a window is the active window it is said to have the focus. Move the mouse cursor slowly to the left. Notice that when the cursor leaves the xterm window, the cursor changes. This is because the xterm window has lost focus.

27. With the mouse cursor over no window, type keys on the keyboard. Notice that they don't appear anywhere on the screen. No window has the focus so the keyboard is not connected to any window.

28. Slowly move the mouse cursor over the xterm window in the lower left of the screen. Note that the cursor changes as the mouse moves over the window. If you type on the keyboard, the characters now appear in the xterm window that has the focus.

29. You can run any graphical application program that's installed on your computer from an xterm window. Just put the xterm window in focus and enter the name of the program. Enter **xcalc &**. A calculator appears. Quit the calculator by entering **killall xcalc**.

30. Put one of the xterm windows in focus and enter **mozilla &**. The Mozilla Web browser appears. To exit this program, click the **File** menu, and select **Quit**. You can leave your computer as is in preparation for the next lab.

Many Linux and UNIX enthusiasts might find this primitive text and graphical interface hybrid quite usable. Nobody would be surprised if you don't.

Certification Objectives

This lab comes close to meeting the CompTIA Linux+ objective "Configuring XFree86." Many Linux distributions, including Fedora Core 2, have moved from XFree86 to Xorg. The two are very similar and their configuration is almost identical.

Review Questions

1. When no window has the focus, the keyboard is connected to the first window that was launched. True or False?
2. When you run only the X server, you can display a menu by right-clicking the desktop. True or False?
3. What key sequence stops the X server?
    a. Alt+F7
    b. Ctrl+Alt+F7
    c. Ctrl+Alt+Backspace
    d. Ctrl+Alt+Escape
4. Which command-line option allows you to specify the size of an application program window and its location on the screen?
    a. **-location**
    b. **-size**
    c. **-geometry**
    d. **-display**
5. When you move the mouse cursor over a window, it becomes the active window. This means that:
    a. The program running in the window runs at a high privilege level. Programs in other windows run slower.
    b. The keyboard is logically connected to the window.
    c. The window can be resized.
    d. The window stays the active window (it's still in focus) even if the mouse cursor leaves the window.

Lab 9.5 Configuring X Programs

Objectives

X programs (X clients) use X libraries. The result is that they tend to understand a common set of command-line options. Examples of options are changing the foreground and background color of windows, as well as setting transparent backgrounds. You can run programs that are automatically minimized, set titles in the title bars, and so forth.

Not all programs implement all of these options, and options may be implemented in somewhat different ways. Programs may also have options that no other programs have. In this lab you try numerous options and see the effects.

Materials Required

This lab requires the following:

- Access as a root user to a computer running Linux
- Completion of Lab 9.4

Estimated completion time: 30 Minutes

LAB ACTIVITY

Activity

1. Switch to the first virtual console by pressing **Ctrl+Alt+F1**. Start an xterm by typing **xterm -display :0 &** and pressing **Enter**. Note that if X Server is not running, then return to the virtual console (press **Ctrl+Alt+F1**) and enter **X &**.
2. Go to the X server screen by pressing **Alt+F7**. Put the xterm window in focus and start the **twm** window manager by entering **twm &**.
3. You're going to start the xclock program. Enter **xclock -title "Pacific Time" &**. Move the odd-looking mouse cursor near where you want the clock to appear on the screen and click the left mouse button. You see the clock appear with Pacific Time in the title bar.

NOTE

Some X documentation suggests that the -T and -title options are equivalent. They're not; the -T option does not always work.

4. When you're running the twm window manager, you can stop a program and delete its window by clicking the desktop (not a window) and selecting **Kill** on the menu. This reveals a skull and crossbones mouse cursor. Position this cursor over the window you want to kill, and click the left mouse button. The program stops and the window disappears. Do this to the clock you just created.
5. Start the clock again, but this time specify that the window background should be red by using the **-bg** command-line option. Enter **xclock -bg red &**. Move the mouse cursor to where you want the clock displayed and right-click. You see the clock appear as before, but the background is now red. Kill the clock window as described in Step 4.
6. Start the clock again, but this time specify that the window background should be red and the foreground should be white by using the **-bg** and **-fg** command-line options, respectively. Enter **xclock -bg red -fg white &**. You

see the clock appear as before, but the background is now red and the foreground is white. The hands of the clock are still black because that's the way the program was written. Kill the clock window as described in Step 4.

7. You can specify reverse video with the **-rv** or **-reverse** command-line option. This exchanges the default foreground and background colors. Enter **xclock -rv &**. The clock now appears in reverse video. The background is black and the foreground is white. Kill the clock window as described in Step 4.
8. Many X programs have their own command-line options that are unique to them. A good example is xterm's **-b** option that sets the margin inside the window. Put the xterm window in focus and type **xterm -b 50 &** and press **Enter**. The xterm window appears (after you click the left mouse button), but there is a 50-pixel border between the window border and the text within the window.
9. Close all windows and programs by pressing Ctrl+Alt+Backspace.

Certification Objectives

This lab comes close to meeting the CompTIA Linux+ objective "Configuring XFree86." Most Linux distributions, including Fedora Core 2, have moved from XFree86 to Xorg. The two are very similar.

Review Questions

1. Which command-line option allows you to set the string that appears in the title bar of a window?
   a. **-display**
   b. **-tb**
   c. **-title**
   d. **-titlebar**
2. Which command-line option allows you to change the background color of a window?
   a. **-display**
   b. **-fg**
   c. **-bg**
   d. **-color**
3. Which command-line option allows you to change the foreground color of a window?
   a. **-display**
   b. **-fg**
   c. **-bg**
   d. **-color**

4. Which command-line option allows you to swap the default foreground and background colors of a window?
   a. **-display**
   b. **-fg**
   c. **-bg**
   d. **-rv**
5. Which xterm command-line option sets a margin between the window border and the text inside the window?
   a. **-b**
   b. **-border**
   c. **-insideborder**
   d. **-ib**

CHAPTER TEN

MANAGING LINUX PROCESSES

Labs included in this chapter

- Lab 10.1 Displaying Parent/Child Relationships
- Lab 10.2 Customizing ps Output
- Lab 10.3 Compiling a Program from Source Code
- Lab 10.4 Experimenting with Scheduling Priority
- Lab 10.5 Determining Who Can Control Processes

CompTIA Linux+ Exam Objectives

Objective		Lab
2.11	Identify, execute, manage and kill processes (e.g., ps, kill, killall, bg, fg, jobs, nice, renice, rc)	10.1, 10.2, 10.4, 10.5
2.12	Differentiate core processes from non-critical services (e.g., PID, PPID, init, timer)	10.2
2.23	Redirect output (e.g., piping, redirection)	10.1, 10.2
3.4	Configure the system and perform basic makefile changes to support compiling applications and drivers	10.3

LAB 10.1 DISPLAYING PARENT/CHILD RELATIONSHIPS

Objectives

The goal of this lab is to investigate the various ways that parent/child relationships between processes can be displayed.

Materials Required

This lab requires the following:

- Access as an ordinary user to a computer running Linux

Activity Background

Chapter 10 in the main text tells you about parent and child processes and shows you how to use the **ps -f** command to see the PID and PPID values. The PPID is the PID of the parent process.

Using the PPID values, you can see the parents of all processes. When child processes have children, the relationships are more complex and difficult to see in the display. In this activity, you explore other commands that more clearly show the relationships between processes.

Estimated completion time: 15 Minutes

ACTIVITY

1. Switch to a command-line terminal (tty2) by pressing **Ctrl+Alt+F2**, and log in to the terminal using any username except root.
2. Enter **ps –eH | more**. The e option selects all processes and the H option produces a process hierarchy display. Child processes appear below their parents and are indented by two spaces. This allows you to more easily see parent/child relationships than with nonhierarchical ps displays. Here's an example of what you'll see:

```
  PID TTY          TIME CMD
    8 ?        00:00:00 kupdated
    7 ?        00:00:00 bdflush
    6 ?        00:00:00 kreclaimd
    5 ?        00:00:02 kswapd
    4 ?        00:00:00 ksoftirqd_CPU0
    1 ?        00:00:04 init
    2 ?        00:00:02   keventd
    3 ?        00:00:00   kapm-idled
    9 ?        00:00:00   mdrecoveryd
   13 ?        00:00:28   kjournald
```

```
  520 ?        00:00:01 syslogd
  525 ?        00:00:00 klogd
  545 ?        00:00:00 portmap
  573 ?        00:00:00 rpc.statd
  722 ?        00:00:00 sshd
  755 ?        00:00:00 xinetd
  786 ?        00:00:00 crond
  836 ?        00:00:51 xfs
  872 ?        00:00:00 atd
  882 ?        00:00:00 miniserv.pl
  886 tty1     00:00:00 log in
  894 tty1     00:00:00   bash
  949 tty1     00:00:00     startx
  956 tty1     00:00:00       xinit
  957 ?        21:22:50         X
  959 tty1     00:00:00         gnome-session
  887 tty2     00:00:00 mingetty
  888 tty3     00:00:00 mingetty
  889 tty4     00:00:00 mingetty
  890 tty5     00:00:00 mingetty
  891 tty6     00:00:00 mingetty
  982 ?        00:00:01 esd
  990 ?        00:00:22 gnome-smproxy
 1005 ?        00:02:26 sawfish
 2972 ?        00:00:00   rep
 1006 ?        00:00:52 xscreensaver
 1010 ?        00:01:08 panel
 1012 ?        00:00:07 gmc
 1019 ?        00:00:00 gnome-name-serv
 1026 ?        00:12:27 deskguide_apple
 1028 ?        00:00:06 another_clock_a
 1030 ?        00:00:00 mini_commander_
 1038 ?        00:00:04 oafd
 1042 ?        00:00:05 wombat
 1046 ?        00:00:01 bonobo-moniker-
 1064 ?        00:00:00 evolution-alarm
 1170 ?        00:07:54 gnome-terminal
 1172 ?        00:00:00   gnome-pty-helpe
 2921 pts/3    00:00:01   bash
18358 pts/3    00:00:00     ps
 1552 ?        00:00:01 gedit
 4770 ?        00:00:00 mount.smbfs
 7089 ?        00:00:00 gconfd-1
 9139 ?        00:01:40 mozilla-bin
 9191 ?        00:00:00   mozilla-bin
 9192 ?        00:00:00     mozilla-bin
 9193 ?        00:00:00     mozilla-bin
 9194 ?        00:00:02     mozilla-bin
 9198 ?        00:00:00     mozilla-bin
```

3. Enter **ps -e f | more**. You see a display similar to the example in Step 2. The -f option causes ps to use graphical characters \ and _ rather than spaces to show the parent/child relationships. Here's an example of a portion of the display:

```
PID TTY      STAT   TIME COMMAND
886 tty1     S      0:00 log in – root
894 tty1     S      0:00  \_ -bash
949 tty1     S      0:00      \_ /bin/sh /usr/X11R6/bin/startx
956 tty1     S      0:00          \_ xinit /etc/X11/xinit/xinitrc --
957 ?        S<  1284:22              \_ /etc/X11/X :0
959 tty1     S      0:00              \_ /usr/bin/gnome-session
```

4. Enter **pstree | more**. A display appears that shows you all the processes on your system arranged in a parent/child hierarchy. Parent processes are to the left of child processes. The example below clearly shows that the init process is the parent or ancestor of all other processes on the system. Some of the children of init have children themselves. The **login** process has a **bash** process as its child. That bash process has the **startx** child process. Startx has an **xinit** child, and so on. Notice the gnome-terminal process that has a **pstree** grandchild that produced this display.

```
init-+-another_clock_a
     |-atd
     |-bonobo-moniker-
     |-crond
     |-deskguide_apple
     |-esd
     |-gconfd-1
     |-gedit
     |-gmc
     |-gnome-name-serv
     |-gnome-smproxy
     |-gnome-terminal-+-bash---pstree
     |                '-gnome-pty-helpe
     |-kapm-idled
     |-keventd
     |-kjournald
     |-klogd
     |-log in---bash---startx---xinit-+-X
     |                                '-gnome-session
     |-mdrecoveryd
     |-5*[mingetty]
     |-mini_commander_
     |-miniserv.pl
```

```
|-mount.smbfs
|-mozilla-bin---mozilla-bin---4*[mozilla-bin]
|-oafd
|-panel
|-portmap
|-rpc.statd
|-sawfish---rep
|-sshd
|-syslogd
|-wombat
|-xfs
|-xinetd
'-xscreensaver
```

NOTE

Note that you're able to see this process information while you're logged in as a nonroot user.

5. Enter **pstree | grep mingetty**. This displays all the **mingetty** processes running on your system. These are your virtual consoles. Instead of listing all of these processes on separate lines, they are grouped together on one line preceded by a number that tells you the number of processes running. You see something similar to this:

   ```
   |-5*[mingetty]
   ```

6. Normally, pstree does not show PIDs for the processes. If you need to see them you can use the -p option. Enter **pstree –p | more**. Here's an example of what you see:

   ```
   init(1)-+-another_clock_a(1028)
           |-atd(872)
           |-bonobo-moniker-(1046)
           |-crond(786)
           |-deskguide_apple(1026)
           |-esd(982)
           |-gconfd-1(7089)
           |-gedit(1552)
           |-gmc(1012)
           |-gnome-name-serv(1019)
           |-gnome-smproxy(990)
           |-gnome-terminal(1170)-+-bash(2921)---pstree(19301)
           |                      '-gnome-pty-helpe(1172)
           |-gpilotd(1014)
           |-kapm-idled(3)
           |-keventd(2)
           |-kjournald(13)
           |-klogd(525)
   ```

```
        |-log in(886)---bash(894)---startx(949)---xinit(956)-+-X(957)
        |                                                    '-gnome-
session(959)
        |-mdrecoveryd(9)
        |-mingetty(887)
        |-mingetty(888)
        |-mingetty(889)
        |-mingetty(890)
        |-mingetty(891)
        |-mini_commander_(1030)
        |-miniserv.pl(882)
        |-mount.smbfs(4770)
        |-mozilla-bin(9139)---mozilla-bin(9191)-+-mozilla-bin(9192)
        |                                       |-mozilla-bin(9193)
        |                                       |-mozilla-bin(9194)
        |                                       '-mozilla-bin(9198)
        |-oafd(1038)
        |-portmap(545)
        |-rpc.statd(573)
        |-sawfish(1005)---rep(2972)
        |-sshd(722)
        |-syslogd(520)
        |-wombat(1042)
        |-xfs(836)
        |-xinetd(755)
            '-xscreensaver(1006)
```

7. Enter **logout** and press **Alt+F7** to go back to your graphical screen.

Certification Objectives

Objectives for the Linux+ exam:

- Identify, execute, manage and kill processes (e.g., ps, kill, killall, bg, fg, jobs, nice, renice, rc) (2.11)
- Redirect output (e.g., piping, redirection) (2.23)

Review Questions

1. Which command shows parent/child process relationships that are most easily apparent?
   a. **ps -eH**
   b. **ps -f**
   c. **ps aux**
   d. **ps**
2. Which column in a ps display identifies the parent process?
   a. PID
   b. PPID

c. TTY

d. COMMAND

3. Which process is the parent or ancestor of all other processes?

a. passwd

b. init

c. anaconda

d. X

4. To see all system processes, you must be logged in as root. True or False?

5. When you use no command-line options with the pstree program, the PIDS of processes are displayed. True or False?

Lab 10.2 Customizing ps Output

Objectives

The goal of this lab is to show you how you can use ps commands to produce customized process display formats. The standard display formats are designed for general use. More information is presented than needed in most cases. You can use command-line options to display any information you like.

Materials Required

This lab requires the following:

- Access as an ordinary user to a computer running Linux

Estimated completion time: 15 Minutes

Activity

1. Switch to a command-line terminal (tty2) by pressing **Ctrl+Alt+F2**, and log in to the terminal using any username except root.

2. Enter **ps -e | more**. The -e option tells ps to display all processes. Notice that there are four columns: PID, TTY, TIME, and CMD. The first few lines of output look similar to this:

```
PID TTY          TIME CMD
  1 ?        00:00:04 init
  2 ?        00:00:02 keventd
  3 ?        00:00:00 kapm-idled
  4 ?        00:00:00 ksoftirqd_CPU0
```

```
    5 ?        00:00:02 kswapd
    6 ?        00:00:00 kreclaimd
    7 ?        00:00:00 bdflush
    8 ?        00:00:00 kupdated
    9 ?        00:00:00 mdrecoveryd
```

3. If the page is full and you see a --More-- prompt at the bottom of the screen, press **q** to get back to the command prompt.

4. Enter **ps ax | more**. The **a** option tells ps to display all processes that were started by terminals (TTYs). The **x** option tells ps to display all processes that were not started by a terminal. This is the logical equivalent of the -e option. Notice that there are five columns: PID, TTY, STAT, TIME, and COMMAND. There are also subtle differences in how data in the columns is displayed. The first few lines of output look similar to this:

```
PID TTY      STAT   TIME COMMAND
  1 ?        S      0:04 init [3]
  2 ?        SW     0:02 [keventd]
  3 ?        SW     0:00 [kapm-idled]
  4 ?        SWN    0:00 [ksoftirqd_CPU0]
  5 ?        SW     0:02 [kswapd]
  6 ?        SW     0:00 [kreclaimd]
  7 ?        SW     0:00 [bdflush]
  8 ?        SW     0:00 [kupdated]
  9 ?        SW<    0:00 [mdrecoveryd]
```

5. If the page is full and you see a --More-- prompt at the bottom of the screen, press **q** to get back to the command prompt.

6. The ps program has many options to change the format. Enter **ps -ef | more**. The -ef option displays all processes in a full listing format. The first few lines of output look similar to this:

```
UID        PID  PPID  C STIME TTY          TIME CMD
root         1     0  0 Oct08 ?        00:00:04 init [3]
root         2     1  0 Oct08 ?        00:00:02 [keventd]
root         3     1  0 Oct08 ?        00:00:00 [kapm-idled]
root         4     0  0 Oct08 ?        00:00:00 [ksoftirqd_CPU0]
root         5     0  0 Oct08 ?        00:00:02 [kswapd]
root         6     0  0 Oct08 ?        00:00:00 [kreclaimd]
root         7     0  0 Oct08 ?        00:00:00 [bdflush]
root         8     0  0 Oct08 ?        00:00:00 [kupdated]
root         9     1  0 Oct08 ?        00:00:00 [mdrecoveryd]
```

7. If the page is full and you see a --More-- prompt at the bottom of the screen, press **q** to get back to the command prompt.

8. Try the following display formats and notice the format of each:

   -f Full listing

   -j Jobs format

   j Job control format

   l Long listing

   s Signal format

   v Virtual memory format

   X i386 register format (use only with an Intel processor-based system)

9. The -o option is for a user-defined format. Enter **ps -eo pid,cmd | more**. The -eo option displays all processes in a user-defined format that includes only the PID and CMD columns. There are two columns that display the data you requested: PID and CMD (or COMMAND). The first few lines of output look similar to this:

```
PID CMD
  1 init [3]
  2 [keventd]
  3 [kapm-idled]
  4 [ksoftirqd_CPU0]
  5 [kswapd]
  6 [kreclaimd]
  7 [bdflush]
  8 [kupdated]
  9 [mdrecoveryd]
```


NOTE

It's important that you have a space after the -o option and no spaces before or after the commas that separate the column names.

10. If the page is full and you see a --More-- prompt at the bottom of the screen, press **q** to get back to the command prompt.

11. Enter **ps -eo pid,ppid,%mem,cmd | more**. This adds the PPID and %MEM columns to the format. The PPID is the process ID of the parent process. The %MEM displays the percentage of system memory that is used by the process. When processes use only a tiny portion of system memory, it is displayed as 0.0. The first few lines of output look similar to this:

```
PID  PPID %MEM CMD
  1     0  0.0 init [3]
  2     1  0.0 [keventd]
  3     1  0.0 [kapm-idled]
  4     0  0.0 [ksoftirqd_CPU0]
  5     0  0.0 [kswapd]
```

```
6     0  0.0 [kreclaimd]
7     0  0.0 [bdflush]
8     0  0.0 [kupdated]
9     1  0.0 [mdrecoveryd]
```

NOTE

Processes whose PPID values are 0 were started by the operating system. Processes whose PPID values are 1 were started by the init program. The Linux+ Certification exam refers to these as core services.

12. Try different or additional columns. Table 10-1 lists many, but not all, of the column names the ps program understands.

Table 10-1 ps command parameters

Name	Description
%cpu	Percentage of CPU time taken by the process
%mem	Percentage of system memory used by the process
args	The command that started the process
cputime	Total CPU time taken by the process
etime	Elapsed time since the process was started
gid	The group ID (GID) of the process; the group that owns the process
group	The name of the group that owns the process
intpri	The priority of the process
lstart	The date and time the process was started
ni	The nice value of the process (scheduling priority)
pid	The process ID
stat	Process status
uid	The user ID (UID) of the process; the user that owns the process
user	The name of the user who owns the process

13. Enter **logout** and press **Alt+F7** to go back to your graphical screen.

Certification Objectives

Objectives for the Linux+ exam:

- Identify, execute, manage and kill processes (e.g., ps, kill, killall, bg, fg, jobs, nice, renice, rc) (2.11)
- Differentiate core processes from non-critical services (e.g., PID, PPID, init, timer) (2.12)
- Redirect output (e.g., piping, redirection) (2.23)

Review Questions

1. Which command displays all processes?
   a. **ps**
   b. **ps a**
   c. **ps x**
   d. **ps -e**
2. Which command is equivalent to ps -e in terms of the processes that are displayed?
   a. **ps**
   b. **ps ax**
   c. **ps -l**
   d. **ps -a**
3. Which command displays a user-defined format?
   a. **ps --option pid,cmd**
   b. **ps -options pid,cmd**
   c. **ps -o pid:cmd**
   d. **ps -o pid,cmd**
4. Which command displays the status of a process?
   a. **ps**
   b. **ps ax**
   c. **ps -l**
   d. **ps -e**
5. Which of these displays the process ID of the parent process?
   a. pid
   b. ppid
   c. parid
   d. parent

Lab 10.3 Compiling a Program from Source Code

Objectives

The goal of this lab is to show you how to compile a program from source code and to build a program needed for Labs 10.4 and 10.5. Those lab exercises need a program that can consistently consume processing time and continuously display data to the screen. We use a prime number generator program to do this. It's unlikely that a prime number generator program comes with your Linux distribution, so you download one from the Internet.

Materials Required

This lab requires the following:

- Access as an ordinary user to a computer running Linux that has access to the Internet
- A Web browser

Estimated completion time: 20 Minutes

LAB ACTIVITY

Activity

1. Start a Web browser on your Linux computer and enter **http://bach.dynet.com/primes/src/gmpprimes/primes.cr.c**. If your Web browser displays a screen asking where you'd like to store the file, choose your home directory. If the Web browser displays the file, click **File**, followed by the command to save the file, and choose your home directory.
2. Switch to a command-line terminal (tty2) by pressing **Ctrl+Alt+F2**, and log in to the terminal using the same username as in Step 1.
3. Make sure that your home directory is your current working directory. If it's not, enter **cd**.
4. Enter **less primes.cr.c**. You're looking at the source code for a C program. (You don't need to understand the C language to complete this exercise.) Press **q** to go back to the command prompt.

NOTE

You should be cautious about any programs you download from the Internet. If you do understand programming and the C language, review the code to see if there's any problem putting this program on your system.

5. Enter **gcc --version**. You should see a version number followed bya copyright notice for the gcc compiler. If you see a `command not found` error message, the compiler is not installed on your computer. In that case you need to install these RPM packages:

   glibc-kernheaders

   glibc-headers

   glibc-devel

   gcc-3.3.3-7

NOTE

Installing RPM packages is covered in the main text.

6. Enter **gcc -O primes.cr.c -lgmp -o primes**. This runs the gcc compiler, tells it to compile the primes.cr.c program into an executable program, uses the GNU precision math library, and places the compiled program in a file called primes.

NOTE

The GNU precision math library is in a file called libgmp.so. The so file suffix stands for shared object. You can find this file in the /usr/lib directory for Fedora Core 2. Other distributions may place the file in /lib.

7. The program is ready to run. Enter **./primes**.
8. The program prompts you with `Enter startoff in base ten:`. It's asking you what number to start with when generating random numbers. Enter **1** (the numeral 1). The program continuously generates random numbers and displays them on the screen. This is useful in the next lab exercise.
9. Stop the program by pressing **Ctrl+C**.
10. The primes program deals with very large numbers and takes more time to generate random numbers as the size of the number increases. You may find this useful in the next lab exercise or later in your Linux career. Enter **./primes**. When prompted for a starting number, enter **10000000000000** (one followed by 13 zeros). You see that it takes much longer to generate prime numbers this large. Type **Ctrl+C** to quit the program.
11. You should keep the primes program on your system for future use. Put it in a directory that holds executable programs. You learned about the Filesystem Hierarchy Standard in a previous chapter. It told you that a suitable directory is /usr/local/bin.You need to be the root user to copy the file. Enter **su**. Enter root's password when prompted. Enter **cp primes /usr/local/bin**.
12. Enter **logout** and press **Ctrl+Alt+F7** to go back to your graphical screen.

Certification Objectives

Objectives for the Linux+ exam:

- Configure the system and perform basic makefile changes to support compiling applications and drivers (3.4)

Review Questions

1. Most or all files in the /lib and /usr/lib directories end in .so. What does this signify?
2. When downloading programs in the form of source code from the Internet, it's best to review the program to see if it contains any hostile code. True or False?
3. In which directories would you expect to find library files? (Choose all that apply.)
   a. /etc
   b. /usr/bin
   c. /usr/lib
   d. /lib
4. Which would be the best directory to store executable programs that did not come with your Linux distribution and that you downloaded from the Internet?
   a. /bin
   b. /usr/bin
   c. /usr/local/bin
   d. /etc
5. Programs that run continually can be stopped with which keyboard key or key sequence?
   a. q
   b. Ctrl+A
   c. Ctrl+C
   d. Escape

Lab 10.4 Experimenting with Scheduling Priority

Objectives

The goal of this lab is to experiment with scheduling priority using the **nice**, **renice**, and **top** programs. Unlike most of the lab exercises you've done so far, in this one you use the graphical user interface so you can have multiple terminal windows, called xterms, displayed at the same time.

Materials Required

This lab requires the following:

- Access as a root user to a computer running Linux
- Completion of Lab 10.3

Estimated completion time: 30 Minutes

Activity

1. You must be logged in as root and in a graphical desktop such as Gnome or KDE. If you're not logged in as root, log out and log back in again as root.
2. You're going to start three terminals and have all three appear on the same screen. You start a terminal by clicking the Red Hat button, then Systems Tools, then Terminal. When you start the first two terminals, resize their windows so they're narrow (about one inch wide on the screen). When you start the third terminal, make it wider—about three inches. Position the windows so they're next to one another. The end result should look similar to the Gnome screen in Figure 10-1.

NOTE

You resize and position windows in Gnome and KDE just as you do in Microsoft Windows.

3. Select each terminal window, and enter **PS1="\w:"** in each. This shortens the shell prompt so it fits in the window. You may recall from Lab 8.3 that \w displays the path of the current working directory.

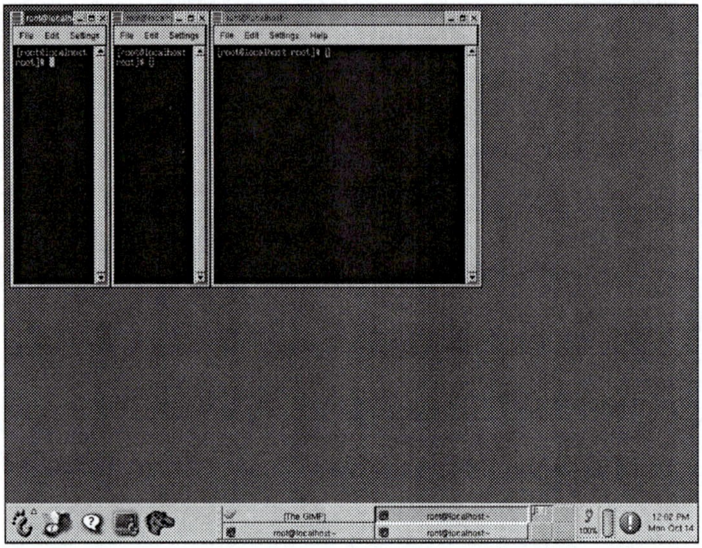

Figure 10-1 Three terminal windows are started

4. All the terminal windows should have your home directory as the current working directory. Because you're logged in as the root user, the directory should be /root and displayed as **~:** in the terminal windows. In each window enter **pwd** to check that you are in the /root directory.
5. Start another terminal window (the fourth) and resize and position it so that your screen now looks similar to Figure 10-2.
6. In the fourth terminal window, enter **top**. The top program appears. Type **i**. Top should now display only active processes. Type **lmt**. Top should no longer display the information at the top of its screen. We refer to this fourth terminal window as the Top window in this exercise.
7. In the far-left terminal window, enter **primes**. When prompted for a starting number, enter **1**.
8. Repeat Step 7 for the center terminal window. Your screen should now look similar to Figure 10-3.
9. Notice that the Top window shows the two primes programs as running processes. Their %CPU values are also similar to one another. This means that they're both consuming about the same amount of processing time and are running about as fast as one another. Notice the PIDs of these two processes. Suppose they're 3148 and 3149. In all the following commands, enter your actual PID numbers in place of 3148 and 3149. Select the far-right terminal window (the one that's not running the primes or top programs), and enter **renice 19 3148**. You've changed the scheduling priority of process 3148 to 19.

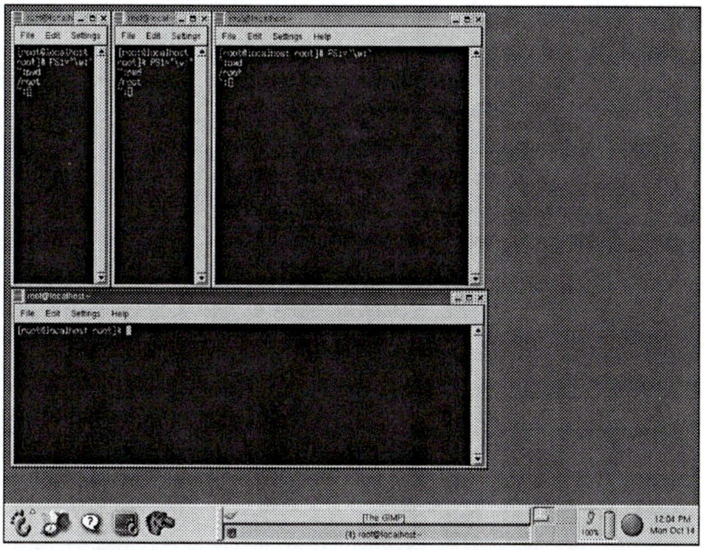

Figure 10-2 Adding a fourth terminal window

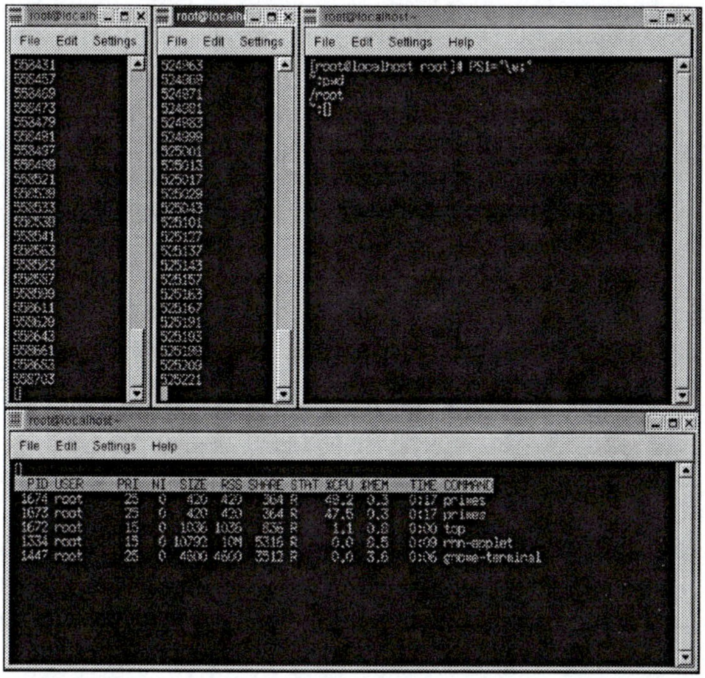

Figure 10-3 Two terminal windows, one running the primes program and one running top

10. Wait a few seconds for the top program to update its display and look at the Top window. You see that the status column shows N for process 3148. This means that the scheduling priority for process 3148 is greater than (slower than) the nominal value of zero. You also see that the %CPU value for process 3149 is larger than process 3148. Process 3149 is running faster. You may be able to observe this by looking at the terminal windows running the primes program. Is one running faster than the other? If you can't notice any difference between the two in terms of how fast they print prime numbers to the screen, you can stop the programs and restart them, this time setting the initial prime number value to a number much higher than 1. Try the same value you used in Step 9 of Lab 10.3, **10000000000000** (one followed by 13 zeros).

11. The top program also gives you the same functionality as the renice program. Select the Top window and press **r**. The top program prompts you with `PID to renice:`. Enter **3148** (remember to replace 3148 with your own PID). The top program prompts you with `Renice PID 3148 to value:`. Enter **-19**.

    Wait a few seconds for top to update its display and notice that the %CPU value for process 3148 is larger than that of process 3149. Now process 3148 is running faster than process 3149. Also note that the status column shows < for process 3148. This indicates that the scheduling priority is less than (faster than) the nominal value of zero.

12. Select the far-right terminal window (the one that's not running the primes or top programs), and enter **nice -n -10 primes.** You are prompted for the starting prime number value. Enter **1**. Wait a few seconds for the top program to update its display and notice that there's a third primes process. Suppose that its PID is 4107. This one shows -10 in the NI (scheduling priority) column. This illustrates that you can set the scheduling priority of a program when you first run it.

13. Take your hands off the mouse and keyboard and wait 10 seconds or so for the system to settle down. Notice that Top displays other active processes besides the primes programs. You see the top process listed but its %CPU value should be small (usually below 1.0) and consistent. You also see processes related to the graphical desktop, such as X, panel, and others that are sporadic.

14. Move the mouse so the cursor is constantly moving on the screen and notice what happens to the top display. Additional processes appear and the %CPU values change as the graphical subsystem is doing more work. The mouse may seem sluggish. One reason is that process 4107 is running at a high scheduling priority. Select the Top window and type **r**. The PID to renice: prompt appears. Enter **4107** (replace 4107 with the PID you derived in Step 12). The Renice PID 4107 to value: prompt appears. Enter **0**. Now move the mouse around the screen. It should be more responsive.

15. Quit all programs by entering **Ctrl+C** in each terminal and then enter **exit** to close each terminal window.

Certification Objectives

Objectives for the Linux+ exam:

- Identify, execute, manage and kill processes (e.g., ps, kill, killall, bg, fg, jobs, nice, renice, rc) (2.11)

Review Questions

1. What command causes top to only display processes that are running?

   a. **a**

   b. **e**

   c. **i**

   d. **o**

2. What program can change the scheduling priority of a process that's already running? (Choose all that apply.)

   a. top

   b. ps

   c. nice

   d. renice

3. Which of the following scheduling priority values (nice values) cause a process to run the fastest?

   a. 0

   b. 1

   c. -19

   d. +19

4. When you use top, what character appears in the STAT column when you set a processes scheduling priority to -15?

   a. <

   b. >

   c. M

   d. N

5. If you're running a Linux server and you want to maximize performance, you should consider not running a graphical desktop on the server. True or False?

Lab 10.5 Determining Who Can Control Processes

Objectives

The goal of this lab is to determine which users can control processes. If you're logged in as the root user, you have full control of processes. If you're logged in as a nonroot user, you have less control. This lab exercise explores this degree of control. Unlike Lab 10.4, you use virtual consoles for this lab.

Materials Required

This lab requires the following:

- Access as both an ordinary user and a root user to a computer running Linux

Estimated completion time: 20 Minutes

Activity

LAB ACTIVITY

1. Switch to a command-line terminal (tty2) by pressing **Ctrl+Alt+F2**, and log in to the terminal as a nonroot user.
2. Switch to the third virtual console (tty3) by pressing **Alt+F3**, and log in as the same nonroot user.
3. Switch to the fourth virtual console (tty4) by pressing **Alt+F4**, and log in as the root user.
4. Switch to the second virtual console (tty2) by pressing **Alt+F2**. Enter **primes**. When you're prompted for a starting value, enter **1**. Prime numbers are now displayed continuously.
5. Switch to the third virtual console (tty3) by pressing **Alt+F3**. Enter **top**. You should see the primes process listed. Notice that the USER column shows the name of your nonroot account and the NI column shows 0 (the nominal scheduling priority). Also notice that the top process is listed and its user is the same nonroot user who is running the primes program.

NOTE: Do not use the i command to have top only display active processes. You'll see the reason for this later.

6. Change the scheduling priority by typing **r**. When you see the `PID to renice:` prompt, enter the PID number of the primes process. When you see the `Renice PID x to value:` prompt, enter **10**.

7. Wait for the top program to update its display and notice that the NI column shows **10** for the primes process. This proves that a nonroot user can change the scheduling priority of a process that he or she owns. However, you used a positive value for the scheduling priority (nice value). What happens if you use a negative value to change the scheduling priority to run faster than the nominal value?

8. Change the scheduling priority by typing **r**. When you see the `PID to renice:` prompt, enter the PID number of the primes process. When you see the `Renice PID x to value:` prompt, enter **-10**. You see an error message appear that says:

   ```
   Renice of PID x to -10 failed: Permission denied.
   ```

   Try other negative values between -1 and -20. The same result should occur. Nonroot users are not allowed to change the scheduling priority to negative values. They cannot make their processes run faster than the nominal value.

9. Switch to the fourth virtual console (tty4) by pressing **Alt+F4**. Enter **top**. You see the primes process that was started by your nonroot user in the second virtual console. You also see two top processes. One top process is running as root and the other is running as the nonroot user.

NOTE Notice that one top process is running (R) while the other is stopped (S). You can never have more than one top process running at the same time. This is why you were asked not to use the i command earlier.

10. Try to change the scheduling priority of the primes process to a negative value. Type **r**. When you see the `PID to renice:` prompt, enter the PID number of the primes process. When you see the `Renice PID x to value:` prompt, enter **-10**. This should succeed because you're using a top program that's running as root. This proves that the root user can change the scheduling priority of any process running as a non-root user.

11. Switch to the third virtual console (tty3) by pressing **Alt+F3**. The top program should still be running there as the nonroot user. To see if the nonroot user can change the scheduling priority of a process running as root, type **r**. When you see the `PID to renice:` prompt, enter the PID number of the top process that's running as root. When you see the `Renice PID x to value:` prompt, enter **10**. This should fail with a message that says:

    ```
    Renice of PID x to 10 failed: Operation not permitted
    ```

    The same thing happens if you specify a negative value. This proves that a nonroot user cannot change the scheduling priority of a process running as root regardless of the scheduling priority value.

NOTE

Everything you've done here with top works the same way when you use the renice program.

12. Type **q** to get back to the command prompt. Enter **logout**.
13. Switch to the fourth virtual console (tty4). The top program should still be running. Type **q**, then enter **logout**.
14. Switch to the second virtual console (tty2). The primes program should still be running. Press **Ctrl+C**. Enter **logout**.
15. Press **Alt+F7** to return to the graphical interface.

Certification Objectives

Objectives for the Linux+ exam:

- Identify, execute, manage and kill processes (e.g., ps, kill, killall, bg, fg, jobs, nice, renice, rc) (2.11)

Review Questions

1. When a user runs a program, what is the nominal scheduling priority value of the process?
   a. 0
   b. 1
   c. 19
   d. -19
2. Nonroot users are able to set the scheduling priority for a process they own to a positive value (the program runs slower). True or False?
3. Nonroot users are able to set the scheduling priority for a process they own to a negative value (the program runs faster). True or False?
4. Nonroot users are not able to set their scheduling priority (nice value) to a negative value with the top program, but they are able to do so with the renice program. True or False?
5. Nonroot users are able to set the scheduling priority for a process owned by the root user to a negative value (the program runs faster). True or False?

CHAPTER ELEVEN

COMMON ADMINISTRATIVE TASKS

Labs included in this chapter

- Lab 11.1 Configuring Virtual Consoles
- Lab 11.2 Testing Your Logging
- Lab 11.3 Using Named Pipes with Logging
- Lab 11.4 Finding Broken Links and Files with No Owners
- Lab 11.5 Understanding File Date and Time Stamps

CompTIA Linux+ Exam Objectives

Objective		Lab
1.11	Select appropriate parameters for Linux installation (e.g., language, time zones, keyboard, mouse)	11.1
2.3	Create files and directories and modify files using CLI commands	11.1, 11.2, 11.3, 11.4, 11.5
2.4	Execute content and directory searches using find and grep	11.4
2.5	Create linked files using CLI commands	11.4
2.6	Modify file and directory permissions and ownership (e.g., chmod, chown, sticky bit, octal permissions, chgrp) using CLI commands	11.4, 11.5
2.9	Access and write data to recordable media	11.1, 11.2, 11.3, 11.4, 11.5
2.10	Manage runlevels and system initialization from the CLI and configuration files (e.g., /etc/inittab and init command, /etc/rc.d, rc.local)	11.1
2.11	Identify, execute, manage and kill processes (e.g., ps, kill, killall, bg, fg, jobs, nice, renice, rc)	11.1, 11.2, 11.3
2.15	Perform text manipulation (e.g., sed, awk, vi)	11.1, 11.2, 11.3, 11.4, 11.5
2.19	Create, modify, and use basic shell scripts	11.1, 11.3
2. 20	Create, modify, and delete user and group accounts (e.g., useradd, groupadd, /etc/passwd, chgrp, quota, chown, chmod, grpmod) using CLI utilities	11.4, 11.5
2.23	Redirect output (e.g., piping, redirection)	11.3
3.10	Configure log files (e.g., syslog, remote logfile storage)	11.2, 11.3

Lab 11.1 Configuring Virtual Consoles

Objectives

The goal of this lab is to become familiar with running a Linux computer via its command-line interface. Using a command-line interface is desirable when the computer functions as a server. In this exercise, you learn how to:

- Start the computer in runlevel 3 (instead of runlevel 5).
- Increase the number of virtual consoles.
- Move between virtual consoles.

Materials Required

This lab requires the following:

- Access as a root user to a computer running Linux

Estimated completion time: 20 Minutes

Activity

1. Switch to a command-line terminal (tty2) by pressing **Ctrl+Alt+F2**, and log in to the terminal as root.
2. Configure the computer so it starts up in runlevel 3 instead of runlevel 5. Enter **vi /etc/inittab**. You should now be looking at the contents of the file. Use the **Down arrow** key to move the cursor down to the line with the `id:5:initdefault:` statement. Press **i**. Notice that the bottom line changes to `INSERT`, telling you that you're in insert mode.
3. Delete the `5` in the `id:5:initdefault:` statement and replace it with a **3**. The line should now read `id:3:initdefault:`. Press the **Escape** key. Notice that `INSERT` is removed from the bottom line. You're back in command mode. Enter **:wq** to save the file and exit the editor.
4. Log out and restart the computer.
5. When the computer has finished rebooting, you see a text-mode login prompt. Log in as the root user.
6. By default, Linux distributions set the number of virtual consoles to six. You can easily add more. This lab is going to have a total of nine virtual consoles. Enter **vi /etc/inittab**. You see the contents of the /etc/inittab file that controls the number of virtual consoles. Using the **Down arrow** key, scroll down to this section of the file:

```
# Run gettys in standard runlevels
1:2345:respawn:/sbin/mingetty tty1
2:2345:respawn:/sbin/mingetty tty2
3:2345:respawn:/sbin/mingetty tty3
4:2345:respawn:/sbin/mingetty tty4
5:2345:respawn:/sbin/mingetty tty5
6:2345:respawn:/sbin/mingetty tty6
```

7. Move the cursor to the line that starts with 6 and press **Y**. You've copied that line into a buffer.
8. Move the cursor down one line and type **3P**. Three additional lines appear. All are exact copies of the one you copied in Step 7.
9. You need to change the new lines so the numbers at the beginning and end of each line are one greater than the previous line. The cursor is already sitting on top of the 6 for the first new line you added in Step 7. Type **r7** to change the 6 to a 7. Move the cursor down to the next line and type **r8**. Move to the next line down and type **r9**.
10. Move the cursor to the end of the line that now begins with 7:. Type **r7**. Move to the next line and type **r8**. Move to the end of the next line and type **r9**.

11. You're finished making changes to the file. Save the file to disk and exit the editor by entering **:wq**.
12. You can put this change into effect without having to reboot the operating system. Enter **kill -HUP 1**. This causes the init process (always process 1) to reread its configuration file (/etc/inittab) and make any needed changes. In this case, it makes three more virtual consoles.
13. Press **Alt+F7**. You should see a login prompt. Log in as any user.
14. Press **Alt+F8**. You should see a login prompt. Log in as any user.
15. Press **Alt+F9**. You should see a login prompt. Log in as any user.
16. Enter **w**. You see a list of all the virtual consoles you're logged in to. The TTY column tells you the virtual console being used, where tty1 is the first virtual console, tty2 is the second, and so on. If you were logged in to all the virtual consoles, it would look similar to this:

```
  1:57pm  up 1:21,  9 users, load average: 2.07, 2.02, 1.77
USER     TTY      FROM      LOG IN@   IDLE   JCPU    PCPU    WHAT
root     tty1     -       12:37pm  35:06   0.14s   0.14s   -bash
root     tty2     -        1:21pm  36:11   8.75s   8.69s   top
root     tty3     -        1:21pm  36:06   0.12s   0.12s   -bash
root     tty4     -        1:21pm  35:57   0.07s   0.07s   -bash
```

```
root     tty5     -     1:21pm  35:47  17:56    17:56    primes
root     tty6     -     1:22pm  35:35  17:40    17:40    primes
root     tty7     -     1:22pm   0.00s  0.13s    0.03s   w
root     tty8     -     1:23pm  34:28   0.09s    0.09s   -bash
root     tty9     -     1:23pm  34:11   0.08s    0.08s   -bash
```

NOTE You can have up to 63 virtual consoles (tty1 to tty63). You can select the first 12 with Alt+Fx, where *x* is one of the 12 function keys and Alt is the left Alt key. You can select the next 12 by using the right Alt key. Beyond 24, you can move from one to the next with Alt+Right arrow and Alt+Left arrow. From a command prompt, you can go to any virtual console by typing chvt *x*, where *x* is a number from 1 to 63.

17. If you want to restore your system so it boots up in a graphical desktop, edit the /etc/inittab file to restore the line you modified in Steps 2 and 3. In case you forgot, the line should now look like this:

    ```
    id:5:initdefault:
    ```

Certification Objectives

Objectives for the Linux+ exam:

- Select appropriate parameters for Linux installation (e.g., language, time zones, keyboard, mouse) (1.11)
- Create files and directories and modify files using CLI commands (2.3)
- Access and write data to recordable media (2.9)
- Manage runlevels and system initialization from the CLI and configuration files (e.g., /etc/inittab and init command, /etc/rc.d, rc.local) (2.10)
- Identify, execute, manage and kill processes (e.g., ps, kill, killall, bg, fg, jobs, nice, renice, rc) (2.11)
- Perform text manipulation (e.g., sed, awk, vi) (2.15)
- Create, modify, and use basic shell scripts (2.19)

Review Questions

1. Which file must you edit to change the runlevel that your computer boots into?
    a. /etc/rc.d/rc
    b. lilo.conf or grub.conf

c. /etc/inittab

d. /etc/rc.local

2. How many virtual consoles are there by default in most Linux distributions?

   a. 4

   b. 6

   c. 8

   d. 12

3. Which file must you edit to have additional virtual consoles?

   a. /etc/inittab

   b. /etc/vc.conf

   c. /etc/vc/init.conf

   d. lilo.conf or grub.conf

4. What is the maximum number of virtual consoles?

   a. 16

   b. 32

   c. 63

   d. 64

5. Which command moves you to any virtual console?

11

Lab 11.2 Testing Your Logging

Objectives

The goal of this lab is to learn how you can easily test your syslog logging to see if it works the way you intended when you created or modified the /etc/syslog.conf file. To test logging, you must cause the logging of events of certain facilities and priorities to occur so you can see how syslog handles them. Fortunately, most Linux distributions include a program called **logger** that makes this testing easy.

Materials Required

This lab requires the following:

- Access as a root user to a computer running Linux

Estimated completion time: 30 Minutes

LAB ACTIVITY

Activity

1. Log in as root in a graphical desktop such as Gnome or KDE.
2. Start three terminals and have all three appear on the same screen. With Fedora Core 2, you start a terminal by right-clicking the desktop and selecting the Open Terminal item. When you start the terminals, resize their windows so they're wide but short (about two inches high on the screen). Position the windows so they're above/below each other as shown in Figure 11-1.

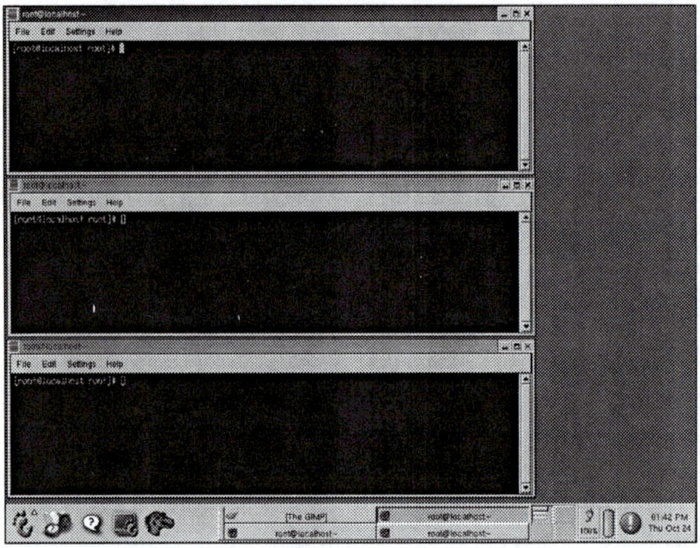

Figure 11-1 Three terminal windows started in Gnome

3. In the first window, enter **less /etc/syslog.conf**. The contents of the syslog-.conf file should appear. You can use the Up and Down arrow keys to see the entire file.
4. Select the second window. Enter **tail -f /var/log/messages**. You're now looking at the end of the messages file. The **-f** option tells the tail program to monitor the file and display any updates to the screen.
5. Select the third window. Enter **logger -p daemon.info This is a test of daemon.info**. This tells the logger program to generate a logging message of **daemon** facility and **info** priority. A line appears in the second window that starts with the current date and time, followed by the name of your computer, the user that logged the message (root), and the text of the message. Note that the facility and priority are not included in the line.
6. Press the **Up arrow** key. Bash recalls the previous line. Press **Enter**. Notice that nothing appears in the second screen. You told the logger program to log an identical message, but it didn't. Press the **Up arrow** key again and press

Enter. Still, nothing appears in the second window. This is because syslog does not print duplicate messages to the log file. However, it does print duplicate messages after a timeout period of a minute or two.

7. Enter **logger -p daemon.warning This is a test of daemon.warning**. This time two lines appear in the second window. The first new line tells you that the last message was repeated two times. These are the log messages you generated in Step 6. The second new line contains the text of the most recent log message:

   ```
   This is a test of daemon.warning.
   ```

8. Enter **logger -p mail.info This is a test of mail.info**. Nothing appears in the second window. This is because this message was for facility mail. Your syslog.conf file is configured to send mail to a different log file. Select the first window and find the line that contains `mail.*`. You can see that any log messages for the mail facility are stored in the /var/log/maillog file.

9. Select the second window and press **Ctrl+C** to get back to the shell prompt. Enter **tail -f /var/log/maillog**. The last line that appears contains the message you sent in Step 8:

   ```
   This is a test of mail.info.
   ```

10. Make syslog do some additional logging. Have it send any log messages of priority err or greater to a file called important. First, select the third window. Next, create the file, because syslog does not do it for you. Enter **touch /var/log/important**. Enter **ls -l /var/log im***. You see the file was created. Notice its length is zero.

11. Now you need to add a line to the syslog.conf file. The line is ***.err /var/log/important**. You can use your favorite text editor program to do this or enter **echo "*.err /var/log/important" >> /etc/syslog.conf**. The syslog daemon does not automatically detect this change. You must tell it that its configuration file has changed. Enter **killall -HUP syslogd**.

12. Select the second window. Press **Ctrl+C** to return to the shell prompt. Enter **tail -f /var/log/important**. Nothing appears because the file is empty.

13. Select the third window. Enter **logger -p mail.err This is a test of mail.err**. Notice that the message appears in the second window.

14. Enter **logger -p mail.warning This is a test of mail.warning**. Nothing appears in the second window. This is because the log message was sent as priority warning, which is a lesser priority than err. Only messages of priority err and greater (crit, alert, and emerg) are sent to the /var/log/important file.

15. Enter **logger -p mail.alert This is a test of mail.alert**. The message appears in the second window because the alert priority is greater than the err priority.

16. Enter **logger -p mail.emerg This is a test of mail.emerg**. The message appears in all three windows. This is because there's a line in the syslog.conf file that sends all messages of emerg priority to all users on the system. The line looks like this:

```
*.emerg      *
```

17. Close all three terminal windows.

Certification Objectives

Objectives for the Linux+ exam:

- Create files and directories and modify files using CLI commands (2.3)
- Access and write data to recordable media (2.9)
- Identify, execute, manage and kill processes (e.g., ps, kill, killall, bg, fg, jobs, nice, renice, rc) (2.11)
- Perform text manipulation (e.g., sed, awk, vi) (2.15)
- Configure log files (e.g., syslog, remote logfile storage) (3.10)

Review Questions

1. You want to monitor the messages log file and have any additional messages written to the log file also displayed on your screen. Which command does this?
   a. **head /var/log/messages**
   b. **head -f /var/log/messages**
   c. **tail /var/log/messages**
   d. **tail -f /var/log/messages**
2. Which command sends a message of mail facility and info priority?
   a. **log mail,info This is a test**
   b. **log -p mail info This is a test**
   c. **logger -p mail.info This is a test**
   d. **logger -w mail:info This is a test**
3. If you make a change to /etc/syslog.conf, you must inform the syslog daemon of the change by sending it a SIGHUP signal. True or False?
4. Which of the following is the highest priority?
   a. crit
   b. alert
   c. debug
   d. warning

5. Which statement, placed in the syslog.conf file, sends all messages of crit priority and higher to the terminal screens of everyone logged in?
    a. mail.crit /var/log/everyone
    b. crit. **
    c. *.crit |/var/log
    d. *.crit *

Lab 11.3 Using Named Pipes with Logging

Objectives

The goal of this lab is to learn how you can use named pipes and simple scripts to add capability to system logging. It's not uncommon for a Linux server to have two or more daemons logging to the same facility. A good example is a server used for e-mail that runs a SMTP daemon and a POP3 daemon. Both log to the mail facility causing the log messages for both daemons to be written to the same log file.

You can't configure syslog to write the log messages for the two daemons to separate files. However, you can use a named pipe and a simple script to send the messages to separate files.

Materials Required

This lab requires the following:

- Access as a root user to a computer running Linux

Estimated completion time: 15 Minutes

Activity

1. Log in as root in a graphical desktop such as Gnome or KDE.
2. Start a terminal.
3. Create the files to which you're going to log SMTP and POP3 messages. Enter **touch /var/log/smtp**. Enter **touch /var/log/pop3**. Enter **ls -l /var/log**. Notice that the two files have been created and are of zero length.
4. Now you need to create a named pipe so that you can use your own program to filter the output of syslogd. Enter **mknod /var/log/mailpipe p**. Enter **ls -l /var/log/mail***. You should see the mailpipe entry in the list of files. Note that the first character in the line is a "p", which stands for "pipe."

5. Add this line to the syslog.conf file so syslogd knows to output to the named pipe: **mail.* |/var/log/mailpipe**. You can use your favorite text editor program to do this or enter **echo "mail.* |/var/log/mailpipe" >> /etc/syslog.conf**. The syslog daemon does not automatically detect this change. You must tell it that its configuration file has changed by entering **killall -HUP syslogd**.

Note that when you specify a named pipe in the syslog.conf file, you must precede the log file path and name with a vertical bar (|).

6. Syslog now logs messages of mail facility to the named pipe. However, nothing is listening to the pipe. You need to build a program to accept messages from the pipe, decide whether they're from the SMTP or POP3 daemons, and send the messages to the appropriate file. Enter the following shell script into a file called mailscript and place it in the /usr/local/bin directory. If you are unsure of what to do, the next few steps show you how to do this with the vi editor.

```
while [ true ]; do
read </var/log/mailpipe
if echo $REPLY | grep "pop3" > /dev/null
then
 echo $REPLY > /var/log/pop3
else
 echo $REPLY > /var/log/smtp
fi
done
```

This program is simple and may need some refinement if you want to use it on a real server. You can write your program in any language, such as Perl or C.

7. Enter **vi /usr/local/bin/mailscript**. Press **i**. Now enter the program shown in Step 6. When you're finished, press the **Esc** key. Type **:wq** and press **Enter**.
8. Make the file executable. Enter **chmod +x /usr/local/bin/mailscript**.
9. You now need to run the program. You can run it in the background by entering **mailscript &**. (Normally, this program would be started from one of the system startup scripts.)
10. Start two other terminals as you did in Step 2 and adjust their sizes and positions so they look similar to Figure 11-1 in the previous lab exercise. Place the window that you've been using for Steps 1 through 9 of this exercise at the top. Refer to this as the first window.
11. Select the second window. Enter **tail -f /var/log/smtp**.
12. Select the third window. Enter **tail -f /var/log/pop3**.

13. Select the first window. Enter **logger -p mail.info This is a message from the pop3 daemon**. The message appears in the third window. The message was written to the /var/log/pop3 log file.
14. Enter **logger -p mail.info This is a message from the smtp daemon**. This message appears in the second window. The message was written to the /var/log/smtp log file.
15. Close all three terminal windows.

Certification Objectives

Objectives for the Linux+ exam:

- Create files and directories and modify files using CLI commands (2.3)
- Access and write data to recordable media (2.9)
- Identify, execute, manage and kill processes (e.g., ps, kill, killall, bg, fg, jobs, nice, renice, rc) (2.11)
- Perform text manipulation (e.g., sed, awk, vi) (2.15)
- Create, modify, and use basic shell scripts (2.19)
- Redirect output (e.g., piping, redirection) (2.23)
- Configure log files (e.g., syslog, remote logfile storage) (3.10)

Review Questions

1. Which command creates a named pipe in the directory in which log files reside?
    a. **mknod /var/log/logpipe p**
    b. **mknod p /var/log/logpipe**
    c. **mknode /usr/log/logpipe**
    d. **mknode np /var/log/logpipe**
2. If you do a long directory listing (ls -l) of a named pipe, the first character on the line is a:
    a. l
    b. n
    c. p
    d. s

3. Which of the following statements in the syslog.conf file is correct if /var/log/logpipe is a named pipe?
   a. a.mail.info /var/log/logpipe
   b. daemon.crit>/var/log/logpipe
   c. c.local1.debug |/var/log/logpipe
   d. d.http.info |var/log/logpipe
4. One reason why a shell script may not run is that it does not have execute (x) permissions. True or False?
5. Which command runs a program called logscript in the background?
   a. **logscript**
   b. **logscript --background**
   c. **logscript &**
   d. **daemon logscript**

Lab 11.4 Finding Broken Links and Files with No Owners

Objectives

The goal of this lab is to learn how to find and fix files with no owners and symbolic links that no longer point to a file. Both of these are common system administration tasks.

Materials Required

This lab requires the following:

- Access as an ordinary user and root user to a computer running Linux

Estimated completion time: 15 Minutes

LAB ACTIVITY

Activity

1. Switch to a command-line terminal (tty2) by pressing **Ctrl+Alt+F2**, and log in to the terminal as root.
2. Create a user account to use for this exercise. Enter **useradd betty**.
3. Log in as user betty by entering **su betty**.

NOTE

When you're the root user and you use the su command to become another user, you don't have to enter the user's password.

4. Go to Betty's home directory. Enter **cd /home/betty**.
5. Create some files in Betty's home directory. Enter **touch file1**. You've created a file called file1. Create a few other files. Use whatever names you like.
6. Enter **ls -l**. You're looking at all the normal files in Betty's home directory. Note that the user owner and group owner of the files is betty. Here's an example of what the ls output might look like:

```
total 0
-rw-rw-r--    1 betty    betty     0 Oct 22 09:48 file1
-rw-rw-r--    1 betty    betty     0 Oct 22 09:48 file2
-rw-rw-r--    1 betty    betty     0 Oct 22 09:48 file3
-rw-rw-r--    1 betty    betty     0 Oct 22 09:48 file4
-rw-rw-r--    1 betty    betty     0 Oct 22 09:48 file5
```


7. Betty wants to make sure that other users can't read the files in her home directory. To do this, take away the read permission for other ordinary users by entering **chmod o-r ***. Enter **ls -l**. You see that the permissions have changed. Now only Betty and the root user can read her files. Here's what this ls output looks like:

```
total 0
-rw-rw----    1 betty    betty     0 Oct 22 09:48 file1
-rw-rw----    1 betty    betty     0 Oct 22 09:48 file2
-rw-rw----    1 betty    betty     0 Oct 22 09:48 file3
-rw-rw----    1 betty    betty     0 Oct 22 09:48 file4
-rw-rw----    1 betty    betty     0 Oct 22 09:48 file5
```

8. Enter **exit**. You're no longer logged in as Betty. You're logged in as root. Enter **cd /home/betty**.
9. Now delete user betty. Enter **userdel betty**.
10. Enter **ls -l**. You're looking at all the files in Betty's home directory. Note that the user owner is now a number, such as 502, instead of betty. The group owner is also a number. This is because every file's owner is stored in the directory as a numeric user ID (the UID). When you delete the user, the ls program prints the UID instead of the user account name. The file no longer has an owner. Here's an example of what ls output might look like for an account with no owner:

```
total 0
-rw-rw----    1 502      502       0 Oct 22 09:48 file1
-rw-rw----    1 502      502       0 Oct 22 09:48 file2
-rw-rw----    1 502      502       0 Oct 22 09:48 file3
-rw-rw----    1 502      502       0 Oct 22 09:48 file4
-rw-rw----    1 502      502       0 Oct 22 09:48 file5
```

11. Create another user. Enter **useradd tom**. Enter **ls -l**. Note that Betty's old files are now owned by Tom. This happened because the useradd program assigned Tom the UID that became available when user betty's account was deleted. Here's an example of what this looks like:

```
total 0
-rw-rw----    1 tom    tom    0 Oct 22 09:48 file1
-rw-rw----    1 tom    tom    0 Oct 22 09:48 file2
-rw-rw----    1 tom    tom    0 Oct 22 09:48 file3
-rw-rw----    1 tom    tom    0 Oct 22 09:48 file4
-rw-rw----    1 tom    tom    0 Oct 22 09:48 file5
```

NOTE

When you delete the account for an existing user and do nothing about the files in the user's home directory, the files become accessible to a future user who is assigned the same UID.

12. Delete user tom. Enter **userdel tom**. The files in Betty's home directory are once again unowned.

13. It's useful to periodically scan your system for files that have no owner. This tells you when there are files that might have been abandoned. If the permissions of the files are set as above to -rw-rw----, the only user who can access them is root. You might want to find these files and assign them to an appropriate user or delete them. To find them, enter **find / -nouser**. This searches the entire filesystem from the root directory on down. Here's an example of what might be displayed:

```
find: /proc/1435/fd/4: No such file or directory
/var/spool/mail/betty
/home/betty
/home/betty/.bash_logout
/home/betty/.bash_profile
/home/betty/.bashrc
/home/betty/.gtkrc
/home/betty/.emacs
/home/betty/file1
/home/betty/file2
/home/betty/file3
/home/betty/file4
/home/betty/file5
/home/betty/.bash_history
```

14. Suppose you want to find and delete unowned files, but you want to be prompted for each file so you can confirm whether to delete it. Enter **find / -nouser -ok rm "{}" "; "**. Each of the files listed in Step 13 as well as files owned by Tom are displayed one by one, followed by a question mark prompt. If you want to delete the file, enter **y**. If you don't want to delete the file, enter **n**.

NOTE You won't be able to delete directories.

15. Another common administrative filesystem-related problem is broken symbolic links. These are links that point to files or directories that no longer exist. They're called dangling links. It's useful to find these dangling links and either repair or delete them. Unfortunately, the find program cannot be used to find dangling links directly. However, the **symlinks** program can find them. To illustrate this task, create and then find a broken symbolic (sym) link. Enter **touch /home/tom /hello**. Enter **ln -s /home/tom/hello hello**. Enter **rm /home/tom/hello**. If necessary, type **y** to confirm the deletion. You now have a dangling link.
16. To find all dangling links, enter **symlinks -r / |grep dangling**. You see a list of dangling symlinks.
17. If you want to delete all dangling symlinks, enter **symlinks -r -d /**.
18. Go back to your graphical desktop by pressing **Ctrl+Alt+F7**. Or, if the three additional virtual consoles you created in Lab 11.1 still exist, press **Ctrl+Alt+F10** to go back.

Certification Objectives

Objectives for the Linux+ exam:

- Create files and directories and modify files using CLI commands (2.3)
- Execute content and directory searches using find and grep (2.4)
- Create linked files using CLI commands (2.5)
- Modify file and directory permissions and ownership (e.g., chmod, chown, sticky bit, octal permissions, chgrp) using CLI commands (2.6)
- Access and write data to recordable media (2.9)
- Perform text manipulation (e.g., sed, awk, vi) (2.15)
- Create, modify, and delete user and group accounts (e.g., useradd, groupadd, /etc/passwd, chgrp, quota, chown, chmod, grpmod) using CLI utilities (2.20)

Review Questions

1. When you're the root user and you use the su command to become another user, you must enter the user's password. True or False?
2. Everyone can read and write unowned files that have -rw-rw---- permissions. True or False?

3. When you list files with the ls -l command, what appears in the user and group owner columns for unowned files?
   a. the name of the user that owned the file last
   b. the name of the user that created the file
   c. the root user
   d. the UID and GID of the user that owned the file last
4. Which command displays any and all files that have no user owners in your filesystem?
   a. **find ./ --nouser**
   b. **find / -nouser**
   c. **locate / -no-user**
   d. **locate --nouser /**
5. Which command finds and displays any broken (dangling) symbolic links in your filesystem?
   a. **find / --dangling**
   b. **find / -links|grep dangling**
   c. **symlinks -c /**
   d. **symlinks -r / |grep dangling**

Lab 11.5 Understanding File Date and Time Stamps

Objectives

Linux system administrators have to do housekeeping (recover disk space by deleting or moving outdated and unnecessary files). Users may have login accounts on the computer and save files in their home directory, or they may use the computer as a file server where they store files in shared directories. When free disk space diminishes to a point where the system is in jeopardy, administrators have to do housekeeping or ask users to do their own housekeeping.

You can recover disk space by deleting old files that are no longer needed or moving old files onto other media (tape, optical media, and so on). To identify old files as such, you look to the date and time stamps on files. Each file has three date and time stamps, and administrators should know how they work if they're to identify old files with precision.

Materials Required

This lab requires the following:

- Access as a root user to a computer running Linux

Activity Background

Linux files have three date and time stamps:

- The creation time or ctime
- The access time or atime
- The modification time or mtime

The creation time is automatically set to the current time and date when the file or directory is created. It is also changed to the current time when a file's permissions, attributes, owners, or contents change. The access time is automatically changed to the current time and date when the file is opened. The modification time is changed when the file is written to and closed.

Estimated completion time: 30 Minutes

Activity

LAB ACTIVITY

1. Switch to a command-line terminal (tty2) by pressing **Ctrl+Alt+F2**, and log in to the terminal using any username, if you aren't already logged in.
2. Go to Betty's home directory that you created in Lab 11.4. Enter **cd/home/betty**.
3. Remove all files in this directory. Enter **rm ***. Answer **y** if you're prompted with an `rm: remove filename` message.
4. Create a new file called file1. Enter **touch file1**.
5. Normally, the ls program displays mtime. Enter **ls -l**. Notice the file's date and time or mtime. Here's an example:

   ```
   -rw-r--r--      1 root      root       0 Oct 23 08:40 file1
   ```

6. The ls program can also display the file's ctime by using the **--time** option. Enter **ls -l --time=ctime**. The date and time is the same as mtime:

   ```
   -rw-r--r--      1 root      root       0 Oct 23 08:40 file1
   ```

7. The ls program can also display atime. Enter **ls -l --time=atime**. The atime should be the same as mtime and ctime:

   ```
   -rw-r--r--      1 root      root       0 Oct 23 08:40 file1
   ```

8. There's no way for the ls program to display atime, ctime, and mtime with only one command. To do this, create an alias that combines three commands. Enter **alias dir="ls -l --time=ctime|grep root;ls -l|grep root;ls -l --time=atime|grep root"**.

9. Enter **dir**. You see three lines. The first line shows the ctime. The second line shows the mtime. The third line shows the atime. Here's what the output looks like:

```
-rw-r--r--    1 root    root     0 Oct 23 08:40 file1
-rw-r--r--    1 root    root     0 Oct 23 08:40 file1
-rw-r--r--    1 root    root     0 Oct 23 08:40 file1
```

NOTE Experienced Linux users or programmers could build a program to display all three times on a single line with little difficulty.

10. Open the file and read from it and see how the time stamps are affected. Enter **cat file1**. Enter **dir**. Only the atime should have changed:

```
-rw-r--r--    1 root    root     0 Oct 23 08:40 file1
-rw-r--r--    1 root    root     0 Oct 23 08:40 file1
-rw-r--r--    1 root    root     0 Oct 23 08:47 file1
```

11. Modify the file. Enter **vi file1**. Type **i**. You're now in insert mode. Type a line of text, such as **This is a test**. Press **Esc**. You're back in command mode. Type **:wq** and press **Enter**.
12. Enter **dir**. Notice that all three times changed. It was expected that mtime would change because you modified the file. It's reasonable that atime would also change because you had to access the file to modify it. But ctime? It seems silly that it should work this way, but it does. Here's what it looks like:

```
-rw-r--r--    1 root    root     0 Oct 23 08:50 file1
-rw-r--r--    1 root    root     0 Oct 23 08:50 file1
-rw-r--r--    1 root    root     0 Oct 23 08:50 file1
```

NOTE This is different than other operating systems, such as NetWare, where a file's creation time does not change just because its contents are modified.

13. If you change a file's permissions, do the date and time change? If so, which of the three times are changed? Enter **chmod 700 file1**. Enter **dir**. You see that only the ctime changes:

```
-rwx------    1 root    root     0 Oct 23 09:04 file1
-rwx------    1 root    root     0 Oct 23 08:50 file1
-rwx------    1 root    root     0 Oct 23 08:50 file1
```

14. What if you change the file's owners? Enter **chown nobody file1**. Enter **dir**. Again, only the ctime changes:

```
-rwx------      1 nobody   root       0 Oct 23 09:06 file1
-rwx------      1 nobody   root       0 Oct 23 08:50 file1
-rwx------      1 nobody   root       0 Oct 23 08:50 file1
```

15. What if you change the file's attributes? Enter **chattr +d file1**. Enter **dir**. As expected, only the ctime changes:

```
-rwx------      1 nobody   root       0 Oct 23 09:08 file1
-rwx------      1 nobody   root       0 Oct 23 08:50 file1
-rwx------      1 nobody   root       0 Oct 23 08:50 file1
```

16. There is an attribute that does affect time and date. It's the A attribute, which affects a file's atime. When the attribute is set, the file's atime is not updated even though the file is accessed. Set the attribute by entering **chattr +A file1**. Now access the file. Enter **cat file1**. Enter **dir**. You see that the atime has not changed:

```
-rwx------      1 nobody   root       0 Oct 23 09:08 file1
-rwx------      1 nobody   root       0 Oct 23 08:50 file1
-rwx------      1 nobody   root       0 Oct 23 08:50 file1
```


NOTE

The practical application for the A attribute is where files are accessed frequently and you don't care about the atime being updated. This saves a little bit of processing time and disk I/O.

17. You can change a file's date and time stamps with the touch program. When you run the touch program with no command-line options, all three date and time stamps are updated. Enter **touch file1**. Enter **dir**. Here's what you see:

```
-rwx------      1 nobody   root       0 Oct 23 09:13 file1
-rwx------      1 nobody   root       0 Oct 23 09:13 file1
-rwx------      1 nobody   root       0 Oct 23 09:13 file1
```

18. The touch man page says that the -a option causes touch to only change the atime. Wait a minute or two then enter **touch -a file1**. Enter **dir**. You see that not only did the atime change but ctime did as well:

```
-rwx------      1 nobody   root       0 Oct 23 09:15 file1
-rwx------      1 nobody   root       0 Oct 23 09:13 file1
-rwx------      1 nobody   root       0 Oct 23 09:15 file1
```

19. The touch man page says that the -m option causes touch to only change mtime. Wait a minute or two and enter **touch -m file1**. Enter **dir**. You see that not only did the mtime change but ctime did as well:

```
-rwx------      1 nobody   root       0 Oct 23 09:18 file1
-rwx------      1 nobody   root       0 Oct 23 09:18 file1
-rwx------      1 nobody   root       0 Oct 23 09:15 file1
```

You should have noticed by now that anything you do to a file, except open it and read from it, causes ctime to change. Therefore, it can only be used as an indication that something happened to cause the file to change in some way.

20. You can take advantage of atime to search for files that have not been accessed recently. Suppose you want to locate files that have not been accessed in one year. Use the command **find / -atime 365**, where 365 is the number of days since the file was last accessed. Because you may be new to Linux and your Linux installation may be recent, use times that are not so long. Enter **find / -atime 7**. This may take a while because the program is searching your entire filesystem. When the program completes, it lists all the files on your filesystem that have not been accessed in seven days.
21. You can also use the find program to search for files based on their mtime. Enter **find / -mtime 5**. This searches for files that have not been modified in five days. There will likely be lots of these files.

NOTE

You can also use the -exec or -ok options with the find command to take some action, such as delete the files or back them up, on those files that you've found as you did in Lab 11.4.

22. Go back to your graphical desktop by pressing **Ctrl+Alt+F7**, or if the three additional virtual consoles you created in Lab 11.1 still exist, press **Ctrl+Alt+F10** to go back.

Certification Objectives

Objectives for the Linux+ exam:

- Create files and directories and modify files using CLI commands (2.3)
- Modify file and directory permissions and ownership (e.g., chmod, chown, sticky bit, octal permissions, chgrp) using CLI commands (2.6)
- Access and write data to recordable media (2.9)
- Perform text manipulation (e.g., sed, awk, vi) (2.15)
- Create, modify, and delete user and group accounts (e.g., useradd, groupadd, /etc/passwd, chgrp, quota, chown, chmod, grpmod) using CLI utilities (2.20)

Review Questions

1. When you open a file and read from it, which time is changed?
   a. ctime
   b. mtime
   c. atime
   d. all of the above

2. When you modify a file's contents, which time is changed?
   a. ctime
   b. mtime
   c. atime
   d. all of the above
3. Which time is changed when you use the command touch file9?
   a. ctime
   b. mtime
   c. atime
   d. all of the above
4. Which command displays mtime?
   a. **ls -l**
   b. **ls -l -m**
   c. **ls -l --time=mtime**
   d. **ls -l --mtime**
5. If you change a file's permissions (using chmod), which time is changed?
   a. ctime
   b. mtime
   c. atime
   d. all of the above

CHAPTER TWELVE

COMPRESSION, SYSTEM BACK-UP, AND SOFTWARE INSTALLATION

Labs included in this chapter

- Lab 12.1 Backing Up to a CD
- Lab 12.2 Compressing Programs with gzexe
- Lab 12.3 Compressing Image Files
- Lab 12.4 Installing and Removing Packages
- Lab 12.5 Detecting and Replacing Missing Package Files

CompTIA Linux+ Exam Objectives

Objective		Lab
1.9	Manage packages after installing the operating systems (e.g., install, uninstall, update) (e.g., RPM, tar, gzip)	12.4, 12.5
2.3	Create files and directories and modify files using CLI commands	12.1, 12.2, 12.3
2.8	Perform and verify backups and restores (tar, cpio, jar)	12.1
2.9	Access and write data to recordable media	12.1
2.13	Repair packages and scripts (e.g., resolving dependencies, file repair)	12.5

Lab 12.1 Backing Up to a CD

Objectives

This lab shows you how you can burn data to a CD-R. There are two parts to this. You must first convert your data into an ISO-9660 image that is compatible with CD media. Then you use your CD burner program to place the image on the CD.

Materials Required

This lab requires the following:

- Access as the root user to a computer running Linux
- An IDE/ATAPI CD burner
- Two blank CD-R discs

Estimated completion time:	30 Minutes

Activity

1. Switch to a command-line terminal (tty2) by pressing **Ctrl+Alt+F2**, and log in as root.
2. Check to see if your system recognizes its CD burner. Enter **cdrecord –scanbus**. You see quite a bit of text appear, ending with something similar to this:

```
scsibus1:
1,0,0100) 'ARTEC    ' 'WRR-52Z ' '1.25' Removable CD-ROM
1,1,0101) *
1,2,0102) *
1,3,0103) *
1,4,0104) *
1,5,0105) *
1,6,0106) *
1,7,0107) *
```

The first line (`scsibus1:`) indicates that Linux sees this drive as a SCSI device. If you're using an IDE/ATAPI drive, this is normal. The second line shows the manufacturer of the drive (ARTEC), the model number (WRR-52Z), and a description of the drive.

NOTE

If your CD burner doesn't appear in this list, you may not be able to complete this lab.

3. You'll use the **mkisofs** program to build the ISO9660 image that will be burned to the CD-R. Become familiar with the program by reviewing its man page. Enter **man mkisofs.** When you have finished reading, press **Q** to exit from the man page.
4. Create an image of the /etc directory by entering **mkisofs –o /tmp/etc.iso –r /etc**. As the program is running you see lines similar to this:

```
36.4% done, estimate finish Mon Sep 13 10:44:28 2004
```

5. Enter **ls –lh /tmp/etc.iso**. You see something similar to this:

```
-rw-r--r--  1 root root  55M  Sep 13 15:32 etc.iso
```

   You've created the image and it's about 55MB.

6. Before you burn the image to a CD-R, you should see if the image was created according to your wishes. You can mount the image as if it were a CD-ROM. Enter **mount –o loop /tmp/etc.iso /mnt/cdrom**. You should see no error messages. The image should be mounted.
7. Enter **ls /mnt/cdrom**. You should see the same files and directories as are in your /etc directory.
8. Insert a blank CD-R into your CD burner. Enter **cdrecord speed=4 dev=/dev/cdrom /tmp/etc.iso**. You see lots of text displayed by the cdrecord program. Some of the text may look like error messages. When the CD-R has been completely burned, you see something similar to this:

```
Track 01: Total bytes read/written: 56578048/
56578048 (27626 sectors)
```

NOTE

The speed=4 parameter in the above command is a conservative value that should work with older and slower CD burners. Your CD burner may be capable of running at a higher speed.

9. You can check to see that the data was recorded to the CD-R by mounting it. Enter **mount /dev/cdrom /mnt/cdrom**. Now enter **ls /mnt/cdrom**. You should see the same files and directories as are in your /etc directory. These should also be the same as you saw in the image file in Step 7.
10. Unmount the CD-R by entering **umount /dev/cdrom**.
11. Eject the CD-R by entering **eject /dev/cdrom**.
12. If you have a computer running Windows available, place the CD-R in that computer and look at the files on the CD-R. Notice that the file names and

directory names are in an 8.3 format (uppercase name truncated to eight characters with a maximum three-character extension). You burned a CD-R that works properly with Linux but not with modern versions of Windows.

13. If you want your Windows computer to see the same file and directory names as Linux, you need to tell the mkisofs program that you want to use Microsoft Joliet (Unicode) names. Enter **mkisofs –o /tmp/etc.iso –r –J /etc**.
14. Place a blank CD-R in the CD burner and enter **cdrecord speed=4 dev=/dev/cdrom /tmp/etc.iso**.
15. Eject the CD-R by entering **eject /dev/cdrom**.
16. Place the CD-R in the Windows computer and examine its file and directory names. They should be the same as you saw with Linux.

Certification Objectives

Objectives for the Linux+ exam:

- Create files and directories and modify files using CLI commands (2.3)
- Perform and verify backups and restores (tar, cpio, jar) (2.8)
- Access and write data to recordable media (2.9)

Review Questions

1. What program is used to create ISO9660 images?
   a. cdrecord
   b. iso9660
   c. mkisofs
   d. mk9660
2. What program is used to write ISO9660 images to a CD burner?
   a. cdrecord
   b. iso9660
   c. mkisofs
   d. mk9660
3. If you want Windows computers to see long file and directory names, what must you do when you have Linux burn a CD-R?
   a. Have the cdrecord program configured for Rock Ridge extensions.
   b. Have the mkisofs program produce Microsoft Joliet names.
   c. Make sure you load the NTFS kernel module.
   d. nothing

4. Which command shows you whether Linux recognizes your CD burner?
   a. **cdrecord devices**
   b. **mkisofs --devices**
   c. **cdrecord –scanbus**
   d. **lsdev**
5. You can mount an ISO9660 image file and view its contents. True or False?

Lab 12.2 Compressing Programs with GZEXE

Objectives

Sometimes it's useful to make data files as small as possible. This may be because the files have to reside on a small disk or because they must be transmitted over a slow network or modem link. Linux binary program files may be compressed for the same reasons. In this lab exercise, you learn how to use the **gzexe** program to compress binary programs.

Materials Required

This lab requires the following:

- Access as an ordinary user to a computer running Linux

Estimated completion time: 15 Minutes

Activity

LAB ACTIVITY

1. Switch to a command-line terminal (tty2) by pressing **Ctrl+Alt+F2**, and log in to the terminal using any username.
2. Ensure that you're in your home directory by entering **cd**.
3. Copy the **rpm** program from the /bin directory into your home directory by entering **cp /bin/rpm ./**.
4. Find the size of the rpm program by entering **ls -l rpm**. You see that the file size is about 81280 bytes.
5. Compress the program by entering **gzexe rpm**. This takes a few seconds, and you see a line similar to this when it finishes:

```
rpm:                    56%
```

NOTE

Linux binary programs tend to compress by about 50%.

6. The rpm program was compressed by 56%. The original was renamed to rpm~, and the new compressed file is called rpm. Enter **ls -l rpm*** to see the new compressed file and the old uncompressed file. There should be a substantial difference in the file sizes, similar to this:

```
-rwxr-xr-x    1 ed     ed       36167   10:22 rpm
-rwxr-xr-x    1 ed     ed       81280   10:21 rpm~
```

7. Both files run the same program. Enter **./rpm --version**. You see this:

```
RPM version 4.3.1
```

8. Enter **./rpm~ --version**. You see something similar to this:

```
RPM version 4.3.1
```

9. When you run the compressed program, it takes longer to start because it must first be uncompressed. You can use the **time** program to compare the time it takes both programs to run. Enter **time ./rpm --version** to see how long it takes to run the compressed program. You see something similar to this:

```
RPM version 4.3.1
real    0m0.309s
user    0m0.100s
sys     0m0.120s
```

NOTE

The time program displays three results in a minutes.seconds format: the real elapsed time from program start to finish, the amount of time the program spent running as the user, and the amount of time the program spent running as the system.

10. Enter **time ./rpm~ --version** to time how long it takes to run the uncompressed program. You see that it takes much less time. You see something similar to this:

```
RPM version 4.3.1
real    0m0.029s
user    0m0.010s
sys     0m0.020s
```

NOTE

The -d command-line option for the gzexe program can be used to return the compressed program to its original uncompressed state.

11. Delete the two rpm files you created in your home directory by entering **rm rpm***. Press **Y** to confirm deletion.

Certification Objectives

Objectives for the Linux+ exam:

- Create files and directories and modify files using CLI commands (2.3)

Review Questions

1. Which program compresses Linux binary programs and allows them to execute in their compressed form?
   a. gzip
   b. compress
   c. gzexe
   d. gunzip
2. Linux binary programs tend to compress by about _______________ %.
3. A compressed binary program loads just as fast as the same uncompressed program. True or False?
4. The gzexe program allows you to convert a compressed program back to its original, uncompressed state. True or False?
5. What result does the time program display if a program takes two hours to run?
   a. 2h.0m0.000s
   b. 1h.60m0.000s
   c. 120m0.000s
   d. 2h.0m

Lab 12.3 Compressing Image Files

Objectives

In this lab, you use the **cjpeg** program to compress bitmap image files and convert them to JPEG format. The bitmap images that you can convert include .bmp files (used on Windows computers) and Targa files. This functionality can be used to post images on a Web page, or just to compress images that you want to send via e-mail or over the Internet. You also use the cjpeg program to convert a .jpeg image file to grayscale rather than color, and you compare file size and image quality of compressed and uncompressed files.

Materials Required

This lab requires the following:

- Access as the root user to a computer running Linux
- A bitmap image file (see steps for details)

Estimated completion time: 20 Minutes

Activity

1. Start an xterm. You should be logged in as root.
2. You need a bitmap image file to use for this lab exercise. This lab uses one that should already be installed on your system. Enter **cd /usr/games/Maelstrom/Images**. This directory has several files with the extension of .bmp. Enter **ls -l *.bmp**.

If you don't have this directory on your system, you can create or capture a bitmap image from a computer running Windows. The Windows Paint program can create bitmap (BMP) images.

3. Some files have a file extension of .bmp but are not really bitmap image files. You can check that a .bmp file is really a bitmap image file by using the file program. Enter **file Maelstrom_Titles#999.bmp**. If the file is a real bitmap image, you see something similar to this:

```
Maelstrom_Titles#999.bmp: PC bitmap data, Windows 3.x format,
128 x 128 x 8
```

4. Now you use the cjpeg program to convert the Maelstrom_Titles#999.bmp bitmap image file to a compressed .jpeg file. The program sends the compressed image to its standard output, so you have to redirect it into a file. Enter **cjpeg Maelstrom_Titles#999.bmp> Maelstrom_Titles#999.jpeg**. The compressed image is now in the **Maelstrom_Titles#999.jpeg** file.
5. Compare the sizes of the .bmp and .jpeg files by entering **ls -l Maelstrom_Titles#999***. You see that the .jpeg file is very small compared to the .bmp file:

```
-r--r--r--
    1 root root 24478 Mar 23 14:24 Maelstrom_Titles #999.bmp
-rw-r--r--
    1 root root 5890 Aug 17 11:46 Maelstrom_Titles #999.jpeg
```

NOTE It's typical for a bitmap image file to compress 15 to 20% of its original size.

6. Did the compression of the image affect the quality of the image? You can find out by looking at both image files with a graphical viewer program. Run the Image Viewer program by selecting it on the Graphics menu. Click the **Open** icon, select **Filesystem** from the list, and select folders until you get to the /usr/games/Maelstrom/Images directory.
7. Click the **Maelstrom_Titles#999.bmp** file. The original uncompressed image appears. Now click the **Open** icon. Another Windows appears. Select the **Maelstrom_Titles#999.jpeg** file. You see that it is very similar to the .bmp file. It may look the same to you. You have compressed the file substantially without significantly affecting the image quality displayed onscreen.
8. Close the Image Viewer windows.
9. You can use the cjpeg program to not only compress the image, but also to convert it to a grayscale image using the -grayscale option. Because the **Maelstrom_Titles#999.bmp** file is already a grayscale image, use the **Maelstrom_Titles#135.bmp** file. First, convert it to a color JPEG file by entering **cjpeg Maelstrom_Titles#135.bmp > Maelstrom_Titles#135.jpeg**.
10. Now convert it to a grayscale image by entering **cjpeg -grayscale Maelstrom_Titles#135.bmp > Maelstrom_Titles#135gray.jpeg**.
11. See how the size of the grayscale file compares to the other files by entering **ls -l Maelstrom_Titles#135***. You see that the grayscale. jpeg file is smaller than the full-color file:

```
-r--r--r--  1 root   root    197686 Jan 26  2003 Maelstrom_Titles#135.bmp
-rw-r--r--  1 root   root    44012 Dec 14 11:46 Maelstrom_Titles#135.jpeg
-rw-r--r--  1 root   root    38203 Dec 14 11:46 Maelstrom_Titles#135gray.jpeg
```

Certification Objectives

Objectives for the Linux+ exam:

- Create files and directories and modify files using CLI commands (2.3)

Review Questions

1. Which program tells you whether a file with the extension of .bmp is really a bitmap image?
   a. ls
   b. lsbmp
   c. file
   d. grep
2. Which program can convert a bitmap image file to a compressed image (.jpeg) file?
   a. file
   b. bmpcvt
   c. cjpeg
   d. jpeg
3. Bitmap images typically compress to about ________________ % of their original size.
4. Which programs typically installed with Red Hat Linux allow you to view image files?
5. The cjpeg program allows you to simultaneously compress a bitmap image file as well as convert it to a grayscale image. True or False?

Lab 12.4 Installing and Removing Packages

Objectives

Most Linux distributions use the Red Hat Package Manager (RPM) program to install and uninstall software. In this lab exercise, you:

- Display all installed packages.
- Install packages from your CD-ROM.
- Uninstall packages.

Materials Required

This lab requires the following:

- Access as a root user to a computer running Linux
- Red Hat Linux CD-ROMs

Estimated completion time: 15 Minutes

LAB ACTIVITY

Activity

1. Switch to a command-line terminal (tty2) by pressing **Ctrl+Alt+F2**, and log in to the terminal as the root user.
2. To see a list of all the packages installed on your computer, enter **rpm -qa**. You see that there are many packages installed, and most of them scroll by on the screen. Note that they are not listed in alphabetic order. To sort them alphabetically and display them a page at a time, enter **rpm -qa | sort | more**. Scroll down the list, and note that there is no listing for a package called rdesktop.
3. Insert the Fedora Core 2 CD-ROM number 3 into your CD-ROM drive. Mount the CD-ROM by entering **mount –t iso9660 /dev/cdrom /mnt/cdrom**. Go to the RPMS directory by entering **cd /mnt/cdrom/Fedora/RPMS**.
4. Find the full name of the **rdesktop** package by entering **ls rdesk***. It's called rdesktop-1.3.1-3.i386.rpm.
5. Install the rdesktop package by entering **rpm -i rdesk***. You can use wildcards instead of typing the entire name as long as there are no name conflicts. Alternatively, you could use the Tab key completion as described in earlier chapters.
6. You can see that the rdesktop package is now installed by entering **rpm -qp rdesk***. This line should appear:

   ```
   rdesktop-1.3.1-3
   ```
7. Get information about the package by entering **rpm -qi rdesktop-1.3.1-3**. Unfortunately, you can't use wildcards here. You see a rather large amount of text that describes the package.
8. Verify that the package was actually installed by entering **whereis rdesktop**. You see this:

   ```
   rdesktop:  /usr/bin/rdesktop /usr/share/rdesktop /usr/
   share/man/man1/rdesktop.1.gz
   ```
9. Now uninstall the package with the -e (erase) command-line option. Enter **rpm -e rdesktop-1.3.1-3**. Nothing is displayed on the screen if uninstallation is successful.

NOTE

RPM, unlike Windows, never gets confused about what files need to be deleted when you uninstall a package. You are never prompted to decide whether a file should be deleted because it may be used by some other package. The package manager already knows this.

10. Verify that the package was uninstalled by entering **whereis rdesktop**. You see this:

    ```
    Rdesktop:
    ```

11. Remove the CD-ROM by entering **cd; umount /dev/cdrom;eject**.

Certification Objectives

Objectives for the Linux+ exam:

- Manage packages after installing the operating systems (e.g., install, uninstall, update) (e.g., RPM, tar, gzip)(1.9)

Review Questions

1. Which command displays all packages installed on your computer?
   a. **rpm --list**
   b. **rpm -q**
   c. **rpm -qa**
   d. **rpm -q all**
2. Which command displays the names of all installed packages that start with x?
   a. **rpm -q x***
   b. **rpm -qa x***
   c. **rpm -qp x***
   d. **rpm –qa | grep x**
3. Which command installs a package called blivet-2.3 if the rpm file in the current directory is called blivet-2.3.rpm?
   a. **rpm -a blivet**
   b. **rpm -a blivet-2.3**
   c. **rpm -a blivet-2.3.rpm**
   d. **rpm -a blivet-2.3.rpm.gz**
4. Which command uninstalls a package called blivet-2.3 if the rpm file on the original CD-ROM is called blivet-2.3.rpm?
   a. **rpm -u blivet**
   b. **rpm -u blivet-2.3**
   c. **rpm -e blivet-2.3**
   d. **rpm -e blivet-2.3.rpm.gz**
5. When you're uninstalling a package, the package manager may sometimes ask whether a file should be deleted because it may be used by another package. True or False?

Lab 12.5 Detecting and Replacing Missing Package Files

Objectives

Sometimes files are erased from a hard disk. This can be because of a mistake or an attack. If these files are part of a package, the programs in the package might not run or might not run properly. You need some way to detect when files are missing and a means to replace them. Package managers can do that for you. This lab exercise shows how the Red Hat Package Manager (RPM) performs these functions.

Materials Required

This lab requires the following:

- Access as a root user to a computer running Linux
- Fedora Core 2 CD-ROMs

Estimated completion time: 20 Minutes

Activity

LAB ACTIVITY

1. Switch to a command-line terminal (tty2) by pressing **Ctrl+Alt+F2**, and log in to the terminal as the root user.
2. One of the packages almost certainly installed on your computer is **gzip**. You can find the package name by entering **rpm -qa | grep gzip**. You see the package name in the list. The package is likely to be gzip-1.3.3-12.
3. Get a description of the package by using the -i command-line option. Enter **rpm -qi gzip-1.3.3-12** (substituting your package name for gzip-1.3.3-12 if necessary). You see something like this:

```
Name        : gzip                     Relocations: (not relocateable)
Version     : 1.3.3                         Vendor: Red Hat, Inc.
Release     : 12                        Build Date: Mon 16 Feb 2004
08:02:51 PM PDT
Install date: Wed 15 Sep 2004 03:54:54 PM PST      Build Host:
tweety.devel.redhat.com
Group       : Applications/File         Source RPM: gzip-1.3.3-12.src.rpm
Size        : 149767                       License: GPL
Packager    : Red Hat, Inc. <http://bugzilla.redhat.com/bugzilla>
```

```
URL         : http://www.gzip.org/
Summary     : The GNU data compression program.
Description :
The gzip package contains the popular GNU gzip data compression
program. Gzipped files have a .gz extension.

Gzip should be installed on your Red Hat Linux system, because it is a
very commonly used data compression program.
```

4. You can see what files are part of the package by using the -l command-line option. Enter **rpm -ql gzip-1.3.3-12**. You see something like this:

```
/bin/gunzip
/bin/gzip
/bin/zcat
/usr/bin/gunzip
/usr/bin/gzexe
/usr/bin/gzip
/usr/bin/zcmp
/usr/bin/zdiff
/usr/bin/zegrep
/usr/bin/zfgrep
/usr/bin/zforce
/usr/bin/zgrep
/usr/bin/zless
/usr/bin/zmore
/usr/bin/znew
/usr/share/doc/gzip-1.3.3
/usr/share/doc/gzip-1.3.3/AUTHORS
/usr/share/doc/gzip-1.3.3/ChangeLog
/usr/share/doc/gzip-1.3.3/NEWS
/usr/share/doc/gzip-1.3.3/README
/usr/share/doc/gzip-1.3.3/THANKS
/usr/share/doc/gzip-1.3.3/TODO
/usr/share/info/gzip.info.gz
/usr/share/man/man1/gunzip.1.gz
/usr/share/man/man1/gzexe.1.gz
/usr/share/man/man1/gzip.1.gz
/usr/share/man/man1/zcat.1.gz
/usr/share/man/man1/zcmp.1.gz
/usr/share/man/man1/zdiff.1.gz
/usr/share/man/man1/zforce.1.gz
/usr/share/man/man1/zgrep.1.gz
/usr/share/man/man1/zless.1.gz
/usr/share/man/man1/zmore.1.gz
/usr/share/man/man1/znew.1.gz
```

NOTE

Note that -l shows you the files that are part of the package. It does not show you the files installed on your hard disk.

5. You can see if all the files that are part of the package are actually installed on your hard disk with the -V command-line option. Enter **rpm -V gzip-1.3.3-12**. If all the files are on your hard disk, you see nothing displayed on the screen.
6. Delete some of these files. Enter **rm /usr/share/man/man1/gzip***. Answer **y** if you're prompted to confirm the file deletions.
7. See how the rpm handles the missing files. Enter **rpm -V gzip-1.3.3-12**. You see something like this:

```
missing    /usr/share/man/man1/gzip.1.gz
```

8. To fix the problem, you need to reinstall the files from the package file on the CD-ROM. Insert the Fedora Core 2 CD-ROM number 1 into your CD-ROM drive. Mount the CD-ROM by entering **mount /dev/cdrom**. Go to the RPMS directory by entering **cd /mnt/cdrom/Fedora/RPMS**.

NOTE

With Linux, package files are not typically stored on the hard disk as Windows .cab files are. You must mount the media (typically a CD-ROM) to install or reinstall a package.

9. Install the missing files from the package file by entering **rpm -i --replacefiles gzip-1.3.3-12**.
10. Enter **rpm -V gzip-1.3.3-12**. You see nothing displayed because there are no missing files.
11. In previous steps, you checked to see if any files in a particular package were missing from your hard disk. You can easily check to see if any files for all the packages installed on your system are missing from your hard disk. Enter **rpm -Va**. This takes a while as all packages are checked.
12. Remove the CD-ROM by entering **cd; umount /dev/cdrom;eject**.

Certification Objectives

Objectives for the Linux+ exam:

- Manage packages after installing the operating systems (e.g., install, uninstall, update) (e.g., RPM, tar, gzip) (1.9)
- Repair packages and scripts (e.g., resolving dependencies, file repair) (2.13)

Review Questions

1. Which command displays information about the words-2-17 package?
    a. **rpm -q words-2-17**
    b. **rpm -qa words-2-17**
    c. **rpm -q --list words-2-17**
    d. **rpm -qi words-2-17**
2. Which command shows you the files that are part of a package?
    a. **rpm -q words-2-17**
    b. **rpm -qa words-2-17**
    c. **rpm -ql words-2-17**
    d. **rpm -qi words-2-17**
3. Which command shows you any files that are part of the package, but not installed on your hard disk?
    a. **rpm -q words-2-17**
    b. **rpm -ql words-2-17**
    c. **rpm -V words-2-17**
    d. **rpm -Z words-2-17**
4. RPM package files are typically stored on your hard disk, similar to Windows .cab files. True or False?

CHAPTER THIRTEEN

TROUBLESHOOTING AND PERFORMANCE

Labs included in this chapter

- Lab 13.1 Using the hdparm Program
- Lab 13.2 Testing Hard Disk Performance
- Lab 13.3 Tuning Hard Disk Parameters
- Lab 13.4 Troubleshooting Performance Problems
- Lab 13.5 Measuring X Server Performance

CompTIA Linux+ Exam Objectives

Objective		Lab
1.11	Select appropriate parameters for Linux installation (e.g., language, time zones, keyboard, mouse)	13.3
1.12	Configure peripherals as necessary (e.g., printer, scanner, modem)	13.3
2.9	Access and write data to recordable media	13.2
6.2	Diagnose hardware issues using Linux tools (e.g., /proc, disk utilities, ifconfig, /dev, knoppix, BBC, dmesg)	13.1, 13.2, 13.3, 13.4, 13.5

Lab 13.1 Using the hdparm Program

Objectives

The goal of this lab is to show you how you can use a program called **hdparm** to get detailed technical information about your hard disks and your computer's interface to the hard disks. You can also use it to conduct simple tests of your hard disk's performance.

Materials Required

This lab requires the following:

- Access as a root user to a computer running Linux

Estimated completion time: 20 Minutes

Activity

LAB ACTIVITY

1. Switch to a command-line terminal (tty2) by pressing **Ctrl+Alt+F2**, and log in to the terminal as the root user.
2. Enter **hdparm**. You see a usage message and a list of command-line options for the hdparm program. Some of the information may scroll off the top of the screen and you'll likely try something like **hdparm | more** to stop the screen from scrolling. This won't work because the hdparm program displays its usage information to the STDERR device instead of the STDOUT device. You can solve this problem by redirecting STDERR to a file and having the more program read the file. Use the command **hdparm 2>/tmp/123;more /tmp/123** to do this.

NOTE

Note the word "(DANGEROUS)" next to a few of the options in the list. You won't be using any of these options in this lab, and you should not practice using these options on a system that contains critical data.

3. You can use the hdparm program to check the general settings for your hard disk just by specifying the device name of your hard disk without command-line options. Enter **hdparm /dev/hda**. If your hard disk is not /dev/hda, substitute the name of your hard disk. You should see something similar to this:

```
/dev/hda:
 multcount     = 16 (on)
 I/O support   =  0 (default 16-bit)
 unmaskirq     =  0 (off)
 using_dma     =  1 (on)
```

```
keepsettings =  0 (off)
readonly     =  0 (off)
readahead    =  8 (on)
geometry     = 3649/255/63, sectors = 58633344,
start = 0
```

You can compute the size of your hard disk from the information in the "geometry" line. Multiply the value of "sectors =" by 512 bytes per sector to get the drive's size. In this case it's 58,633,344 times 512 or 30,020,272,128—a 30-GB hard disk.

4. The hdparm program lets you query the hard disk for its internal details. Enter **hdparm -i /dev/hda**. You see lots of information that is technical and detailed. You may not understand what most of it means, but some of it is obvious. It's easy to spot the hard disk manufacturer, model number, firmware revision level, and serial number. This output is from a Western Digital WD400 drive:

```
/dev/hda:

 Model=WDC WD400BB-22FJA0, FwRev=13.03G13, SerialNo=WD-WCAJA1908104
 Config={ HardSect NotMFM HdSw>15uSec SpinMotCtl Fixed DTR>5Mbs FmtGapReq }
 RawCHS=16383/16/63, TrkSize=0, SectSize=0, ECCbytes=58
 BuffType=unknown, BuffSize=2048kB, MaxMultSect=16, MultSect=16
 CurCHS=16383/16/63, CurSects=16514064, LBA=yes, LBAsects=78165360
 IORDY=on/off, tPIO={min:120,w/IORDY:120}, tDMA={min:120,rec:120}
 PIO modes:  pio0 pio3 pio4
 DMA modes:  mdma0 mdma1 mdma2
 UDMA modes: udma0 udma1 udma2 udma3 udma4 *udma5
 AdvancedPM=no WriteCache=enabled
 Drive conforms to: device does not report version:

 * signifies the current active mode
```

There is other useful information in this output. For example, this hard disk has a 2 MB internal disk cache. You can tell from the string "BuffSize=2048kB."

5. If the level of detail in Step 4 is too much for you, you can produce friendlier output. Enter **hdparm -I /dev/hda | more**. Examine the following output:

```
/dev/hda:

ATA device, with non-removable media
        Model Number:       WDC WD400BB-22FJA0
```

13

```
        Serial Number:       WD-WCAJA1908104
        Firmware Revision:  13.03G13
Standards:
        Supported: 6 5 4 3
        Likely used: 6
Configuration:
        Logical         max     current
        cylinders       16383   16383
        heads           16      16
        sectors/track   63      63
        --
        CHS current addressable sectors:    16514064
        LBA    user addressable sectors:    78165360
        device size with M = 1024*1024:        38166 MBytes
        device size with M = 1000*1000:        40020 MBytes (40 GB)
Capabilities:
        LBA, IORDY(can be disabled)
        bytes avail on r/w long: 58Queue depth: 1
        Standby timer values: spec'd by Standard, with device specific minimum
        R/W multiple sector transfer: Max = 16       Current = 16
        Recommended acoustic management value: 128, current value: 254
        DMA: mdma0 mdma1 mdma2 udma0 udma1 udma2 udma3 udma4 *udma5
             Cycle time: min=120ns recommended=120ns
        PIO: pio0 pio1 pio2 pio3 pio4
             Cycle time: no flow control=120ns  IORDY flow control=120ns
Commands/features:
        Enabled Supported:
           *    READ BUFFER cmd
           *    WRITE BUFFER cmd
           *    Host Protected Area feature set
           *    Look-ahead
           *    Write cache
           *    Power Management feature set
           *    SMART feature set
           *    Mandatory FLUSH CACHE command
           *    Device Configuration Overlay feature set
Automatic Acoustic Management feature set
SET MAX security extension
           *    DOWNLOAD MICROCODE cmd
           *    SMART self-test
           *    SMART error logging
HW reset results:
         CBLID- above Vih
         Device num = 0 determined by CSEL
Checksum: correct
```

6. The hdparm program lets you perform simple nondestructive read tests of the hard disk's performance. Enter **hdparm -t /dev/hda**. This runs a read test and minimizes the effect of the disk cache on the results. The results produce

a speed rating in MB/sec, which is the number of megabytes per second the hard disk was able to read. You see output similar to this:

```
/dev/hda:
 Timing buffered disk reads:  142 MB in  3.01 seconds = 47.18 MB/sec
```

7. The next read test makes use of the disk cache and produces results that show the hard disk capable of faster read performance. Enter **hdparm -T /dev/hda**. You see results similar to this:

```
/dev/hda:
 Timing buffer-cache reads:   720 MB in  2.00 seconds = 359.69 MB/sec
```

8. Log out and return to your graphical interface by pressing **Alt+F7**.

Certification Objectives

Objectives for the Linux+ exam:

- Diagnose hardware issues using Linux tools (e.g., /proc, disk utilities, ifconfig, /dev, knoppix, BBC, dmesg) (6.2)

Review Questions

1. The hdparm program displays its usage information to the STDERR device rather than the STDOUT device; so it does not work with programs such as more or less. How do you solve this problem? > file

2. To compute the total storage capacity of your hard disk, display the hard disk's geometry information and multiply the total number of sectors by:
   a. 128
   b. 256
   c. 512
   d. 1024

3. Which command shows you a hard disk's serial number and firmware revision level?
   a. **hdparm -t /dev/hda**
   b. **hdparm -T /dev/hda**
   c. **hdparm -V /dev/hda**
   d. **hdparm -I /dev/hda**

4. Which command displays the results of a simple read test where the effect of the disk cache is minimized?
   a. **hdparm -t /dev/hda**
   b. **hdparm -T /dev/hda**

c. **hdparm -V /dev/hda**

d. **hdparm -I /dev/hda**

5. Which command displays the results of a simple read test that includes the effects of the disk cache?

   a. **hdparm -t /dev/hda**

   b. **hdparm -T /dev/hda**

   c. **hdparm -V /dev/hda**

   d. **hdparm -I /dev/hda**

Lab 13.2 Testing Hard Disk Performance

Objectives

The hdparm program can be used to configure your hard disk and its interface in your computer. In this lab, you download a hard disk benchmarking program called **bonnie** that goes beyond the simple performance measurement capability of hdparm. You see how to use bonnie to check the read and write speed of your hard disk.

Materials Required

This lab requires the following:

- Access as a root user to a computer running Linux
- At least 100 MB of free space on one of your Linux filesystems

Estimated completion time: 30 Minutes

NOTE

This activity might take you more or less time, depending on the speed of your computer.

LAB ACTIVITY

Activity

1. Switch to a command-line terminal (tty2) by pressing **Ctrl+Alt+F2**, and log in to the terminal as the root user.
2. Create a directory called bonnie below your home directory by entering **mkdir bonnie**.
3. Go back to the graphical desktop by pressing **Alt+F7**.

4. Start a Web browser on your Linux computer. Enter the following into the URL or Address line:

   http://www.textuality.com/bonnie/bonnie.tar.gz

5. When you're prompted where you'd like to store the file, choose your bonnie directory.

NOTE Your Windows program may rename the file to a different name, such as bonnie.tar.tar. If this happens, you should restore the file to its original name using the Linux mv command. For example, enter **mv bonnie.tar.tar mv bonnie.tar.gz**.

6. Switch to the command-line terminal (tty2) by pressing **Ctrl+Alt+F2**.
7. Go to the bonnie directory by entering **cd bonnie**. Uncompress the file by entering **tar xzvf bonnie.tar.gz.**
8. Compile the bonnie program by entering **make**. It should compile quickly, and there should be no errors. The bonnie program is called Bonnie (note the uppercase B). Change the program name to all lowercase letters by entering **mv Bonnie bonnie**. Assume you've done this for the remainder of this exercise.

NOTE If you want to keep the bonnie program on your system permanently, you should move it to a more appropriate directory, such as /usr/local/bin. You can also copy the bonnie man page file, called bonnie.1, to an appropriate man page directory, such as /usr/local/man/man1. These directories are compatible with the Filesystem Hierarchy Standard that was covered in Chapter 5.

9. Check to see how much free disk space you have by entering **df -h**. You need at least 100 MB of free space, and more is better. In this example, /dev/hda1 has 1.9 GB available:

```
Filesystem            Size  Used Avail Use% Mounted on
/dev/hda1             3.7G  1.6G  1.9G  46% /
none                   62M     0   61M   0% /dev/shm
/dev/fd0              1.4M   23k  1.3M   2% /mnt/floppy
```

10. Check to see how much memory is installed in your system by entering **free**. In this example, there is about 128 MB total RAM:

```
             total       used       free     shared    buffers     cached
Mem:        126572      16044     110528          0        916       4520
-/+ buffers/cache:      10608     115964
Swap:        52408        316      52092
```

11. Run the bonnie program by entering **./bonnie**. This may take a long time on a slow computer. Do not run any other programs during the test that will

write to or read from the hard disk and skew the results. When you run the bonnie program with no command-line parameters, it uses a 100 MB file for its testing. The file is automatically created in the current directory. It is deleted when the test is complete. You should see results similar to this:

```
File './Bonnie.9995', size: 104857600
Writing with putc()...done
Rewriting...done
Writing intelligently...done
Reading with getc()...done
Reading intelligently...done
Seeker 1...Seeker 2...Seeker 3...start 'em...done...done...

              -------Sequential Output-------- ---Sequential Input-- --Random--
              -Per Char- --Block--- -Rewrite-- -Per Char- --Block--- --Seeks---
Machine    MB K/sec %CPU K/sec %CPU K/sec %CPU K/sec %CPU K/sec %CPU  /sec %CPU
          100 2845 98.2 14205 47.2  6202 46.6  2621 99.3 119979 99.6 6259.9 98.6
```

The results show that the Sequential Output performance for block writes was 14205 KB/s or about 14.2 MB/s. This result is significant for applications that write an entire file to disk, such as a word processor. The number of random seeks is 6259 per second. This result is significant for applications that either write many small files or modify many records in a database file. You can learn how to interpret this and all the results by visiting this Web site: *www.textuality.com/bonnie*.

12. When you run bonnie with no command-line parameters, as you did in the previous step, it uses a 100 MB file for its testing. This is bad if your computer has 128 MB of memory, because the test does not test true hard disk speed if your computer caches some or all of the 100 MB file. The size of the test file should be several times larger than the amount of memory in your computer. If you have the disk space, run the test again, but this time use a larger file to reduce the effects of the disk cache. For example, use a 400 MB file by entering **./bonnie -s 400**. You should see results similar to this:

```
File './Bonnie.9983', size: 419430400
Writing with putc()...done
Rewriting...done
Writing intelligently...done
Reading with getc()...done
Reading intelligently...done
Seeker 1...Seeker 2...Seeker 3...start 'em...done...done...
```

```
                -------Sequential Output-------- ---Sequential Input-- --Random--
                -Per Char- --Block--- -Rewrite-- -Per Char- --Block--- --Seeks---
Machine      MB K/sec %CPU K/sec %CPU K/sec %CPU K/sec %CPU K/sec %CPU  /sec %CPU
            400  2494 97.5  4857 19.7  1408 11.4  2256 89.2  5902  8.7  54.2  1.9
```

NOTE The results show that the Sequential Output performance for block writes was 4857 KB/s or about 4.8 MB/s. This is far lower than the previous results where a 100 MB test file was used. Using a 400 MB test file clearly reduces the effects of the disk cache. This tells you that having excess memory that Linux can use as a disk cache significantly improves disk performance. It also comes closer to your disk's true performance.

NOTE When you use a larger file for the test, you obtain accurate results but the test runs longer.

13. Log out and return to your graphical interface by pressing **Alt+F7**.

Certification Objectives

Objectives for the Linux+ exam:

- Access and write data to recordable media (2.9)
- Diagnose hardware issues using Linux tools (e.g., /proc, disk utilities, ifconfig, /dev, knoppix, BBC, dmesg) (6.2)

Review Questions

1. If you run the bonnie program with no command-line parameters, what size test file is used?
   a. 10 MB
   b. 50 MB
   c. 100 MB
   d. 400 MB
2. Which bonnie command uses a 500 MB test file?
   a. **bonnie -f 500**
   b. **bonnie -l 500**
   c. **bonnie -m 500**
   d. **bonnie -s 500**

3. When you use the bonnie program, the size of the test file should be:
   a. equal to the amount of memory in your computer
   b. equal to amount of free space on your hard disk
   c. several times greater than the amount of memory in your computer
   d. equal to the amount of memory and the size of your swap partition
4. While the bonnie test is running, it's important that no other programs write to the hard disk being tested, but it's okay if programs read from the disk. True or False?
5. The Random Seeks result of the bonnie test is significant for database applications. True or False?

Lab 13.3 Tuning Hard Disk Parameters

Objectives

In Labs 13.1 and 13.2, you learned how to use the hdparm and bonnie programs to get information about hard disks. In this lab, you use both programs to configure your hard disk settings and measure the resulting performance. You'll see that by making relatively simple and safe changes, you can improve your hard disk's performance.

Materials Required

This lab requires the following:

- Access as the root user to a computer running Linux
- At least 100 MB of free space on one of your Linux filesystems

Activity Background

The hdparm program can be used to change many of the settings relating to your hard disk. Some of these settings were determined when you installed Linux on your computer, or may be controlled by your computer's BIOS. The hard disk settings may already be optimized for your computer, or you may be able to improve the performance of your hard disk by adjusting these settings. In this lab exercise, you change hdparm settings so you can see the effects these settings have on performance as measured by the bonnie program. You can easily restore your original settings by rebooting Linux.

NOTE In this exercise, the results of testing using the bonnie program are shown for a sample computer. Your results will likely be different.

Estimated completion time: 40 Minutes

NOTE

This activity might take you more or less time, depending on the speed of your computer.

LAB ACTIVITY

Activity

1. Switch to a command-line terminal (tty2) by pressing **Ctrl+Alt+F2**, and log in to the terminal as the root user.
2. Use the hdparm program to change your hard disk settings to values that ensure *minimum* hard disk performance. Your computer is not likely to be set like this now. Assume that your hard disk is /dev/hda. If it's not, substitute the correct device name for hda. Enter **hdparm -c0 -d0 -m0 /dev/hda**. The -c0 parameter sets the hard disk to 16-bit data transfers. Most modern-day hard EIDE disks support 32-bit transfers. The -d0 parameter turns off DMA data transfers, thus requiring your processor to get more involved with the transfers. The -m0 parameter turns off the multiple-sector I/O, also called IDE Block Mode. Refer to the hdparm man page for more detail on the available parameters.
3. Move to the bonnie directory by typing **cd bonnie**. Run the bonnie program with a 400 MB test file by entering **./bonnie -s 400**. This is appropriate for a computer with 128 MB of memory or less. If you have more memory, you should choose a larger test file. If, for example, you have 256 MB of memory, you need about a 1 GB file. The results for the sample computer show that the Sequential Output Per Block is 3461 KB/s (3.4 MB/s), and that 97.3% of the CPU was used during that test. The number of Random Seeks is 49.3 and 20.8% of CPU time was used. These are poor results for any modern computer.
4. Now run the hard disk using 32-bit data transfers by entering **hdparm -c3 /dev/hda**. Run the bonnie program again by entering **./bonnie -s 400**. The results show that the Sequential Output Per Block is 5051 KB/s (5.1 MB/s), and that 34.9% of the CPU was used during that test. The number of Random Seeks is 53.1 and 11.6% of CPU time was used. This is a significant improvement for both tests in two ways. The performance of the disk operations is improved and it takes far less of the CPU's time, allowing the CPU to do other work.
5. Next, enable multiple sector I/O (IDE Block Mode) and use 16 sectors by entering **hdparm -m16 /dev/hda**. Note that you're still using 32-bit data transfers. Run the bonnie program again by entering **./bonnie -s 400**. The

13

results show that the Sequential Output Per Block is 4829 KB/s (4.8 MB/s), and that 20.8% of the CPU was used during that test. The number of Random Seeks is 51.2 and 2% of CPU time was used. This reduced the performance of the hard disk a bit, but also reduced the amount of work the CPU must perform. The amount of CPU time for Random Seeks was reduced substantially while suffering only a minor reduction in performance. If your computer were running primarily as a database server with many processes running concurrently, this would likely result in substantially improved performance.

NOTE

Interpreting the results of benchmark testing is difficult. Determining how the results relate to your system and applications comes with experience, and is part science and part art. The bonnie Web site (*www.textuality.com/bonnie*) covers these considerations to a degree.

6. Now turn on DMA by entering **hdparm -d1 /dev/hda**. Note that you're still using 32-bit data transfers and multiple sector I/O (IDE Block Mode). Run the bonnie program again by entering **./bonnie -s 400**. The results show that the Sequential Output Per Block is 5015 KB/s (5.0 MB/s), and that 7.3% of the CPU was used during that test. The number of Random Seeks is 55.2 and 1.4% of CPU time was used. The most significant improvement was in the reduction of CPU time for both Sequential Output and Random Seeks.
7. Now that you're using DMA, see how turning off other hard disk settings affects performance. Turn off multiple sector I/O (IDE Block Mode) by entering **hdparm -m 0 /dev/hda**. Run the bonnie program again by entering **./bonnie -s 400**. The results show that the Sequential Output Per Block is 4878 KB/s (4.9 MB/s), and that 7.2% of the CPU was used during that test. The number of Random Seeks is 57 and 1.3% of CPU time was used. There was a slight decrease in CPU time for both tests and a slight improvement in Random Seeks but a slight reduction in Sequential Output Per Block performance. Was this worth doing? You decide.

NOTE

There are other hdparm parameters you can experiment with, such as the IDE transfer mode (-X), but the hdparm man page says they're dangerous. Only experiment with such parameters on a system where you can live with crashing your hard disk and having to reinstall Linux.

8. Restore your original hard disk settings by rebooting your computer. Switch to a command-line terminal (tty2) by pressing **Ctrl+Alt+F2**, and log in to the terminal as the root user. Run the bonnie program with a 400 MB test file by entering **./bonnie -s 400**. How do the results compare to those in the earlier steps?
9. Log out and return to your graphical interface by pressing **Alt+F7**.

Certification Objectives

Objectives for the Linux+ exam:

- Select appropriate parameters for Linux installation (e.g., language, time zones, keyboard, mouse) (1.11)
- Configure peripherals as necessary (e.g., printer, scanner, modem) (1.12)
- Diagnose hardware issues using Linux tools (e.g., /proc, disk utilities, ifconfig, /dev, knoppix, BBC, dmesg) (6.2)

Review Questions

1. Which command sets your hard disk to use 32-bit data transfers?
   a. **hdparm --32 /dev/hda**
   b. **hdparm -m32 /dev/hda**
   c. **hdparm -d32 /dev/hda**
   d. **hdparm -c3 /dev/hda**
2. Which command sets your hard disk so it implements multiple sector I/O (IDE Block Mode)?
   a. **hdparm --16 /dev/hda**
   b. **hdparm -m16 /dev/hda**
   c. **hdparm -d32 /dev/hda**
   d. **hdparm -c0 /dev/hda**
3. Which command sets your hard disk so it performs DMA data transfers?
   a. **hdparm --16 /dev/hda**
   b. **hdparm -m16 /dev/hda**
   c. **hdparm -d1 /dev/hda**
   d. **hdparm -c0 /dev/hda**
4. Increasing the performance of Random Seeks significantly improves the performance of word-processing applications. True or False?
5. When you enable DMA data transfers, the biggest improvement tends to be the reduction of CPU time. True or False?

Lab 13.4 Troubleshooting Performance Problems

Objectives

The previous three lab exercises focused on hard disk performance because that tends to be the performance bottleneck for disk I/O-intensive applications. Another bottleneck is the processor for compute-intensive applications. You cannot use a program such as hdparm to "tune" the processor as you can for a hard disk. However, you can apportion the processor time so that important applications receive more attention from the processor than less important applications. Essentially, you can make some applications run faster than others. You experimented with setting priorities in Lab 11.4. This lab exercise explores the subject in more detail.

Materials Required

This lab requires the following:

- Access as the root user on a computer running Linux
- Access as an ordinary user to a computer running Linux
- The primes program you compiled in Lab 10.3

Estimated completion time: 30 Minutes

Activity

1. If you have not already performed Lab 10.3, complete it now to compile the primes program.
2. Switch to the second virtual console (tty2) by pressing **Ctrl+Alt+F2**, and log in as the root user.
3. Switch to the third virtual console (tty3) by pressing **Alt+F3**, and log in as the same user you used in Lab 10.3. In the examples in this lab, we'll use john as the username. Run the primes program by entering **./primes**. Enter **1** in response to the `Enter startoff in base ten:` prompt.
4. Switch to the fourth virtual console (tty4) by pressing **Alt+F4**, and log in as john. Run the primes program by entering **./primes**. Enter **1** in response to the `Enter startoff in base ten:` prompt.
5. Switch to the fifth virtual console (tty5) by pressing **Alt+F5**, and log in as john. Run the primes program by entering **./primes**. Enter **1** in response to the `Enter startoff in base ten:` prompt.

6. Switch to the sixth virtual console (tty6) by pressing **Alt+F6**, and log in as the root user. Run the primes program by entering **./primes**. Enter **1** in response to the `Enter startoff in base ten:` prompt.
7. Switch to the second virtual console (tty2) by pressing **Alt+F2**. Run the top program by entering **top**. Notice that the top four running processes are the primes programs. Each is running at about the same %CPU value. Assuming that no other processes are running, the value should be about 24%. Three of the primes processes are running as user john and one is running as user root.
8. If you want to reduce the performance of the processes that john is running, you have to change the scheduling priority for john's processes. You can do this within top as you did in Lab 11.4. However, there's an easier way. Exit the top program by pressing **q**. You use the renice program with the -u option to specify the user. Enter **renice 10 -u john**. This sets the scheduling priority on all of john's running processes to 10, which causes them to run slower.
9. Enter **top**. You see that the three primes processes running as john are now down to about 20% of CPU time, and the primes process running as root is up to about 40%.
10. Suppose that you want the primes process running as root to have very little CPU time. You want it to allow other processes run by any user to have much higher priority. You can set its scheduling priority to 19 (the lowest priority possible). Press **r**. At the `PID to renice:` prompt, enter the PID of the primes process that's running as root. At the `Renice PID x to value:` prompt, enter **19**. Wait a few seconds for the top display to stabilize. Notice that the process is now running at about 4% CPU time and the three primes processes running as john are all running at about 31% CPU time.
11. Exit the top program by pressing **q**. Enter **renice 0 -u john**. You've changed the scheduling priority on all of john's processes back to 0, the nominal value. Enter **top**. Notice that all the primes processes running as john are now running at about 32% and the primes process running as root is down to about 2%.
12. Stop all of john's primes processes. Press **k**. At the `PID to kill:` prompt, enter the PID of one of john's primes processes. Press **Enter** at the Kill PID x with signal [15]: prompt. Notice that the remaining two primes processes running as john are up to about 48% CPU time, and the primes process running as root is up to about 3%.
13. Press **k**. At the `PID to kill:` prompt, enter the PID of one of john's primes processes. Press **Enter** at the `Kill PID x with signal [15]:` prompt. Notice that the remaining primes process running as john is up to about 94% CPU time and the primes process running as root is up to about 6%.
14. Press **k**. At the `PID to kill:` prompt, enter the PID of the remaining primes process running as john. Press **Enter** at the `Kill PID x with`

13

`signal[15]:` prompt. Notice that the primes process running as root shoots up to about 99% CPU time. By setting the scheduling priority for a process to 19, you ensure that it runs fast when no other processes are running, but it allows any other processes to steal its CPU time for more important jobs.

15. Press **q** to quit the program, and log out of terminals 2, 3, 4, and 5. Press **Ctrl+C** in terminal 6 to stop primes from running under root and log out. Return to the graphical interface.

Certification Objectives

Objectives for the Linux+ exam:

- Diagnose hardware issues using Linux tools (e.g., /proc, disk utilities, ifconfig, /dev, knoppix, BBC, dmesg) (6.2)

Review Questions

1. When you're running the top program, you can change the scheduling priority of more than one process at a time. True or False?
2. Which program allows you to change the scheduling priority of all the processes running as a certain user?
   a. ps
   b. top
   c. nice
   d. renice
3. If you want a process to always run fast when no other processes are running, but run slowly when any other process is running, you set its scheduling priority to ________________ .
4. Suppose there are three running processes on your system, and they are all running at nominal scheduling priority (0). They all run at about 32% CPU time. What happens when you change the scheduling priority of all three processes to the same new value?
5. Suppose you want to stop all the processes of the same name regardless of which user they are running as. What program would you use?
   a. ps
   b. top
   c. kill
   d. killall

Lab 13.5 Measuring X Server Performance

Objectives

When you use a Linux computer for graphical applications you must run an X server. The video hardware and X server software in that computer can often be a bottleneck. There are numerous performance benchmark programs for X servers. One reason you would want to run these benchmarks is if you wanted to compare video (display) hardware to see which performs better. Another use for a video benchmark program is to see how different video drivers perform. A good example is to measure the performance difference between using frame buffers versus using a driver that's specific to the video hardware. You likely discover that, in all cases, frame buffers don't perform as well as drivers specific to the video hardware.

Materials Required

This lab requires the following:

- Access as a root user to a computer running Linux

Estimated completion time: 15 Minutes

Activity

LAB ACTIVITY

1. Start an xterm. If you're using the Gnome desktop, click the terminal icon with the footprint in front of it. If you're running the KDE desktop, click the terminal icon. If there is no icon on the desktop, click the **Red Hat** icon, select **System Tools**, and click **Terminal**.
2. The XFree86 X server includes a performance benchmark program called **x11perf**. This program can run many tests of video performance. If you're unsure of which test to run, you can run them all. Enter **x11perf -all**. A new window appears and all the tests are performed in that window. The results of each test are displayed on the xterm you used to run the program.
3. Running all the tests takes a long time. How long depends on the performance of your video hardware. Allow the tests to run for a while to get an idea of how the program works, then stop the program with **Ctrl+C**. In the xterm window, you see the results of the test. Here's what the results of one of the tests look like. Yours should be similar:

```
x11perf - X11 performance program, version 1.5
The XFree86 Project, Inc server version 3360 on :0.0
from red
Mon Dec  9 20:55:11 2003

Sync time adjustment is 0.1293 msecs.
```

```
30000000 reps @   0.0002 msec (4890000.0/sec): Dot
30000000 reps @   0.0002 msec (4860000.0/sec): Dot
30000000 reps @   0.0002 msec (4930000.0/sec): Dot
30000000 reps @   0.0002 msec (4870000.0/sec): Dot
30000000 reps @   0.0002 msec (4860000.0/sec): Dot
150000000 trep @   0.0002 msec (4880000.0/sec): Dot
```

NOTE

The test results show the number of graphical operations per second in parentheses. In the above example, the test was able to display 4.8 million dots per second.

4. By default, the x11perf program runs each test five times. You can change the number of times each test runs with the -repeat command-line option. Enter **x11perf -all -repeat 1**. Allow the tests to run for a while to get an idea of how it works, then stop the program with **Ctrl+C**.
5. You can also control how long each test runs with the -time command-line option. Enter **x11perf -all -repeat 1 -time 2**. All tests run once and last for about two seconds. Again, allow the tests to run for a while, then press **Ctrl+C**.
6. You can run individual tests by specifying them on the command line instead of using the -all option. Enter **x11perf -eschertilerect100**. The tests will take a few minutes. Press **Ctrl+C** after a while to end if necessary
7. You can run numerous tests by specifying them on the command line. Enter **x11perf -move -resize**. You see both tests run.

NOTE

If you have another video card for your computer, you can replace the existing video card and run these steps again to see the difference in performance. Remember to guard against static electricity when working on your computer by wearing a grounding strap.

8. When you have finished, log out.

Certification Objectives

Objectives for the Linux+ exam:

- Diagnose hardware issues using Linux tools (e.g., /proc, disk utilities, ifconfig, /dev, knoppix, BBC, dmesg) (6.2)

Review Questions

1. What performance benchmark program comes with XFree86?
2. Using frame buffers yields better video performance than using drivers that are specific to certain video hardware. True or False?

3. The ________________ command runs all x11perf tests.

4. What command-line option allows you to control the number of times each x11perf test runs?

    a. -1 or -2 or -3, etc.

    b. -n

    c. -repeat

    d. -dup

5. You can run more than one x11perf test by specifying each one on the command line. True or False?

CHAPTER FOURTEEN

LINUX NETWORKING

Labs included in this chapter

- Lab 14.1 Configuring Ethernet Interfaces
- Lab 14.2 Creating IP Aliases
- Lab 14.3 Installing and Configuring NcFTPd
- Lab 14.4 Using the mii-tool Program
- Lab 14.5 Configuring and Using NTP

CompTIA Linux+ Exam Objectives

Objective		Lab
3.1	Configure client network services and settings (e.g., settings for TCP/IP)	14.1, 14.2, 14.3, 14.4, 14.5
3.2	Configure basic server network services (e.g., DNS, DHCP, SAMBA, Apache)	14.3, 14.5
3.3	Implement basic routing and subnetting (e.g., /sbin/route, ip forward statement)	14.1, 14.2
3.7	Configure a Network Interface Card (NIC) from a command line	14.1, 14.2, 14.4
6.2	Diagnose hardware issues using Linux tools (e.g., /proc, disk utilities, ifconfig, /dev, knoppix, BBC, dmesg)	14.1, 14.4

Lab 14.1 Configuring Ethernet Interfaces

Objectives

This lab exercise shows you how to change any interface parameter in real time without having to reboot Linux. In particular, it shows you how to change the IP address, subnet mask, broadcast address, or MAC address of your Ethernet card. It also shows you how to set the default route for packets going outside the local network segment.

Materials Required

This lab requires the following:

- Access as a root user to a computer running Linux
- An Ethernet network interface card (NIC) installed in your computer
- A connection to a local area network

Activity Background

The main program you work with when dealing with interfaces and IP addresses is **ifconfig**. This stands for "interface configuration." In this lab you configure the Ethernet interface (Ethernet NIC). Your first Ethernet card is called eth0 by default. If you have a second Ethernet card, it is called eth1.

NOTE

Windows has a similar program called ipconfig, so it may be confusing if you work with both Linux and Windows.

You also learn to use the **route** command to set the default gateway, the router that acts as a default exit point for communications to networks outside of a local network segment.

Estimated completion time: 15 Minutes

LAB ACTIVITY

Activity

1. Switch to the second virtual console (tty2) by pressing **Ctrl+Alt+F2**, and log in as root.
2. When you run ifconfig with no command-line parameters, it displays a status message of all your interfaces. Enter **ifconfig**. You see a status display similar to this when your only interface is a single Ethernet card (eth0):

```
eth0      Link encap:Ethernet HWaddr 00:07:95:BB:A3:6A
   inet     addr:192.168.0.1 Bcast:192.168.0.255 Mask:255.255.255.0
            UP BROADCAST RUNNING MULTICAST MTU:1500 Metric:1
            RX packets:1611 errors:0 dropped:0 overruns:0 frame:0
        TX packets:1712 errors:0 dropped:0 overruns:0 carrier:0
        collisions:0 txqueuelen:100
        RX bytes:243068 (237.3 Kb) TX bytes:382677 (373.7 Kb)
        Interrupt:11 Base address:0xde00

   lo   Link encap:Local Loopback
        inet addr:127.0.0.1 Mask:255.0.0.0
        UP LOOPBACK RUNNING MTU:16436 Metric:1
        RX packets:12 errors:0 dropped:0 overruns:0 frame:0
        TX packets:12 errors:0 dropped:0 overruns:0 carrier:0
        collisions:0 txqueuelen:0
        RX bytes:1101 (1.0 Kb) TX bytes:1101 (1.0 Kb)
```

NOTE

The "lo" in the output above refers to the local loopback network device, which you learn more about in Lab 14.2.

3. You can change the IP address of the card by passing the new address as a parameter on the ifconfig command line. Enter **ifconfig eth0 192.168.0.2**.

4. You can view the status of a single interface by specifying the interface name on the command line. Enter **ifconfig eth0**. You see something similar to this:

```
eth0  Link encap:Ethernet HWaddr 00:07:95:BB:A3:6A
      inet addr:192.168.0.2 Bcast:192.168.0.255 Mask:255.255.255.0
      UP BROADCAST RUNNING MULTICAST MTU:1500 Metric:1
      RX packets:1611 errors:0 dropped:0 overruns:0 frame:0
      TX packets:1712 errors:0 dropped:0 overruns:0 carrier:0
      collisions:0 txqueuelen:100
      RX bytes:243068 (237.3 Kb) TX bytes:382677 (373.7 Kb)
      Interrupt:11 Base address:0xde00
```

5. You can change the subnet mask by specifying it on the command line. Enter **ifconfig eth0 netmask 255.255.255.240**.

6. Again display the status of eth0 by entering **ifconfig eth0**. You see something like this:

```
eth0  Link encap:Ethernet HWaddr 00:07:95:BB:A3:6A
      inet addr:192.168.0.2 Bcast:192.168.0.255 Mask:255.255.255.240
      UP BROADCAST RUNNING MULTICAST MTU:1500 Metric:1
      RX packets:1611 errors:0 dropped:0 overruns:0 frame:0
      TX packets:1712 errors:0 dropped:0 overruns:0 carrier:0
      collisions:0 txqueuelen:100
      RX bytes:243068 (237.3 Kb) TX bytes:382677 (373.7 Kb)
      Interrupt:11 Base address:0xde00
```

7. If you know about IP subnets, you notice that the previous display shows the broadcast address as 192.168.0.255. This is clearly wrong. The correct broadcast address is 192.168.0.15. This tells you that ifconfig can't compute the broadcast address properly, even though it has all the information (IP address and subnet mask) required. You have to enter the appropriate broadcast address yourself. Enter:

   ifconfig eth0 broadcast 192.168.0.15

   Whenever you have to change the subnet mask of an interface, always specify the broadcast address as well, for example:

   ifconfig eth0 netmask 255.255.255.240 broadcast 192.168.0.15

8. You can display only the line that shows the broadcast address and subnet mask. Enter **ifconfig eth0 | grep inet**. You see a display similar to this:

   ```
   inet addr:192.168.0.2 Bcast:192.168.0.15 Mask:255.255.255.240
   ```

9. It's sometimes necessary to change the MAC address of your Ethernet card, for example, if your company uses locally administered MAC addresses. In the above output displays, the MAC address is 00:07:95:BB:A3:6A. You can change it, but first you must take the interface down. Enter **ifconfig eth0 down**.

NOTE

While the interface is down your computer cannot send or receive packets on the interface.

10. Change the MAC address by entering **ifconfig eth0 hw ether 00:00:0B:AD:F0:0D**.

11. Bring the interface back up by entering **ifconfig eth0 up**. You can see that the MAC address has changed by entering **ifconfig eth0 | grep eth0**. You see this:

    ```
    eth0  Link encap:Ethernet HWaddr 00:00:0B:AD:F0:0D
    ```

12. An important IP parameter cannot be controlled by ifconfig. This is the default route or default gateway. You must use the **route** program to set this parameter. If you run route without command-line options, it displays your routing table. However, it tries to resolve IP addresses in the table to names using DNS. The -n option disables the DNS lookup. Enter **route -n**. Your routing table looks similar to this:

    ```
    Kernel IP routing table
    Destination    Gateway     Genmask         Flags   Metric Ref   Use Iface
    192.168.0.0    0.0.0.0     255.255.255.240 U       0      0       0 eth0
    ```

    The routing table is used by the Linux internal router to determine where packets need to be sent so they arrive at their destinations. The route program is useful for troubleshooting network-related problems.

13. Add a default route (default gateway) of a router or device with the IP address of 192.168.0.14 by entering **route add default gw 192.168.0.14**. See how your routing table was affected by again entering **route -n**. There should be an entry for the new gateway.

```
Kernel IP routing table
Destination  Gateway       Genmask          Flags Metric Ref Use Iface
192.168.0.0  0.0.0.0       255.255.255.240  U     0      0     0 eth0
0.0.0.0      192.168.0.14  0.0.0.0          UG    0      0     0 eth0
```

14. Leave your computer configured as it is now to go on to Lab 14.2.

Certification Objectives

Objectives for the Linux+ exam:

- Configure client network services and settings (e.g., settings for TCP/IP) (3.1)
- Implement basic routing and subnetting (e.g., /sbin/route, ip forward statement) (3.3)
- Configure a Network Interface Card (NIC) from a command line (3.7)
- Diagnose hardware issues using Linux tools (e.g., /proc, disk utilities, ifconfig, /dev, knoppix, BBC, dmesg) (6.2)

Review Questions

14

1. What is the name of the first Ethernet interface?
   a. eth0
   b. eth1
   c. etha
   d. eth0:0
2. Which Linux program allows you to change the subnet mask?
   a. netmask
   b. ifconfig
   c. ipconfig
   d. route
3. An Ethernet card's MAC address may be changed with the ifconfig program. True or False?
4. To change the MAC address of an interface, you must first shut down the interface. True or False?
5. Whenever you change the subnet mask with the ifconfig program, you should also set the broadcast address. True or False?

6. Which program allows you to set your default route (default gateway)?
   a. netmask
   b. ifconfig
   c. ipconfig
   d. route

Lab 14.2 Creating IP Aliases

Objectives

Lab 14.1 showed you how to use the basic functions of the ifconfig program, such as setting the IP address, subnet mask, and broadcast address of an Ethernet interface. This lab covers a more advanced use of ifconfig, creating IP aliases (assigning more than one IP address to a single physical interface). You also examine the ifconfig status display in a little more detail.

Materials Required

This lab requires the following:

- Access as a root user to a computer running Linux
- An Ethernet card installed in your computer
- A connection to a local area network
- Your computer set up as you left it at the end of Lab 14.1

Activity Background

Each physical interface in your computer can have more than one IP address assigned to it. When you assign another IP address to a physical interface, you are creating an IP alias. You can create up to 256 IP aliases for each physical interface in your computer. You can also assign IP aliases to the local loopback interface. The local loopback (lo) interface is a special logical device (it doesn't exist physically) used to move network packets within a single host. The loopback interface can be useful in testing networking functions without having to have network access to another computer. Creating IP aliases for the local loopback interface can be very useful in advanced networking applications, such as building an Internet server.

Estimated completion time: 15 Minutes

Activity

LAB ACTIVITY

1. Switch to the second virtual console (tty2) by pressing **Ctrl+Alt+F2**, and log in as the root user.

2. You're going to create an IP alias. To do this, you must create an interface based on the name of the physical interface. Your first Ethernet interface is called eth0 by default, so you create an IP alias called eth0:0. Enter **ifconfig eth0:0 1.1.1.1**.

NOTE These steps show you how to create IP aliases. The actual IP addresses you use depend on your network.

3. If you run the ifconfig program with no command-line parameters, you see the new interface. Enter **ifconfig**. You see something similar to this:

```
eth0      Link encap:Ethernet HWaddr 00:07:95:BB:A3:6A
          inet addr:192.168.0.2 Bcast:192.168.0.255 Mask:255.255.255.0
          UP BROADCAST RUNNING MULTICAST MTU:1500 Metric:1
          RX packets:1611 errors:0 dropped:0 overruns:0 frame:0
          TX packets:1712 errors:0 dropped:0 overruns:0 carrier:0
          collisions:0 txqueuelen:100
          RX bytes:243068 (237.3 Kb) TX bytes:382677 (373.7 Kb)
          Interrupt:11 Base address:0xde00

eth0:0    Link encap:Ethernet HWaddr 00:07:95:BB:A3:6A
          inet addr:1.1.1.1 Bcast:1.255.255.255 Mask:255.0.0.0
          UP BROADCAST RUNNING MULTICAST MTU:1500 Metric:1
          Interrupt:11 Base address:0xde00

lo        Link encap:Local Loopback
          inet addr:127.0.0.1 Mask:255.0.0.0
          UP LOOPBACK RUNNING MTU:16436 Metric:1
          RX packets:12 errors:0 dropped:0 overruns:0 frame:0
          TX packets:12 errors:0 dropped:0 overruns:0 carrier:0
          collisions:0 txqueuelen:0
          RX bytes:1101 (1.0 Kb) TX bytes:1101 (1.0 Kb)
```

4. Next, you create another IP alias. Enter **ifconfig eth0:5 1.2.3.4**. You should now have two IP aliases. You can tell ifconfig to list only a single interface by specifying the name on the command line. Enter **ifconfig eth0:0**. You see this:

```
eth0:0   Link encap:Ethernet HWaddr 00:07:95:BB:A3:6A
         inet addr:1.1.1.1 Bcast:1.255.255.255 Mask:255.0.0.0
         UP BROADCAST RUNNING MULTICAST MTU:1500 Metric:1
         Interrupt:11 Base address:0xde00
```

5. Enter **ifconfig eth0:5**. You see this:

```
eth0:5   Link encap:Ethernet HWaddr 00:07:95:BB:A3:6A
         inet addr:1.2.3.4 Bcast:1.255.255.255 Mask:255.0.0.0
         UP BROADCAST RUNNING MULTICAST MTU:1500 Metric:1
         Interrupt:11 Base address:0xde00
```

6. The convention is to use numbers following the base interface name (eth) and colons for IP aliases, but you can use anything you like. Enter **ifconfig eth0:abc 1.2.3.5**. Enter **ifconfig eth0:abc**. You see this:

```
eth0:abc Link encap:Ethernet HWaddr 00:07:95:BB:A3:6A
         inet addr:1.2.3.5 Bcast:1.255.255.255 Mask:255.0.0.0
         UP BROADCAST RUNNING MULTICAST MTU:1500 Metric:1
         Interrupt:11 Base address:0xde00
```

7. Now create two IP aliases for the local loopback (lo) interface. Enter **ifconfig lo:0 127.0.0.2**, and then enter **ifconfig lo:1 127.0.0.3**. Now enter **ifconfig | more**. You see all the interfaces you've created so far.
8. You can shut down any of these IP aliases. Enter **ifconfig eth0:5 down**. Now enter **ifconfig | more**. You see that the eth0:5 interface is no longer listed.
9. If you try to bring an IP alias back up that's been shut down, you can't. You must re-create IP aliases after shutting them down. Enter **ifconfig eth0:5 up**. You see an error message similar to this:

   SIOCSIFFLAGS: Cannot assign requested address
10. To return to your original network settings, reboot your computer.

Certification Objectives

Objectives for the Linux+ exam:

- Configure client network services and settings (e.g., settings for TCP/IP) (3.1)
- Implement basic routing and subnetting (e.g., /sbin/route, ip forward statement) (3.3)
- Configure a Network Interface Card (NIC) from a command line (3.7)

Review Questions

1. Which of these commands configures an IP alias?
   a. **ifconfig -alias 192.168.0.50**
   b. **ifconfig eth0-alias 192.168.0.50**
   c. **ifconfig eth0:0 192.168.0.50**
   d. **ifconfig 192.168.0.50 -alias eth0:0**
2. You can assign IP aliases to the local loopback (lo) interface. True or False?
3. How many IP aliases can be created?
   a. up to 64 per physical interface
   b. up to 256 per physical interface
   c. up to 64 regardless of the number of physical interfaces
   d. up to 256 regardless of the number of physical interfaces

4. When you shut down a physical interface, you must specify the IP address, subnet mask, and broadcast address again when you bring up the interface. True or False?

5. When you shut down an IP alias, you must specify the IP address, subnet mask, and broadcast address again when you bring up the interface. True or False?

Lab 14.3 Installing and Configuring NcFTPd

Objectives

FTP is a popular method of transferring files over a network. The most popular FTP server for Linux is WuFTP. It is included with nearly all Linux distributions. However, it can be difficult to configure and has had security issues. Experienced Linux users and administrators often use other FTP server software. One such alternative is NcFTPd. In this exercise, you download, install, and configure NcFTPd.

Materials Required

This lab requires the following:

- Access as a root user to a computer running Linux that also has an ordinary user account
- A Web browser and access to the Internet

NOTE

This lab explores information on the World Wide Web. Because Web pages can change without notice, what you see may not exactly match the terminology described in this lab. You may have to use your judgment to find the best match for links described here. When in doubt, check with your instructor.

Estimated completion time:	45 Minutes

Activity

LAB ACTIVITY

1. Start your Web browser and enter **http://www.ncftp.com/ncftpd** in your Web browser's Address line.

2. Read the home page to see the benefits of using this FTP server. Pay attention to the fact that NcFTPd does not use inetd or xinetd, which results in higher performance. NcFTPd also does not have to call other programs, such as /bin/ls, to do its job.

3. Click the **security** link to learn why NcFTPd is more secure than WuFTP.

4. Go back to the home page, and click the **Download Now!** link.
5. You need to choose the software version for your computer and operating system. This lab assumes that you're running Linux on an Intel-based computer. Click the **NcFTPd Server 2.8.1 for Linux (x86)** or whatever the latest version is.
6. You're downloading a compressed file (tarball). Save this file to your home directory.
7. Switch to the second virtual console (tty2) by pressing **Ctrl+Alt+F2**, and log in as root.
8. If necessary, go to your home directory by entering **cd**.
9. Uncompress and untar the file by typing **tar xzvf ncftpd** and pressing the **Tab** key to fill out the rest of the long file name. Now press **Enter** to start the **tar** program.
10. To go to the new subdirectory that was created, type **cd ncftpd**, and press the **Tab** key to fill out the rest of the directory name. Press **Enter** to go to the subdirectory.
11. Install the software by entering **./install_ncftpd.pl**. You see text similar to this:

```
Created /etc/ftpusers
Using /var/ftp for ftp-home
No FTP server is running.
/etc/xinetd.conf does not appear to be handling the "ftp" service.
/etc/xinetd.d does not appear to be handling the "ftp" service.
NcFTPd is not currently running.
Installing configuration files.
Installing new NcFTPd config files.
Created /usr/local/etc/ncftpd/general.cf.
Looking up IP address and hostname for this machine.
Created /usr/local/etc/ncftpd/domain.cf.
Installing programs.
Configuring your system so NcFTPd starts automatically at system boot.
Starting NcFTPd: OK
Checking if the FTP service has started.

CONGRATULATIONS! NcFTPd has been successfully installed.
Your next step is to customize your installation by editing:

  /usr/local/etc/ncftpd/general.cf
  /usr/local/etc/ncftpd/domain.cf

Be sure to run /usr/local/sbin/restart_ncftpd after  doing that.

Installation log saved as /usr/local/etc/ncftpd/install_ncftpd.log.
```

The above text tells you that you must run the **restart_ncftpd** program whenever you make changes to NcFTPd. Normally, programs reconfigure themselves when you send them a SIGHUP signal.

12. You can see that NcFTPd is running by displaying its processes. Enter **ps ax | grep ncftpd**. You see lines similar to these:

```
15108 ? S< 0:00 ncftpd d  /usr/local/etc/ncftpd/general.cf /usr/local
15109 ? SN 0:00 ncftpd -d /usr/local/etc/ncftpd/general.cf /usr/local
15110 ? S< 0:00 ncftpd -d /usr/local/etc/ncftpd/general.cf /usr/local
15111 ? S< 0:00 ncftpd -d /usr/local/etc/ncftpd/general.cf /usr/local
15112 ? S< 0:00 ncftpd -d /usr/local/etc/ncftpd/general.cf /usr/local

15113 ? S< 0:00 ncftpd -d /usr/local/etc/ncftpd/general.cf /usr/local
15114 ? S< 0:00 ncftpd -d /usr/local/etc/ncftpd/general.cf /usr/local
```

13. Enter **ps aux | grep ncftpd**. Notice that all the ncftpd processes are running as the root user.

14. When an ordinary user logs in, the current working directory is set to the user's home directory. When an anonymous user logs in, the current working directory is set to /var/ftp. Place files in these directories so you can quickly recognize when you're in these directories. Create a file in the /var/ftp directory. Enter **touch /var/ftp/free_willy**. Look at how the file was created. Enter **ls -l /var/ftp/free_willy**. Note that the file is owned by the root user and group:

```
-rw-r--r-- 1 root    root        0 Nov 17 10:20 free_willy
```

14

15. Log in as a non-root user. Create a file with an unusual name. Enter **touch save_the_whales**.

16. Connect to the FTP server by entering **ftp localhost**. You see something similar to this:

```
Connected to localhost (127.0.0.1).
220 red NcFTPd Server (unregistered copy) ready.
Name (localhost:root):
```

17. Log in as an anonymous user. Enter **anonymous**. You see this:

```
331 Guest login ok, send your complete e-mail address as password.

Password:
```

18. Enter an e-mail address. Enter **none.of.your@business.com**. You see this:

```
230-You are user #1 of 50 simultaneous users allowed.
230-
230 Logged in anonymously.
Remote system type is UNIX.
Using binary mode to transfer files.
ftp>
```

NOTE

By default, NcFTPd requires that you log in within 15 seconds. If you do not, you see an error message and an ftp> prompt. You can log in again by entering **open localhost**.

19. Because you logged in as an anonymous user, the directory should be /var/ftp. See if this is true. Enter **ls**. You see the free_willy file that you created in the /var/ftp directory in Step 14, except that the owner is now ftpuser. The NcFTPd server hides the real owner of the file from FTP clients:

```
-rw-r--r-- 1 ftpuser ftpusers   96 Nov 17 10:08 README
-rw-r--r-- 1 ftpuser ftpusers    0 Nov 17 10:20  free_willy
```

20. Disconnect from the FTP server, but do not exit the FTP client program by entering **close**. You see this:

```
221 Goodbye.
ftp>
```

21. Now log in as your user account. First connect to the FTP server by entering **open localhost**. You are prompted for your username. Enter your username. (The user account must already exist on this system.) If your username was john, you'd see this:

```
331 User john okay, need password.
Password:
```

22. Enter the password for the user account. If you entered it correctly, you see this:

```
230-You are user #1 of 50 simultaneous users allowed.
230-
230 Restricted user logged in.
Remote system type is UNIX.
Using binary mode to transfer files.
ftp>
```

23. Because you logged in as an ordinary user, the directory should be the user's home directory. See if this is true. Enter **ls**. You see the save_the_whales file that you created in Step 15:

```
-rw-r--r-- 1 john   john     0 Nov 17 10:20 save_the_whales
```

The owner of files in your home directory is different than the owner of the files in the /var/ftp directory.

24. Exit the ftp program with the **quit** command.

Certification Objectives

Objectives for the Linux+ exam:

- Configure client network services and settings (e.g., settings for TCP/IP) (3.1)
- Configure basic server network services (e.g., DNS, DHCP, SAMBA, Apache) (3.2)

Review Questions

1. Which of the following is *not* a reason why NcFTPd performs better than WuFTP?
    a. It does not spawn child processes when users connect.
    b. It does not use the FTP protocol.
    c. It is not started from inetd or xinetd.
    d. It does not have to run programs such as /bin/ls.
2. When a user logs in as an ordinary (nonanonymous) user, the working directory is the user's home directory. True or False?
3. When a user logs in as anonymous, the working directory is /usr/local/ftp. True or False?
4. What command do you use to disconnect from the FTP server, but not leave the FTP client?
    a. **disconnect**
    b. **exit**
    c. **quit**
    d. **close**
5. When anonymous users look at files in the /var/ftp directory, they see files owned by whomever placed them there. True or False?

Lab 14.4 Using the mii-tool Program

Objectives

Linux includes a program, called **mii-tool**, that solves an interesting problem that occurs when you work with Ethernet. Most Ethernet cards support dual speeds; they can run at either 10 Mb/s or 100 Mb/s depending on the switch or hub to which they connect. (These cards are often called Ethernet 10/100 cards.) Many operating systems have no easy way to determine which speed is used. The mii-tool program can tell you.

NOTE For the mii-tool program to work properly, your Ethernet card needs to have Media Independent Interface circuitry. Older or inexpensive cards may not have this circuitry, and your results will not be the same as indicated in this lab exercise.

Materials Required

This lab requires the following:

- Access as the root user to a computer running Linux
- An Ethernet card installed in your computer and connected to an Ethernet hub or switch or to another computer using a crossover cable

Estimated completion time: 10 Minutes

Activity

1. Switch to the second virtual console (tty2) by pressing **Ctrl+Alt+F2**, and log in as root.
2. Ensure that your Ethernet card is connected by cable to an Ethernet hub or switch. You can connect directly to another computer's Ethernet card by using a crossover cable.
3. If you run mii-tool with no command-line parameters, it displays the status of all the Ethernet cards in your computer. Enter **mii-tool**. Here's an example of what the output looks like with one Ethernet card installed:

```
eth0: negotiated 100baseTx-FD, link ok
```

   Here's what it might look like with three Ethernet cards installed:

```
eth0: negotiated 100baseTx-HD, link ok
eth1: negotiated 100baseTx-FD, link ok
eth2: negotiated 10baseT, link ok
```

4. If you have more than one Ethernet card and you want to display the MII status of only one, specify the name on the command line. Enter **mii-tool eth0**. You see something like this:

```
eth0: negotiated 100baseTx-HD, link ok
```

5. You can get greater detail by using the **-v** command-line option. Enter **mii-tool -v**. Here's an example of what you see:

```
eth0: negotiated 100baseTx-HD, link ok

  product info: Intel 82555 rev 4
  basic mode:  autonegotiation enabled
```

```
basic status: autonegotiation complete, link ok
capabilities: 100baseTx-FD 100baseTx-HD 10baseT-FD 10baseT-HD
advertising: 100baseTx-FD 100baseTx-HD 10baseT-FD 10baseT-HD
link partner: 100baseTx-HD 10baseT-HD
```

NOTE

If you're using an Ethernet hub instead of a switch, you always run in half-duplex regardless of whether the Ethernet devices connected to it can run in full-duplex.

6. You can have the mii-tool program monitor the Ethernet card and tell you when its status changes by using the **-w** command-line option. Enter **mii-tool -w**. The output is similar to this:

   ```
   10:38:55 eth0: negotiated 100baseTx-FD, link ok
   ```

7. Disconnect the cable from the Ethernet card. This message appears every few seconds:

   ```
   10:39:10 eth0: no link
   ```

8. Reconnect the cable. A message similar to this appears once when the link is reestablished:

   ```
   10:40:05 eth0: negotiated 100baseTx-FD, link ok
   ```


9. You can override your Ethernet card's capabilities and have it advertise only certain capabilities. For example, you can tell it to advertise that it can only run at 10 Mb/s. Press **Ctrl+C** to return to the command prompt, then enter **mii-tool -A 10baseT**. The card begins to autonegotiate and tell its link partner that it can support only the 10 Mb/s speed.
10. You can force an Ethernet card to disable its autonegotiation and run at a certain speed and duplex mode. Enter **mii-tool -F 100baseTx-HD**. (In actuality, there is no practical reason to run in half-duplex when your Ethernet card and its link partner are capable of full-duplex. This step just illustrates that it's possible to change the configuration.)
11. Reset your Ethernet card back to its default configuration by entering **mii-tool -R**.

Certification Objectives

Objectives for the Linux+ exam:

- Configure client network services and settings (e.g., settings for TCP/IP) (3.1)
- Configure a Network Interface Card (NIC) from a command line (3.7)
- Diagnose hardware issues using Linux tools (e.g., /proc, disk utilities, ifconfig, /dev, knoppix, BBC, dmesg) (6.2)

Review Questions

1. If all the computers on your network are capable of full-duplex, they can all run full-duplex regardless of whether they're connected to hubs or switches. True or False?
2. What command monitors your Ethernet cards and displays link status changes?
   a. **mii-tool**
   b. **mii-tool -F**
   c. **mii-tool -R**
   d. **mii-tool -w**
3. What command displays details about your Ethernet card's MII status?
   a. **mii-tool**
   b. **mii-tool -status**
   c. **mii-tool -v**
   d. **mii-tool -V**
4. What command restarts autonegotiation?
   a. **mii-tool -auto**
   b. **mii-tool -F**
   c. **mii-tool -r**
   d. **mii-tool -V**
5. What command can force your Ethernet card into a certain speed and duplex mode?
   a. **mii-tool -A 100BaseTx-HD**
   b. **mii-tool -F 100BaseTx-HD**
   c. **mii-tool -R 100BaseTx-HD**
   d. **mii-tool -w 100BaseTx-HD**

Lab 14.5 Configuring and Using NTP

Objectives

The NTP protocol allows any computer on the Internet to synchronize to precision time servers. The software that makes this possible is the **ntpd** time server. Most Linux distributions include and install ntpd by default. You simply need to configure it. This lab shows you how to synchronize your computer with international time servers using the nptd daemon, and how to check that your computer is synchronized with the **ntptrace** command.

Materials Required

This lab requires the following:

- Access as a root user to a computer running Linux
- A Web browser and Internet connection
- If there is a firewall between your Linux computer and the Internet, it must allow TCP packets on port 123 to pass in order to successfully complete this exercise

NOTE

This lab explores information on the World Wide Web. Because Web pages can change without notice, what you see may not exactly match the terminology described in this lab. You may have to use your judgment to find the best match for links described here. When in doubt, check with your instructor.

Estimated completion time: 30 Minutes

Activity

LAB ACTIVITY

1. Switch to the GUI (tty7) by pressing **Ctrl+Alt+F2**, and log in as root.
2. Run your Web browser and enter:

   http://www.eecis.udel.edu/~mills/ntp/clock2b.html

   in the Address line. The page that appears lists the public NTP time servers that you may access.
3. Choose three time servers from the list that are geographically closest to you and note their names and IP addresses.
4. Using your favorite text editor, edit the /etc/ntp.conf file. Add three server lines to the file that contain the names or IP addresses of the time servers you selected in Step 3. Here's an example of these three lines:

```
server  montpelier.caltech.edu
server  bigben.cac.washington.edu
server  tick.ucla.edu
```

NOTE

You can specify the IP addresses of the time servers instead of their names. This saves a DNS lookup each time your time server needs to contact the remote time servers. However, if the IP address of a remote time server changes, your server will not be able to contact it.

5. Save the file and exit the editor.

6. The ntpd daemon does not work properly if your computer's time is off by more than 1000 seconds (about 17 minutes). Check to see that your computer's time is within this limit. Enter **date** to display the current date and time. If the time is not within the 1000-second limit, set your computer's current time so it is within this limit. You can change your system time with the date program. To set your computer's time to 12:00 noon, enter **date -s 12:00**.

7. Start the ntpd daemon by entering **/etc/rc.d/init.d/ntpd start**. You should see the following line:

   ```
   Starting ntpd:                              [ OK ]
   ```

8. When the ntpd daemon starts, it writes messages to the /var/log/messages log file. Enter **tail -f /var/log/messages**. You see lines similar to this:

   ```
   Nov 19 23:59:33 red ntpd[2071]: ntpd 4.1.0 Wed Sep 5 06:54:30 EDT 2003(1)
   Nov 19 23:59:33 red ntpd: ntpd startup succeeded
   Nov 19 23:59:33 red ntpd[2071]: precision = 9 usec
   Nov 19 23:59:33 red ntpd[2071]: kernel time discipline status 0040
   Nov 19 23:59:33 red ntpd[2071]: frequency initialized -24.206 from
   /etc/ntp/drift
   ```

9. It takes several minutes before ntpd synchronizes to the remote time servers you have specified. You can tell when synchronization occurs with the ntptrace program. Enter **ntptrace**. Before synchronization occurs, you see lines similar to this:

   ```
   red: stratum 16, offset 0.000083, synch distance 0.00003
   0.0.0.0:         *Not Synchronized*
   ```

   After synchronization occurs, you see lines similar to this:

   ```
   red: stratum 3, offset 0.000083, synch distance 0.11951
   igor.alcpress.com: stratum 2, offset 0.000869, synch distance 0.05373
   usno.pax.dec.com: stratum 1, offset 0.001123, synch distance 0.01474,
   refid 'USNO'
   ```

10. If you want the ntpd daemon to run every time you boot up your system, enter **chkconfig ntpd on**. This starts the ntpd daemon whenever your system enters runlevels 3, 4, and 5.

NOTE

In the unlikely event you want the ntpd daemon to run when you enter runlevel 1, enter **chkconfig -level 1 ntpd on**.

11. If you decide to run the ntpd daemon as a permanent part of your system, read the Rules Of Engagement on the *http://ntp.isc.org/bin/view/Servers/WebHome* Web page. It tells you how you should notify the administrators of the remote time servers that you'll be using their time servers.

Certification Objectives

Objectives for the Linux+ exam:

- Configure client network services and settings (e.g., settings for TCP/IP) (3.1)
- Configure basic server network services (e.g., DNS, DHCP, SAMBA, Apache) (3.2)

Review Questions

1. The ntpd daemon does not work correctly if your computer's current time is off by more than 60 seconds. True or False?
2. You configure the ntpd daemon by editing the /etc/ntp.conf file. True or False?
3. When you start the ntpd daemon, it immediately synchronizes to remote time servers. True or False?
4. What program can be used to tell when your time server is synchronized to remote time servers?
   a. date
   b. time
   c. ntpd
   d. ntptrace
5. What should you do if you decide to run the ntpd daemon permanently and you're synchronizing to remote public time servers?

CHAPTER FIFTEEN

CONFIGURING NETWORK SERVICES AND SECURITY

Labs included in this chapter

CompTIA Linux+ Exam Objectives		
Objective		**Lab**
2.23	Redirect output (e.g., piping, redirection)	15.1, 15.4
4.3	Given security requirements, implement appropriate encryption configuration (e.g., blowfish, 3DES, MD5)	15.1, 15.2, 15.3, 15.4, 15.5
4.10	Identify whether a package or file has been corrupted or altered (e.g., checksum, Tripwire)	15.1

NOTE

All of these lab exercises use encryption technology. Before performing these labs, you should check to be sure these actions are legal in your country. One resource for legal information is *http://rechten.uvt.nl/koops/cryptolaw/*.

Lab 15.1 Validating Files

Objectives

This lab exercise shows you how to validate files as genuine using cryptographic hashes. The md5sum program is one way of achieving this.

Materials Required

This lab requires the following:

- Access as an ordinary user to a computer running Linux

Activity Background

Linux provides a few ways of ensuring that files are genuine, such as the **sum**, **cksum**, and **md5sum** programs. You should avoid the sum and cksum programs because they are cryptographically weak. The md5sum program is much stronger. It uses the MD5 message digest to create a cryptographic hash of a file you specify. You make this hash available to anyone to whom you transmit a copy of the file. The person receiving the file also uses the md5sum program to compute a hash on the received file. If the hash generated at the transmitting location agrees with the hash generated at the receiving location, the file is genuine. If the hashes disagree, the file has been tampered with.

The hash consists of 32 characters. Fortunately, you don't have to visually compare two long sequences of characters. The md5sum program does the comparison for you with its --check option.

Estimated completion time: 10 Minutes

LAB ACTIVITY

Activity

1. Switch to the second virtual console (tty2) by pressing **Ctrl+Alt+F2**, and log in as any user.
2. Become familiar with the md5sum man page. Enter **man md5sum**. Read the page, though you shouldn't be concerned if you don't understand everything on the page. Press **q** to exit the man page.
3. Copy an arbitrary program file into your home directory. Enter **cp /bin/bash /root**.

4. Generate a cryptographic hash of the file and display the output to the screen by entering **md5sum -b bash**. Because the bash file is a binary program, use the -b option. You'll see something similar to this:

```
20b6100fa713bbd5591a74073fe622bca *bash
```

NOTE The first 32 characters is the MD5 hash. The name of the file the hash was computed against follows.

5. Generate the hash again, but this time send the output to a file. Enter **md5sum --b bash>bash.md5**.
6. Check that the bash file is genuine by checking it against the bash.md5 file. Enter **md5sum --check bash.md5**. You see this:

```
bash: OK
```

7. Change the bash file by writing a few characters to the end of it. Enter **echo "123" >> bash**.
8. Check the bash file again by entering **md5sum --check bash.md5**. Because the file has been modified since the hash was created you see this:

```
bash: FAILED
md5sum: WARNING: 1 of 1 computed checksum did not match
```


NOTE The md5sum program uses the generic term "checksum" instead of the more precise term "hash."

9. Erase the bash file by entering **rm bash** and enter **y**.
10. Enter **logout** and press **Alt+F7** to go back to your graphical desktop.

Certification Objectives

Objectives for the Linux+ exam:

- Identify whether a package or file has been corrupted or altered (e.g., checksum, Tripwire) (4.10)
- Given security requirements, implement appropriate encryption configuration (e.g., Blowfish, 3DES, MD5) (4.3)
- Redirect output (e.g., piping, redirection) (2.23)

Review Questions

1. One disadvantage of using the md5sum program is that you must compare two 43-character hashes visually. True or False?
2. The md5sum program outputs its hash to STDOUT. True or False?
3. The md5sum program produces a cryptographic result that consists of how many characters?
   a. 16
   b. 32
   c. 64
   d. 128
4. The md5sum program does not use the term "hash." It uses which generic term?
   a. parity
   b. checksum
   c. block check character
   d. crc
5. The md5sum program can only ensure that binary files are genuine. True or False?

Lab 15.2 Using SSH

Objectives

This lab has you use SSH to communicate with another Linux computer.

Materials Required

This lab requires the following:

- Two computers running Linux with a network connection between them
- A user account on both computers

Activity Background

One of the exercises in the main text is to configure and use telnet. Telnet can be a significant security concern if you use it over a public network. Telnet produces an unencrypted packet stream that, if intercepted, easily reveals the communications taking place. Using **SSH** (secure shell) is a far better way to communicate because the packet stream is encrypted using a cryptographically strong cipher.

Estimated completion time: 20 Minutes

LAB ACTIVITY

Activity

1. On one of the computers, switch to the second virtual console (tty2) by pressing **Ctrl+Alt+F2**, and log in as any user. The other computer must be running the sshd daemon. Fedora Core 2 normally starts up sshd upon booting, so in most cases you can safely assume that it's running.
2. Connect to the other computer using SSH. Assuming the IP address of the other computer is 192.168.1.12 and your user account on the other computer is kenny, enter **ssh kenny@192.168.1.12** (substitute the other computer's IP address and your username as appropriate throughout the rest of the lab). You see something similar to this:

```
The authenticity of host "192.168.1.12" can't be established.
RSA key fingerprint is 3d:c1:c4:b4:24:df:f2:ef:ca:8f:f2:
62:34:51:5a:0b.
Are you sure you want to continue connecting (yes/no)?
```

NOTE

The RSA key fingerprint is a 128-bit number expressed as 32 hexadecimal digits.

15

3. Enter **yes**. You see this:

```
Warning: Permanently added "192.168.1.12" (RSA) to the
list of known hosts.
Kenny@192.168.1.12's password:
```

4. Enter the password for the user account. You see something similar to this:

```
Last login: Wed Sep 29 11:44:55 2004 from 192.168.1.11
Linux 2.4.20
```

5. Disconnect from the other computer by entering **exit**. You'll see something similar to this:

```
Connection to 192.168.1.12 closed.
```

6. When you told SSH that you wanted to continue connecting in Step 3, you implied that you trusted the other computer to be genuine. The host's key was then placed in your known_hosts file. This file is in your .ssh directory (below your home directory). Enter **cd .ssh**. Enter **ls -l**. You see something similar to this:

```
-rw-r--r--  1 kenny users  682  2004-09-
29 13:07 known_hosts
```

7. Examine the contents of the known_hosts file by entering **cat known_hosts**. You see something similar to this:

```
192.168.1.12, 192.168.1.12, ssh-rsa
AAAAB3NzaC1yc2EAAAABIwAAAIEA8qHgdWqbvt3c82W1jCbOcF18tkxw
OmbHO
RnKS2188g4UsLLT/
BYHsyenWNt+o5yS9u1WD3oGQ85Yb9Z1cNW1xpX7x9Seg7I1b
+O2j478qdO/vvFWYwZWOihUnt73gTeM1xdGmRRLUdZT+g6Lw/
16ww8rL0wAzVD
HSLtdCyEqkV8=
```

NOTE

The first field is the name of the host, the second field is the IP address of the host, and the third field is the host key. In this example, the host has no name, so its IP address is used as the name.

8. If you have access to another computer running an sshd daemon and you have a user account on it, connect to it as you did in Steps 2 through 5. Examine the known_hosts file again. Now you see a second entry in the file that looks similar to this:

```
192.168.1.12, 192.168.1.12, ssh-rsa
AAAAB3NzaC1yc2EAAAABIwAAAIEA8qHgdWqbvt3c82W1jCbOcF18tkxw
OmbHO
RnKS2188g4UsLLT/
BYHsyenWNt+o5yS9u1WD3oGQ85Yb9Z1cNW1xpX7x9Seg7I1b
+O2j478qdO/vvFWYwZWOihUnt73gTeM1xdGmRRLUdZT+g6Lw/
16ww8rL0wAzVD
HSLtdCyEqkV8=

192.168.1.13, 192.168.1.13, ssh-rsa
AAAAB3NzaC1yc2EAAAABIwAAAIEAs8DCchAum+53De5Fo9WGQSSHEu
EsUZ/E
qySK8wtmGUnqw+oxVRJz7iDUxT9nUqbWx7Z6A69f4/
obH2pVxFsp2y21fK+PQPvC1
0CjExOVP3t96Jo/5h46Gxwjzn81z0urkFOQ/
mFURD0EnluD1N+u9oK5dyikdPbu09p7a
m1SycU=
```

9. SSH protects you from connecting to a computer that masquerades as the legitimate one. To simulate this, change the known_hosts file so the host key is different. Using your favorite text editor, change a host key so one of its characters is different. Choose a character about midway through the key. Save the file.

10. Try to connect to the host. Enter **ssh kenny@192.168.1.12**. You see something similar to this:

```
@@@@@@@@@@@@@@@@@@@@@@@@@@@@@@@@@@@@@@@@@@@@@@@@@@@@@@@@@@@
@    WARNING: REMOTE HOST IDENTIFICATION HAS CHANGED!     @
@@@@@@@@@@@@@@@@@@@@@@@@@@@@@@@@@@@@@@@@@@@@@@@@@@@@@@@@@@@
IT IS POSSIBLE THAT SOMEONE IS DOING SOMETHING NASTY!
Someone could be eavesdropping on you right now (man-in-
the-middle attack)!
It is also possible that the RSA host key has just been
changed.
The fingerprint for the RSA key sent by the remote host
is 3d:c1:c4:b4:24:db:f2:ef:ca:8f:f2:62:34:51:5a:db.
Please contact your system administrator.
Add correct host key in /home/ed/.ssh/
known_hosts to get rid of this message.
Offending key in /home/ed/.ssh/known_hosts:3
RSA host key for igor has changed and you have requested
strict checking.
Host key verification failed.
```

11. A host key may change as a result of an administrator regenerating the key. When this occurs, you need to update the key in your known_hosts file. The easiest way to do this is to delete that host's key in the file. Then connect to the host as you did in Steps 2 and 3.
12. If numerous users on your computer connect to other computers with SSH, you can maintain a single known_hosts file instead of all users maintaining their own. This shared file is called ssh_known_hosts and is kept in the /etc/ssh directory. Log in as root by entering **su** and enter the password for the root user. Enter **cp known_hosts/etc/ssh_known_hosts**. Enter **exit**. Delete your known_hosts file by entering **rm ~/.ssh/known_hosts**.
13. Connect to the other computer with SSH by entering **ssh kenny@192.168.1.12**. You're prompted for the password. Enter your password. You're connected even though you have no known_hosts file.
14. Enter **logout** and press **Alt+F7** to go back to your graphical desktop.

15

Certification Objectives

Objectives for the Linux+ exam:

- Given security requirements, implement appropriate encryption configuration (e.g., Blowfish, 3DES, MD5) (4.3)

Review Questions

1. To establish a SSH connection, the other computer must be running the sshd daemon. True or False?

2. The RSA key fingerprint is how large a value?
    a. 32 bits
    b. 64 bits
    c. 128 bits
    d. 256 bits
3. Where is your known_hosts file?
    a. /etc/ssh
    b. ~/ssh
    c. ~/.ssh
    d. /var/ssh
4. If a host key changes, what's the easiest way to place the new key in your known_hosts file?
5. All users can share a common known_hosts-like file. True or False?

Lab 15.3 Generating Public and Private Keys

Objectives

This lab exercise shows you how to generate public and private keys using the GNU Privacy Guard program, called **gpg**.

Materials Required

This lab requires the following:

- Access as a root user to a computer running Linux

Estimated completion time:	30 Minutes

Activity

1. Switch to the second virtual console (tty2) by pressing **Ctrl+Alt+F2**, and log in as root.
2. When a nonroot user runs the gpg program, it displays error messages about insecure memory. To suppress these messages and make gpg operation a bit more secure, you can set the SUID bit on the gpg program. Enter **chmod u+s /usr/bin/gpg**.
3. Enter **logout**. Log in as a nonroot user. Assume you're logging in as user Diana for the remainder of this lab.

4. Generate the public and private keys by entering **gpg --gen-key**. You see this appear:

```
gpg (GnuPG) 1.2.4; Copyright (C) 2003 Free Software
Foundation, Inc.
This program comes with ABSOLUTELY NO WARRANTY.
This is free software, and you are welcome to redistribute
it under certain conditions. See the file COPYING for details.

Please select what kind of key you want:
   (1) DSA and ElGamal (default)
   (2) DSA (sign only)
   (3) RSA (sign only)
Your selection?
```

5. You want both DSA and ElGamal. Accept the default by pressing the **Enter** key. You see this:

```
DSA keypair will have 1024 bits.
About to generate a new ELG-E keypair.
                    Minimum size is  768 bits
                   Default keysize is 1024 bits
   Highest suggested keysize is 2048 bits
What keysize do you want? (1024)
```

6. Accept the default 1024-bit keysize by pressing the **Enter** key. You see this:

```
Please specify how long the key should be valid.
       0= key does not expire
      <n>  = key expires in n days
    <n>w = key expires in n weeks
    <n>m = key expires in n months
     <n>y = key expires in n years
Key is valid for? (0)
```


7. Accept the default by pressing the **Enter** key. You see this:

```
Key does not expire at all
Is this correct (y/n)?
```

8. Enter **y** to confirm that you want a perpetual key. You see this:

```
You need a User-ID to identify your key; the software
constructs the user id
From Real Name, Comment and Email Address in this form:
          "Heinrich Heine (Der Dichter) heinrich@
duesseldorf.de"

Real Name:
```

9. Enter your full name. You see this:

```
Email address:
```

10. Enter your e-mail address. You see this:

```
Comment:
```

11. Enter some text that might describe you, your family, your company, and so on. This comment is visible to anyone who has your public key. You see something similar to this:

```
You selected this USER-ID:
     "Diana Williams (Eat right) <dw@example.com>"

Change (N)ame, (c)omment, (E)mail or (O)kay/(Q)uit?
```

12. You can change any of the information you entered in Steps 9 and 11. When you're finished, enter **O**. You see this:

```
You need a Passphrase to protect your secret key.

Enter passphrase:
```

13. Enter a passphrase (password). The most secure passphrases consist of combinations of numbers, lowercase letters, uppercase letters, and symbols. You see this:

```
Repeat passphrase:
```

14. Enter the same passphrase again. Immediately start pressing the Shift keys repetitively until the following screen output is displayed. You see something similar to this:

```
We need to generate a lot of random bytes. It is a good
idea to perform Some other action (type on the keyboard,
move the mouse, utilize the disks) during the prime
generation; this gives the random number generator a
better chance to gain entropy.+++++++++++++++++++++++++
...+++++.++++..+++++++++++++++++....>++++++++++++++++
.......................................++++++^^^
gpg: /home/diana/.gnupg/trustdb.gpg: trustdb created
public and secret key created and signed.
Key marked as ultimately trusted.

pub  1024D/86B9D4C4 2003-09-
29 Diana Williams (Eat right) <dw@example.com>
      Key fingerprint = 47BD 21F7 AFFC D1BE E4DD 9D88
D7D7 B1B8 86B9 8866 D4C4
sub   1024g/3CE44EBD 2004-09-29
```

15. You've created your key pair. In the previous example, the key specifier is 86B9D4C3. Make a note of it. A new directory, called .gnupg, was created below your home directory. Go there by entering **cd ~/.gnupg**.

16. Enter **ls --l**. You see something similar to this:

```
total 24
-rw------- 1 diana users 8075 2004-09-28 17:46 gpg.conf
-rw------- 1 diana users  932 2004-09-28 18:50 pubring.gpg
-rw------- 1 diana users    0 2004-09-28 17:46 pubring.gpg~
-rw------- 1 diana users  600 2004-09-28 18:50 random_seed
-rw------- 1 diana users 1069 2004-09-28 18:50 secring.gpg
-rw------- 1 diana users 1240 2004-09-28 18:50 trustdb.gpg
```

The pubring.gpg file is your public key. The secring.gpg file is your private or secret key. These are binary files so you can't view them.

17. In case you forget your passphrase or if your private key is lost or compromised, you need to have a revocation certificate that you can publish to others. Generate this revocation certificate by entering:

    gpg --output revoke.asc --gen-revoke *key*,

    where *key* is the key specifier. You see this:

    ```
    sec 1024D/86B8D4C4 2004-09-
    29  Diana Williams (Eat right) <dw@example.com>

    Create a revocation certificate for this key?
    ```

18. Enter **y**. You see this:

    ```
    Please select the reason for the revocation:
      0 = No reason specified
      1 = Key has been compromised
      2 = Key is superseded
      3 = Key is no longer used
      Q = Cancel
    (Probably you want to select 1 here)
    Your decision?
    ```

19. Enter **1**. You see this:

    ```
    Enter an optional description; end it with an empty line:
    >
    ```

20. Enter **Key has been lost or compromised**. Press the **Enter** key a second time. You see this:

    ```
    Reason for revocation: Key has been compromised
    Key has been lost or compromised.
    Is this okay?
    ```

21. Enter **y**. You see something similar to this:

    ```
    You need a passphrase to unlock the secret key for
    User: "Diana Williams (Eat right) <dianaw@example.com>
    1024-bit DSA key, ID 86B9D4C4, created 2004-09-29

    Enter passphrase:
    ```

15

22. Enter the passphrase you used when you generated your key pair in Step 13. You see this:

```
ASCII armored output forced.
Revocation certificate created.

Please move it to a medium which you can hide away; if
Mallory gets Access to this certificate he can use it
to make your key unusable. It is smart to print this
certificate and store it  away, just in case Your
media becomes unreadable. But have some caution: The
print system of your machine might store data and make
it available to others!
```

23. Enter **ls -l**. You'll see a file called revoke.asc has been added to your directory. This is a plaintext file that you can view. Enter **cat revoke.asc**. You see something similar to this:

```
-----BEGIN PGP PUBLIC KEY BLOCK-----
Version: GnuPG v1.2.4 (GNU/Linux)
Comment: A revocation certificate should follow

iGoEIBECACoFAkFaS1QjHQJLZXkgaGFzIGJlZW4gbG9zdCBvciBjb2
1wcm9taXNl
ZC4ACgkQ19exuIa51MQYDwCeMn0GIQjP98N05nGEFJpXed7R2PQAnj
POfhTkBJLo
N7+nD8tgqg8L17vQ
=GaeG
-----END PGP PUBLIC KEY BLOCK-----
```

24. Enter **logout**. Log in as another nonroot user and repeat Steps 4 through 23.

25. Enter **logout** and press **Alt+F7** to go back to your graphical desktop.

Certification Objectives

Objectives for the Linux+ exam:

- Given security requirements, implement appropriate encryption configuration (e.g., Blowfish, 3DES, MD5) (4.3)

Review Questions

1. If you lose your key or you think it has been compromised, what should you do?
   a. Generate a new key.
   b. Notify the Webmaster of the gpg Web site and generate a new key.
   c. Submit a revocation certificate (that you've prepared in advance) to a key server and generate a new certificate.
   d. Generate a new key using a different e-mail address.

2. Which is the minimum size key you can generate with the gpg program?
   a. 512
   b. 768
   c. 1024
   d. 2048
3. Which is the default size key you generate with the gpg program?
   a. 512
   b. 768
   c. 1024
   d. 2048
4. By default, keys expire in one year. True or False?
5. The comment that you enter when you generate your key is only visible to you. True or False?

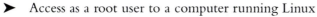

Lab 15.4 Exchanging and Signing Keys

Objectives

This lab exercise shows you how to exchange keys with other users and to sign their keys, thus creating a "web of trust."

Materials Required

This lab requires the following:

- Access as a root user to a computer running Linux

Estimated completion time: 30 Minutes

Activity

LAB ACTIVITY

1. Switch to the second virtual console (tty2) by pressing **Ctrl+Alt+F2**, and log in as one of the users you used in the previous lab. This lab assumes that these are users Diana and Danny and you're logging in as Diana now. Substitute your usernames as appropriate in the examples.
2. Diana and Danny want to exchange encrypted data with each other. They must place each other's public keys on their key rings. Diana needs to export her public key to a file so Danny can import it. Enter **gpg -a --export**

***86B9D4C4* >~/dianakey** where *86B9D4C4* is the key specifier you determined in Step 15 of the previous lab.

3. Using the -a option exports the key in plaintext (ASCII) format so it's readable. Enter **cat ~/dianakey**. You should see something similar to this:


```
-----BEGIN PGP PUBLIC KEY BLOCK-----
Version: GnuPG v1.2.4 (GNU/Linux)

mQGiBEFaFO8RBAD9j4kkJjNRAAcIlJymGRB1DUZfwFadZwvPV7yjx0
V3tRpQ+2wa
IXvLDYB5rwHkwlFJhaRYwXALHld6PJ6jOAzwkCBtPwCvkCKFl+FS6N
X+UNxFYyIr
psky7VF5DRzq07YMj0Pk+3o6FGDTOTQ1+ajXONr4xN0STwD57ggOh4
dHmwCgqTv5
ebGOcFaOavJhPBqO885jtlED/iprEsL/
DF0rM1+A4q+3wb2ItocDGJbsgX4/8znR
19+7an7uvJ2eocIPRK2+tqZU06ig7k5q6tyvGT13/GiojxjNhSAejii/
HbIyllLE
/HA5cB8qr8YPpX2FJdiKR8mohzLpu9HFLMrYQFFYz8aA/
ccWa3tRXuPCPjGKIvAg
g94UA/9grvEFPLe2+nfChMfqQuxQgXBO4+4gwokzqQ4trHxsV3dg6D/
y2BRYHclX
C1DJ6ue0JKGJNvMxtPr5oER1tIHDQuenieF0K3uSOqTbR/
EPC8ELNJSIOIIjuK8U
Nu0vJhuC5E9qCPy7+Ble6kbYSXkZ757Nkl1mu2/SlWE/
b4kpL7Q6RWQgU2F3aWNr
aSAoQWNjZWxlcmF0ZWQgTGVhcm5pbmcgQ2VudGVyKSA8ZWRAYWxjcH
Jlc3MuY29t
PoheBBMRAgAeBQJBWhTvAhsDBgsJCAcDAgMVAgMDFgIBAh4BAheAAA
oJENfXsbiG
udTEBtsAn1QPnfh5oVdnUz6nv5rXXyJmWLH8AKCMbvbOSxixAGFI7Y
jFgLfBEviH
87kBDQRBWhTyEAQAxFaSgAl2UzhFVUbEnnQwvtzoGwsbJMuTq/
taernHW0g6TOsR
+oD6mfB2nYh3CDvu1veplLM3GGw4yePciZGA0TRpmEuTArgsOPl46
1NP/VRLOc9a
BIF9y6rSTRqv2RKMigjqHnCN2Le6qfypA1e39YUGlUk+JS1zDxcWG
CgLvNsAAwUD
/ja4BD6ip6rpUd9SMyWiAmLDr54O7HSb/f4lvek3WptZNKqbZ0/
BSqOc4vB2zvJp
P0glFrWgkejL1Vpjz0OoAos3tpGpxn6XTWlZFZcYqzfzRyhj0Ph5a
r3gzcHE7Jxf
ejCDW80n9GvnDs6TsWx7Kxmjsz1Efp7E+XYNTkwxNPX3iEkEGBECA
AkFAkFaFPIC
GwwACgkQ19exuIa51MSejACgnF0BwzGbwnvierOadR6NH7pOppgAn
Av7s0FS/TZd
CAA50dC41tC1I9A6
=6YRd
-----END PGP PUBLIC KEY BLOCK-----
```

4. Ensure that Danny can read the file by entering **chmod 644 ~/dianakey**.
5. Enter **logout**. Log in as Danny. Examine Danny's key ring by entering:

   gpg --list-keys.

   You see something similar to this:

```
/home/danny/.gnupg/pubring.gpg
----------------------------------------
pub  1024D/E6016194 2004-09-
29 Danny Williams (NYFD) <daw@example.com>
sub  1024g/220814ED 2004-09-29
```

6. Danny needs to export his public key to a file so Diana can import it. Enter **gpg -a -export *E6016194* >~/dannykey** where *E6016194* is the key specifier you determined in Step 15 of the previous lab.
7. Ensure that Diana can read the file by entering **chmod 644 ~/dannykey**.
8. Danny can import Diana's key. Enter **gpg --import /home/diana/dianakey**. You see something similar to this:

```
gpg: key 86B9D4C4: public key "Diana Williams (Eat
right) <dw@example.com>" imported
gpg: Total number processed: 1
gpg:               imported: 1
```

NOTE

This step requires that Danny has read permissions to Diana's file. Diana may have to give Danny those permissions by entering chmod o+r /home/diana/dianakey

9. Danny's key ring now has Diana's key. You can see this by entering **gpg --list-keys**. You see something similar to this:

```
/home/danny/.gnupg/pubring.gpg
----------------------------------------
pub  1024D/E6016194 2004-09-
29 Danny Williams (NYFD) <daw@example.com>
sub  1024g/220814ED 2004-09-29

pub  1024D/86B9D4C4 2004-09-
29 Diana Williams (Eat right) <dw@example.com>
sub  1024g/12B8E56D 2004-09-29
```

10. Enter **logout**. Log in as Diana.
11. Import Danny's key by entering **gpg --import /home/danny/dannykey**.
12. Diana's key ring now has Danny's key. You can see this by entering **gpg --list-keys**. You see something similar to this:

```
/home/diana/.gnupg/pubring.gpg
----------------------------------------
pub  1024D/86B9D4C4 2004-09-
29 Diana Williams (Eat right) <dw@example.com>
sub  1024g/12B8E56D 2004-09-29

pub  1024D/E6016194 2004-09-
29 Danny Williams (NYFD) <daw@example.com>
sub  1024g/220814ED 2004-09-29
```

13. If Diana is certain that Danny's key is genuine, she can sign it. Enter:

    gpg --edit-key "Danny Williams"

    You see something similar to this:

```
gpg (GnuPG) 1.2.4; Copyright © 2003 Free Software
Foundation, Inc.
This program comes with ABSOLUTELY NO WARRANTY.
This is free software, and you are welcome to
redistribute it
Under certain conditions. See the file COPYING for
details.

Pub  1024D/E6016194  created: 2004-09-
29 expires: never    trust: -/-
Sub  1024g/220814ED  created: 2004-09-29 expires: never
(1). Danny Williams (NYFD) daw@example.com

Command>
```

14. To sign Danny's key, enter **sign**. You see something similar to this:

```
pub 1024D/E6016194  created: 2004-09-
29 expires: never    trust: -/-
Primary key fingerprint: 63F9 F685 0C33 94EF 9DA2 0034
4885 159D E601 6194

      Danny Williams (NYFD) <daw@example.com>

How carefully have you verified the key you are about
to sign actually belongs
To the person named above?  If you don't know the
 answer, enter "0".

    (0) I will not answer. (default)
    (1) I have not checked at all.
    (2) I have done casual checking.
    (3) I have done very careful checking.

Your selection? (enter '?' for more information):
```

15. Assume that Diana knows that Danny's key is genuine. Enter **3**. You see something similar to this:

```
Are you really sure that you want to sign this key
with your key: "Diana Williams (Eat right) <dw@example.
com>"  (86B9D4C4)

I have checked this key very carefully.

Really sign?
```

16. Enter **y**. You'll see something similar to this:

```
You need a passphrase to unlock the secret key for
user: "Diana Williams (Eat right) <dw@example.com>"
1024-bit DSA key, ID 86B9D4C4, created 2004-09-29

Enter passphrase:
```

17. Enter Diana's passphrase. If you enter the correct passphrase, you see this:

```
command>
```

18. Enter **q**. You see this:

```
Save changes?
```

19. Enter **y**. You're back at the shell's command prompt.
20. Enter **logout**. Log in as Danny. Danny can now sign Diana's key by using Steps 13 through 18 as a guide.
21. Enter **logout**. Press **Alt+F7** to go back to your graphical desktop.

Certification Objectives

Objectives for the Linux+ exam:

- Given security requirements, implement appropriate encryption configuration (e.g., Blowfish, 3DES, MD5) (4.3)
- Redirect output (e.g., piping, redirection) (2.23)

Review Questions

1. Which command generates a new key?
   a. **gpg --key**
   b. **gpggen**
   c. **gpg --gen-key**
   d. **gpg --new**

2. Which command displays your key ring?
   a. **gpg --list=keys**
   b. **lskeys**
   c. **gpg --show-key**
   d. **pkikey**
3. Users that want to exchange data with one another using public key encryption must have each other's private keys on their key ring. True or False?
4. When you use the gpg --export command, you are exporting private keys. True or False?
5. Signing other user keys is the way to achieve a "web of trust." True or False?

Lab 15.5 Encrypting Files

Objectives

This lab exercise shows you how to encrypt files using public key encryption.

Materials Required

This lab requires the following:

- Access as a root user to a computer running Linux

Estimated completion time: 15 Minutes

Activity

LAB ACTIVITY

1. Switch to the second virtual console (tty2) by pressing **Ctrl+Alt+F2**.
2. Log in as one of the users you used in the previous lab. This lab assume that these are users Diana and Danny and you're logging in as Diana now. Substitute your usernames as appropriate in the examples.
3. Create a plaintext file, called secret, using your favorite text editor. Place some text in the file that you want to share with Danny but nobody else. The lab assumes you entered **The sky is blue**.
4. Encrypt the file by entering **gpg --recipient "Danny Williams" --encrypt secret**. You've created an encrypted file called secret.gpg without destroying the original file called secret. Enter **ls -l secret***. You see something similar to this:

```
-rw-r--r---  1 diana users  17 2004-09-29  13:44  secret
-rw-r--r---  1 diana users  17 2004-09-29  13:44  secret
```

NOTE

Normally, Diana would send the encrypted file to Danny via e-mail or some other way. Because Diana and Danny's home directories are on the same computer and Danny can read files in Diana's directory, skip these additional steps.

5. Enter **logout** and log in as Danny.
6. Decrypt the secret.gpg file by entering **gpg --decrypt /home/diana/secret.gpg**. You see something similar to this:

```
You need a passphrase to unlock the secret key for
User: "Danny Williams (NYFD) daw@example.com
1024-bit ELG-E key, ID 220814ED, created 2004-09-
29 (main key E6016194)

Enter passphrase:
```

7. Enter Danny's passphrase for his key. You see something similar to this:

```
gpg: encrypted with 1024-bit ELG-
E key, ID 12B8E56D, created 2004-09-29
      "Diana Williams (Eat right) <dw@example.com>"
The sky is blue.
```

   You've successfully decrypted the file and displayed the file's contents.

8. If you want to send the contents to a file, use the --output option. Enter **gpg --decrypt /home/diana/secret.gpg --output secret**. You should have a file called secret in your current directory whose contents is the decrypted file.
9. Enter **logout**. Press **Alt+F7** to go back to your graphical desktop.

Certification Objectives

Objectives for the Linux+ exam:

- Given security requirements, implement appropriate encryption configuration (e.g., Blowfish, 3DES, MD5) (4.3)

Review Questions

1. When you encrypt a file to send to another user, you use your private key to encrypt the file. True or False?
2. When you encrypt a file, gpg automatically deletes the original (nonencrypted) file. True or False?

3. Which command encrypts a file?
    a. **gpg --encrypt secret**
    b. **gpgencrypt --recipient "Danny Williams"**
    c. **gpg --recipient "Danny Williams" --encrypt secret**
    d. **gpgencrypt --encrypt secret**
4. Which command decrypts a file?
    a. **gpg --decrypt secret.gpg**
    b. **gpgdecrypt secret.gpg**
    c. **gpg --sender "Diana Williams" secret.gpg**
    d. **gpg --recipient "Danny Williams" secret.gpg**
5. When you decrypt a file, you can send it to a file with the --file option. True or False?